THE POLITICAL ECONOMY OF
REVOLUTIONARY NICARAGUA

THEMATIC STUDIES IN LATIN AMERICA

Series editor: Gilbert W. Merkx, Director, Latin American Institute, University of New Mexico

---

THE POLITICAL ECONOMY OF REVOLUTIONARY NICARAGUA
by Rose J. Spalding

WOMEN ON THE U.S.–MEXICO BORDER*
edited by Vicki L. Ruiz and Susan B. Tiano

JEWISH PRESENCE IN LATIN AMERICA*
edited by Judith L. Elkin and Gilbert W. Merkx

PINOCHET: THE LOGIC OF POWER*
by Genaro Arriagada

THE CHILEAN POLITICAL PROCESS*
by Manuel Antonio Garreton

LATIN AMERICAN AGRICULTURE AND REFORM*
by William C. Thiesenhusen

LATIN AMERICA: ITS CITIES AND IDEAS*
by Luis Alberto Romero

LABOR AND POLITICS IN LATIN AMERICA*
by Edward Epstein

LAND, POWER, AND POVERTY: ROOTS OF CONFLICT
IN RURAL CENTRAL AMERICA*
by Charles D. Brockett

THE PUERTO RICAN EXPERIENCE IN THE UNITED STATES*
by Clara Rodriguez

THE UNITED STATES, HONDURAS, AND THE CRISIS
IN CENTRAL AMERICA*
by Donald E. Schulz

in preparation.

THE POLITICAL ECONOMY OF REVOLUTIONARY NICARAGUA

Edited by

ROSE J. SPALDING

Political Science Department
DePaul University
Chicago, Illinois

Boston
Allen & Unwin, Inc.
London   Sydney

Cover/jacket photo by William Denton.
Cover/jacket design by Jean Morley.

Allen & Unwin, Inc.
8 Winchester Place, Winchester, MA 01890, USA

George Allen & Unwin (Publishers), Ltd
40 Museum Street, London, WC1A 1LU, UK

George Allen & Unwin (Publishers), Ltd
Park Lane, Hemel Hempstead, Herts HP2 4TE, UK

George Allen & Unwin Australia Pty Ltd
8 Napier Street, North Sydney, NSW 2060, Australia

First Published in 1987

Library of Congress Cataloging-in-Publication Data

The Political economy of revolutionary Nicaragua.

   (Thematic studies in Latin America)
   Bibliography: p.
   Includes index.
   1. Nicaragua—Economic policy.   2. Nicaragua—
Economic conditions—1979–   . I. Spalding, Rose J.
HC146.P65   1986   338.9'7285   86-14095
ISBN   0–04–497014–5   (alk. paper)
ISBN   0–04–497015–3   (alk. paper :   pbk.)

British Library Cataloguing in Publication Data

Political economy of revolutionary Nicaragua.
   1. Nicaragua—Economic Conditions—
1979.   2. Nicaragua—Politics and
government—1979–
I. Spalding, Rose J.
330.97285'053   HC146

   ISBN 0–04–497014–5
   ISBN 0–04–497015–3   Pbk

Contents

Acknowledgments

Editing a book is a much more challenging, time-consuming and costly venture than I had ever imagined. This collection would not have been possible without the support and assistance of many people. Two acknowledgments are especially important. The University Research Council of DePaul University provided two grants that covered most of the costs of producing the manuscript. And Laura J. Enriquez generously gave time and advice to this project, helping to organize the panel where the idea for the book was born and finding ways to get correspondence back and forth between the U.S. and Nicaragua. Were it not for the demands of her thesis, this would have been a co-edited work. I would also like to acknowledge the help and advice I received from Richard R. Fagen, Thomas Walker, Martin Diskin, Marcos Wheelock, Sofía Clark, Susan Ramirez, Emilio Pantojas, Jean Enriquez, and my husband William Denton.

The production of this book also drew heavily on the professional skills of many people. Bob Holden translated the chapters by Pizarro and Vilas; Chris Mauro provided secretarial support; Russell H. Till provided design and production services; and Rachel J. Wark coordinated the production process. John Michel of Allen & Unwin, Inc. and Latin American series editor Gilbert W. Merkx provided friendly support and expert advice throughout the process. My sincere thanks to them all.

About the Authors

CLAES BRUNDENIUS
  Research Policy Institute, University of Lund, Sweden.

Brundenius is a Swedish economist who has worked for the OECD in Paris and the Food and Agriculture Organization (FAO) and the United Nations in Peru. In 1983 he worked in Nicaragua at the Ministry of Industry on assignment from the United Nations, and at the Instituto de Investigaciones Económicas y Sociales (INIES). He is the author of *Revolutionary Cuba: The Challenge of Economic Growth with Equity* (Boulder, Colo.: Westview Press, 1984) and co-editor of *Development Strategies and Basic Needs in Latin America* (Boulder, Colo.: Westview Press, 1982).

MICHAEL E. CONROY
  Department of Economics, University of Texas at Austin

Conroy is a U.S. economist who began working in Central America as a Peace Corp volunteer in the 1960s. He has traveled regularly to Nicaragua since 1980. In 1983 he was a Visiting Scholar at the Kellogg Institute, Notre Dame University. His work on Nicaragua includes "External Dependence, External Assistance, and Economic Aggression Against Nicaragua," *Latin American Perspectives*, 12, 2 (1985): 39−68; "False Polarization? Differing Perspectives on the Economic Strategies of Post-Revolutionary Nicaragua," *Third World Quarterly*, 6, 4 (1984): 993−1032; and a chapter in Thomas Walker's edited collection, *Nicaragua: The First Five Years* (New York: Praeger, 1985). Conroy co-chairs the Latin American Studies Association Task Force on Scholarly Relations with Nicaragua and coedits (with Laura J. Enriquez) the *LASA−NICA Scholars News.*

LAURA J. ENRIQUEZ
Programa Alimentario Nicaragüense, Ministerio de Desarrollo Agropecuario y Reforma Agraria (MIDINRA), Nicaragua.

Enriquez is a U.S. sociologist whose Ph.D. thesis entitled "Social Transformation in Latin America: Tensions between Agro-Export Production and Agrarian Reform in Revolutionary Nicaragua" was completed in 1985. During her three years of field work in Nicaragua, she was a research associate at the Centro de Investigación y Asesoría Socio-Económica (CINASE) in Managua. Her written work has been published in Thomas Walker's edited collection, *Nicaragua: The First Five Years*. Enriquez also coedits (with Michael E. Conroy) the *LASA—NICA Scholars News*. She now works for the Nicaraguan Food Program in Managua.

E.V.K. FITZGERALD
Institute of Social Studies, The Hague; Economic Advisor, Ministry of the Presidency, Nicaragua.

FitzGerald is a British development economist who worked in the Planning Ministries of Peru (1972—1975), Mexico (1975—1979), and Nicaragua (1980—1983) before becoming an economic advisor to Junta Coordinator (now President) Daniel Ortega in 1983. He is the author of *The Political Economy of Peru, 1956—1977* (Cambridge: Cambridge University Press, 1980); *Public Sector Investment Planning for Developing Countries* (New York: Holmes & Meier, 1978); and *The State and Economic Development: Peru Since 1968* (Cambridge: Cambridge University Press, 1976). His most recent work includes a chapter in Thomas Walker's edited volume *Nicaragua in Revolution* (New York: Praeger, 1982) and "The Problem of Balance in the Peripheral Socialist Economy: A Conceptual Note," *World Development* 13, 1 (1985):5—14.

BILL GIBSON
Department of Economics, University of Vermont.

Gibson is a U.S. economist whose work in macromodel building and marxian economic theory has been published in the *Journal of Development Economics*, *Review of Radical Political Economics*, and *Journal of Development Studies*. Since 1982 he has been an economic advisor to the Centro de Investigación y Estudios de la Reforma Agraria (CIERA) in Nicaragua. His published work on Nicaragua includes "A Structural Macromodel for Post-Revolutionary Nicaragua," *Cambridge Journal of Economics*, 9 (1985): 347—369.

ROBERTO PIZARRO
Advisor, Ministerio de Comercio Exterior in Nicaragua.

Pizarro is a Chilean economist who has worked in Nicaragua since 1980. Before coming to Nicaragua he held academic positions in Chile as Director of the Centro de Estudios Socio-Económicos and Dean of the Facultad de Economía Política at the Universidad de Chile, and in Argentina as Professor of the Facultad de Economía at the Universidad de Buenos Aires.

DAVID F. RUCCIO
Department of Economics and Helen Kellogg Institute for International Studies, University of Notre Dame.

Ruccio is a U.S. economist whose work on socialist planning and theories of development has appeared in *World Development* and elsewhere. His recent work includes a coedited volume entitled *Debt and Development in Latin America*. He is currently working on an economic history of Nicaragua during the period 1850 to 1979. In the Summers of 1985 and 1986 he worked as a visiting researcher at the Instituto de Investigaciones Económicas y Sociales in Nicaragua (INIES).

ROSE J. SPALDING
Department of Political Science, DePaul University.

Spalding is a U.S. political scientist who has worked in Mexico and Nicaragua. She began field work in Nicaragua in 1982 with financial support from the National Endowment for the Humanities. Her published work on Nicaragua includes "La expansión económica del estado en Nicaragua después de la revolución," *Foro internacional*, 25, 1 (1984):14–32; and "Food Politics and Agricultural Change in Revolutionary Nicaragua, 1979–1982" in John C. Super and Thomas C. Wright (eds.), *Food, Politics, and Society in Latin American* (Lincoln: University of Nebraska Press, 1985):199–227.

RICHARD STAHLER-SHOLK
Research Associate, Coordinadora Regional de Investigaciones Económicas y Sociales (CRIES), Nicaragua.

Stahler-Sholk is a Ph.D. candidate at the University of California, Berkeley. He has been working at CRIES in Nicaragua since October 1984. His published work includes an article on the Nicaraguan bourgeoisie in *Comparative Politics*; a chapter on the external economic constraints on the Nicaraguan revolution in Thomas Walker's collection *Nicaragua: The First Five Years*; and an article on organized labor in Nicaragua in Sheldon L. Maram and Gerald Michael Greenfield's forthcoming edited volume, *Latin American Labor Organizations*.

PETER UTTING
*Research Associate, Centro de Investigación y Estudios de la Reforma
Agraria (CIERA), Nicaragua.*

Utting is an Australian rural sociologist who has worked in Nicaragua at
CIERA since 1980. As an advisor to CIERA's food policy research group, he
has contributed to several CIERA documents on food production and distribution problems in Nicaragua. In 1986 he also worked at the United Nations
Research Institute for Social Development (UNRISD) in Geneva, Swizterland.

CARLOS M. VILAS
*Research Coordinator, Centro de Investigaciónes y Documentación de la
Costa Atlántica, Nicaragua.*

Vilas is an Argentine social scientist who has lived and worked in Nicaragua
since 1980. Before moving to Nicaragua he held academic positions in
Argentina, the Dominican Republic and Honduras, and worked for two years
in the ECLA office in Argentina. In Nicaragua he has worked for the Ministry of
Planning and CIDCA, and has served as a consultant for projects sponsored
by UNESCO, the ILO, and the OAS. His major recent publications on Nica-
ragua include *Perfiles de la Revolución Sandinista* (La Habana: Casa de las
Américas, 1984) [published in English as *The Sandinista Revolution: National
Liberation and Social Transformation in Central America* by Monthly Review
Press, 1986]; and *La Revolución en Nicaragua* (México: Ediciones ERA,
1985), coedited with Richard Harris [published in English as *Nicaragua: A
Revolution Under Siege* by Zed Books Ltd, 1985].

JOHN WEEKS
Department of Economics, American University.

Weeks is a U.S. economist who has published widely in the field of political
economy, with particular attention to Peru and Central America. In
1981–1982, he served as a consultant for several international development
agencies while working at the Ministry of Planning in Nicaragua. His most
recent published work on the region includes *The Economies of Central
America* (New York: Holmes & Meier, 1985); a chapter on the industrial
sector in Thomas Walker's collection, *Nicaragua: The First Five Years*; and
"Las elecciones nicaragüenses de 1984," *Foro internacional*, 26, 1 (1985).

Introduction

ROSE J. SPALDING

[I]deologically oriented leaderships in revolutionary crises . . . have typically ended up accomplishing very different tasks and furthering the consolidation of quite different kinds of new regimes than those they originally (and perhaps ever) ideologically intended. This should not seem surprising once we realize and reflect upon a straightforward truth: Revolutionary crises are *not* total breakpoints in history that suddenly make anything possible if only it is envisaged by willful revolutionaries!

Theda Skocpol, *States and Social Revolutions* (p. 171).

Men make their own history, but they do not make it just as they please.

Karl Marx, *The Eighteenth Brumaire of Louis Bonaparte* (p. 103).

Revolutions are distinguished from other social upheavals by the deeper aura of possibility that surrounds them. They focus human energy and vision on consciously changing the course of a nation's development. The established order gets turned on its head, and sweeping institutional change is unleashed. Pursuing social change, revolutions expand the state apparatus and deepen state penetration of civil society. If successful, this process promises both political transformation and a socioeconomic metamorphosis.

Efforts to transform a society, however, are riddled with complications. The experience of past revolutions shows that actual outcomes defy easy prediction or rigorous planning. The authors of a revolution may design a course of action, but the prospects for change remain bounded by the legacy of the past. Careful analysis of the process of transition reveals shifts and vacillations, as leaders and followers alike struggle with the complexities of profound social change. Recognizing this, we can begin to appreciate the complex ways in which the structural inheritance and immediate circumstances inform transitional options.

1

An array of factors delimits the possibilities for societal restructuration. The productive capacity that remains in the wake of revolutionary upheaval forms the first major constraint facing the revolutionary leaders. An impoverished and atomized economic order obviously limits the prospects for rapid transformation. Simultaneously, the structure and capacity of the state apparatus inherited from the deposed regime also shape the process of transition. A lopsided, underdeveloped state structure, plagued by a perennial scarcity of human and material resources, undercuts even modest planning aspirations. When the inherited bureaucratic infrastructure and fiscal base are inadequate, a long period of programmatic disarray and financial imbalance can result.

Established class relations also counter the revolution's redistributive impulse. The degree of control by the dominant class varies with the character of its resources and the pattern of its alliances. If control over wealth is concentrated and the economic elite is highly organized, this sector can use powerful material and organizational assets to impede change. Its capacity to confront the revolution is further heightened when it has forceful international and domestic alliances. International allies can provide psychological and material support for a sustained struggle over class hegemony; domestic allies allow the elite to claim representativeness, lending legitimacy to their opposition.

Vulnerabilities to and dependence on the international market further shape the course of revolutionary change. The depth of a country's insertion into the international economy, the degree of product or market specialization, and the level of dependence on external financing all affect its capacity for autonomous development. In countries with highly open, internationally penetrated economies, the revolutionary leadership faces special problems exercising control over the direction of change. Situational factors also affect the transition. The intensity of the imperialist impulse fluctuates over time, suggesting that the moment of the transition influences its outcome. In phases of heightened imperialist activism, interventions of regional powers seeking to impose their own definition on the revolution or, indeed, to destroy it undermine the development of any coherent revolutionary model. These and other factors influence the ultimate redefinition of the social order that transpires during the course of a revolution.

This book illustrates these tensions in the case of the recent Nicaraguan revolution. It looks beyond the highly general, simplistic arguments about the Sandinista ideology that have characterized much public discussion of Nicaragua. Hurled charges of "totalitarianism," "communism," and indeed even "Marxist-Leninism" have served more to mislead than to inform the debate about Nicaragua. Likewise, laudatory proclamations, derived from a sympathetic reading of the Sandinista vision, offer little insight into the concrete dynamics of change in Nicaragua. It is important now to raise the level of the discussion.

This book moves beyond the war of rhetoric to explore concretely the process of economic change in Nicaragua during the 1979—1985 period. Although the theoretical orientations, research methods, and emphases of the contributors vary, they have a shared commitment to a careful, empirical analysis of the revolutionary process. This collection describes both the revolution's plans and its short-term economic outcomes. In the process, it highlights both achievements and limitations and attempts to understand the dynamics of both.

In so doing, this work shows how the past intrudes on the present, delimiting options and shaping choices. It captures the tensions within and between various parts of the economic project and outlines the limitations on state economic capacity. It illustrates the powerful constraints rendered by the international political and economic context in which Nicaragua is embedded. The highly destructive impact of the U.S.-backed counterrevolutionary war is discussed repeatedly throughout the collection. In sum, this work attempts to clarify the internal and external obstacles that the revolution confronts daily. Ultimately, this book calls attention to the continuing debates within, and the enormous flexibility of, Nicaragua's political leadership, as it struggles to define and defend its revolutionary model.

Among the central questions that this work addresses are the following:

What theory of economic transformation did the Sandinistas embrace? What were the broad outlines of their new development model, and how did it differ from the economic model of the Somoza era? How has the model evolved in actual practice?

By the beginning of the twentieth century, the Nicaraguan economy was characterized by its openness to forces of the international market and its growing dependence on agricultural exports. Although Nicaragua's trade was somewhat more diversified and its land distribution less skewed than that of some other Central American nations, the country was still plagued by many of the problems common to the agroexport economic model. Cotton and coffee remained Nicaragua's dominant exports; these two crops generated between roughly 40 and 60% of total export earnings during the 1960s and 1970s, and fluctuating prices for these commodities took an economic toll. The urban, industrial expansion associated with the creation of the Central American Common Market in the 1960s did little to address economic imbalances. The new industries were not well integrated into the national economy and reinforced Nicaragua's vulnerability to external market forces.

Under control of the Somoza family (1936—1979), the Nicaraguan government took little responsibility for stimulating national economic development. In the first chapter of this book, entitled "A Structural Overview of the Nicaraguan Economy," Bill Gibson analyzes state economic policy during the Somoza era. This policy is found to be "classically liberal" and grounded on the theory of "comparative advantage," even in the face of recurring external shocks. The spasmodic economic intervention in which the government indulged had essentially private, nondevelopmental objectives. According to Gibson, it served either to fuel the Somoza "kleptocracy" or to maintain the regime's political control in the face of rising opposition. Indeed, Gibson concludes that, given the extreme openness of the economy, interventionist and countercyclical economic policies would probably have failed, producing only rising inflation and capital flight.

In contrast, the Sandinistas have pursued a policy of economic self-determination and redistribution. To achieve these objectives, they have attempted to reduce their susceptibility to external economic pressures by nationalizing the banking system and the commercialization of exports, introducing a system of import and exchange controls, and expanding their domestic tax base. Gibson concludes, however, that the structural economic constraints inherited from the Somoza period, combined with the massive destruction caused by the counterrevolutionary (*Contra*) war, have undermined this model. Instead, raging inflation, declining real wages, and rising foreign debt have confounded the transition process.

In the chapter entitled "The Mixed Economy in Nicaragua: The Economic Battlefield," John Weeks also analyzes the Sandinista economic model and the tensions that have emerged from it. The Sandinistas endorsed the concept of a "mixed economy" for Nicaragua and called for an eventual transition to socialism. Weeks looks first at the historical development of the "mixed economy" concept and then outlines the Nicaraguan variant of this model. He notes that, in most of Europe and Latin America, mixed economies have functioned, not as an impediment to capitalism, but at the behest of capital, sustaining and stimulating capitalist accumulation. In contrast, the mixed economy in revolutionary Nicaragua was designed to subordinate capital to "popular hegemony," acceding to capital's narrowest economic goals while denying its political objectives. The model permitted substantial private ownership and private profit, but it denied the capitalist class control over the state. Instead, the state was to function in a deliberately redistributive manner, according to the "logic of the majority."

Unlike analysts who focus on the variation within the Nicaraguan private sector, Weeks sees the Nicaraguan bourgeoisie as a highly cohesive class that quickly rejected this arrangement. Distrustful about the Sandinistas' willingness to control workers, hostile to restrictions on access to foreign currency, and resentful of competition for resources with expanding state enterprises, private capital withdrew from the model. He argues that the bourgeoisie turned to Washington for direction, as it had repeatedly throughout the nation's history, and joined forces with the CIA-backed counterrevolutionary forces (Contras) attempting to overthrow the Sandinista government. Although Weeks suspends judgment on the theoretical question of whether this confrontation was the inevitable result of the model or was simply an artifact of the particular character of the Nicaraguan bourgeoisie, he concludes that the Nicaraguan experience with the mixed economy model has been an unambiguous failure.

David Ruccio's chapter, "The State and Planning in Nicaragua," continues this effort to locate the Sandinista economic model within a larger theoretical context. He shifts the focus from the private sector toward the state itself and poses questions about the nature of a socialist transition. Ruccio rejects the a priori conclusion that Nicaragua has embarked on a transition to socialism. Although noting that the size of the state sector has expanded and that planning has been introduced, he argues that socialism is not easily reducible to these two ingredients and calls attention to the complex and contradictory effects that such changes may have.

Through a careful study of the economic planning process in Nicaragua, Ruccio identifies a series of problems that have impeded the development of coherent planning. Among them are ministerial "feudalism"; declining labor productivity (particularly in the state enterprises); continuing capital flight; and growing external and internal imbalances. The state's ability to act as the "center of accumulation" was further vexed by the extreme variability of the surplus (which fluctuated with international market conditions) and the state's weak extractive capacity. Thus the state is unable to play a directive role; indeed, it is increasingly preoccupied with simple survival. Given these circumstances, Ruccio finds that precise definition of the model and nature of economic transition in Nicaragua remains elusive.

What have been the development priorities of the Sandinista state? How did the new government respond to the classic dilemmas facing economic policymakers, such as the tension between industrial and agricultural development, domestic and export-oriented production, and accumulation versus distribution?

The Sandinistas came to power with a commitment to promote vigorous and sustained economic development, diminish foreign dependence, and reduce inequality in the distribution of resources. Yet how these goals were to be achieved was neither clear nor self-evident.

One issue to be resolved was the relative importance of industrial, as opposed to agricultural, development. As Claes Brundenius points out in his essay, "Industrial Development Strategies in Revolutionary Nicaragua," the industrial sector had been seriously damaged during the insurrection. Because of the importance of industry, both as a source of jobs and of productive output, state planners initially attempted to revive the sector. Yet they soon recognized that simple reactivation would only renew the structural imbalances that traditionally characterized the sector. A more fundamental reorientation was proposed that would strengthen forward and backward linkages and better integrate industry and agriculture.

Such structural transitions, however, were not easily achieved. Because it was heavily dependent on imported technology and raw materials, the industrial sector remained vulnerable to external crisis. The recent collapse of the Central American Common Market and the persistence of acute balance of payments problems seriously undercut industrial development. Although Brundenius remains optimistic about the medium and long-term prospects for industrial development and increased industrial trade with Cuba, the recent contraction of the sector and the erosion of ambitious agroindustrial projects complicate this transition.

As the primary source of food and foreign exchange, the agricultural sector gained renewed significance in the planning process. Still, questions remained about how resources were to be allocated within this sector. How much attention, for example, should be given to the long-neglected basic grain producers, who provided most of the national food supply, as opposed to the historically favored agroexport producers, who were the source of vital foreign exchange? How should resources (land, credit, foreign exchange, etc.) be allocated between the state farms and the private producers or between large and small private producers? Should price incentives for those who attained high levels of productivity be emphasized, or should the goal be to sustain those most marginalized?

In "Banking Systems and Revolutionary Change: The Politics of Agricultural Credit in Nicaragua," Laura J. Enriquez and Rose J. Spalding assess changing agricultural development priorities by examining shifts in the distribution of bank resources. Following the nationalization of the banking system in 1979, credit distribution became an important tool for state economic policymaking. Enriquez and Spalding show how the expansionary credit policy adopted by the state transformed an elite-oriented banking system into a mechanism for "democratizing" the distribution of credit. Individual peasants, cooperative members, and the newly established state farms absorbed a large and growing portion of the bank's resources. In contrast, the portion of credit received by larger private producers declined steadily with each passing year, reflecting changes in the economic structure and tensions in the mixed economic model.

Enriquez and Spalding identify two growing problems in the new credit program: (a) the continuing inability of the banking system to penetrate fully into the peasant economy; and (b) the bank's inability to regenerate adequate internal resources for its continued operation. As low interest rates, problems with loan recuperation, and periodic debt clearings limited the bank's funds, continuing credit expansion was increasingly financed by emissions from the Central Bank of Nicaragua. The results were inflationary, with increasingly destabilizing consequences for the national economy.

Concern about tensions and trade-offs that characterize revolutionary economic policy also undergirds Peter Utting's essay, "Domestic Supply and Food Shortages." Utting's central question is: How is it that food shortages and rising food prices have become such prominent features of Nicaraguan life, when the Sandinista government appears committed to a "basic needs" approach? He provides a multifaceted answer, analyzing changes in both food supply and demand. In terms of supply, government efforts to dismantle the old credit, labor, and marketing systems, before it was capable of replacing them, led to a disarticulation of the peasant production process. Furthermore, the lure of expanded opportunities combined with the dislocations of war and military service led to massive urban migration and acute agricultural labor shortages. Along with growing trade imbalances and decreased access to food imports, these factors contributed to a reduced supply of several basic foods.

Simultaneously, government commitments to address the basic needs of the population led to programs favoring increased consumption. The state established hefty food subsidies, improved food distribution systems, and created an array of nutrition programs. The resulting disjuncture between supply and demand gave rise to speculation, hoarding, bottlenecks, and shortages. Ultimately this undermined the state distribution system and triggered spiraling food costs. Utting's essay, like those of Enriquez and Spalding and of Brundenius, illustrates the immense complexity of the effort to restructure subsystems of the national economy in the context of ingrained poverty, intersectoral disarticulation, deepening resource shortages, and external pressures.

What impact has the international context had on the political economy of the revolution? How have the Sandinistas grappled with the problems of foreign dependence? What options have been created, and what pressures brought to bear?

The Sandinistas inherited a national economy that was acutely dependent on trade, highly vulnerable to international economic pressures, and strongly tied to the United States. A central theme in their revolutionary program was the importance of increased national autonomy. This commitment to reduce Nicaragua's external vulnerability presented them with a major challenge.

The new government launched a series of infrastructural development projects that it hoped, in the long run, would raise agricultural production, reduce dependence on imported energy, and increase the domestic process- ing of agricultural products. Once completed, these projects had the potential to produce a more nationally centered economic model. In the short run, however, reduced dependence could only mean diversified dependence. To achieve what autonomy they could, the Sandinistas began the search for new exchange and alliance relations.

As Richard Stahler-Sholk notes in his essay, "Foreign Debt and Economic Stabilization Policies in Revolutionary Nicaragua," the Somoza government had engaged in heavy foreign borrowing. Indeed, on coming to power, the Sandinistas inherited the highest debt/GDP ratio in Latin America. In the first three years under the revolutionary government, much of that debt was renegotiated, and both multilateral and bilateral lenders provided substantial new development assistance. The Sandinistas succeeded in securing bilateral financing that crossed geopolitical lines, drawing on resources from Western Europe and Latin America as well as the socialist countries.

Yet Stahler-Sholk finds that intense pressure from the Reagan administra- tion soon undercut new multilateral and private bank loans, just as continued capital flight and trade imbalances provoked a liquidity crisis. New bilateral loans also declined and soon proved to be insufficient to sustain productive expansion. As problems mounted, Stahler-Sholk notes that foreign assistance came increasingly in the form of lines of credit from friendly governments rather than liquid foreign exchange, making it more difficult to cover priority needs as they were defined by the Sandinista government. He also finds a heightened lending role for a declining number of countries, with Mexico and, more recently, the socialist countries playing a key part. Describing the contracting investment and production bottlenecks that resulted, Stahler- Sholk highlights the deep dilemmas associated with the search for adequate external financing in the context of revolutionary change.

Michael Conroy, in his "Patterns of Changing External Trade in Revolu- tionary Nicaragua: Voluntary and Involuntary Trade Diversification," also explores the Sandinista quest for autonomy, examining the push for increased diversification of both markets and products. He finds that the revolutionary government made significant progress toward the diversification of its trade markets in the first three years. The previous concentration of trade with the United States and the Central American Common Market was reduced; markets in other Latin American countries and socialist nations expanded.

After 1982, however, as pressures from the United States built, progress toward diversification was halted. Conroy finds that increased agroindustrial production and the cultivation of new export crops proved unobtainable. Export patterns tended to reconcentrate around a small number of products (particularly cotton and coffee) and markets (now with Japan playing a prominent role). In the face of escalating rhetoric about the neutrality and efficiency of a laissez-faire international market system, Conroy's work presents harsh evidence of the international market's highly politicized and coercive nature. This essay highlights the immense complexity of structural trade change in a small, open, and peripheral economy.

Evidence of these and other economic costs of the Reagan administration's policies toward Nicaragua is compiled systematically in E. V. K. FitzGerald's "An Evaluation of the Economic Costs to Nicaragua of U.S. Aggression: 1980–1984." His essay draws heavily on the documentation gathered by the Nicaraguan government for its case against the United States in the International Court of Justice at the Hague. Using quantitative data from the Economic Commission on Latin America, the World Bank, and the Nicaraguan Secretariat of Planning and the Budget, FitzGerald makes counterfactual projections to estimate what Nicaragua's investment rate, production, balance of payments, foreign loans, and inflation rate would have been in the absence of U.S. hostility.

According to these estimates, under "normal" circumstances, the Nicaraguan economy would now be functioning with a healthy rate of growth and without serious economic imbalances. This suggests that the Sandinistas' inability to realize development objectives was not the inevitable result of the country's poverty nor inherent contradictions in the planning model nor the routine workings of an unfavorable international market. Instead, FitzGerald argues that the primary explanation for Nicaragua's current economic problems is the illegal intervention of the United States. Responsiblity for the disequilibrium that now characterizes the Nicaraguan economy is located squarely in the White House.

What is the outlook for the Sandinista development project? How might the government respond to the legacy of economic imbalances, the knotty tensions that arise from recent policy developments, and the devastating pressures that emanate from abroad? What might the future bring?

All of the essays in this collection raise and address the preceding questions, but two chapters focus on them most directly. Roberto Pizarro's "The New Economic Policy: A Necessary Readjustment" analyzes the controversial economic adjustment measures announced in February 1985, arguing that this package of policy changes was an important first step toward addressing the imbalances in the system. He notes that economic policies adopted in the first five years frequently had negative side effects that exacerbated inefficiency or undermined production. An exchange rate policy that overvalued the national currency artificially cheapened many imports (thus encouraging waste), while reducing earnings for export crops (thus discouraging production). Subsidies and price controls fed the explosive growth of a "parasitic economy" in which street vendors selling candies or soft drinks made more money than the heads of government ministries.

The 1985 adjustment was, he argues, vital for national economic stability. The new emphasis on efficiency, tying wages to production, cutting government spending, eliminating subsidies on basic consumer goods, raising taxes, and adjusting the exchange rate were all measures that were long overdue. Pizarro concludes, however, that although these changes were positive, economic imbalances have become deeply entrenched in Nicaragua and will now be very difficult to eliminate.

Finally, Carlos Vilas reflects on the array of problems found in the Nicaraguan economy in his chapter, "Troubles Everywhere: An Economic Perspective on the Sandinista Revolution." He argues that, other than the broad commitment to national unity, a mixed economy, and international nonalignment, the Sandinistas seem to have "no principled commitments to particular economic policies nor to courses of specific action." This creates a capacity for sharp policy change and pragmatic reversals.

Vilas finds that the general economic strategy, with its continued emphasis on export agriculture, has made the system vulnerable to external pressures and private sector sabotage and may eventually lead to an erosion of the social base of the revolution. He recommends that the Sandinistas now shift toward a more nation-centered development model, giving greater priority to domestic self-sufficiency, the needs of the peasantry, local-level planning, and mass participation in economic decisions. Evidence of increased attention to the peasantry in 1985 and 1986 in the form of additional land redistribution and rural wage and price adjustments is presented as a desirable development. Yet Vilas concludes that revolutionary economies during the period of transition are ultimately not viable economies; their survival depends on their ability to secure substantial external support from friendly governments for a considerable period of time.

Although the analysts contributing to this collection offer numerous observations and suggestions, none offers magical solutions to the multiple conundrums facing the Nicaraguan revolution. There is a broad agreement that the cessation of the counterrevolutionary war is a central starting point for any measure of economic progress. Beyond that, the reigning contradictions and dislocations must be a matter of internal discussion and negotiation, as the revolutionary leadership continues its search for a viable economic strategy.

These essays together shed considerable light on the process of economic change in Nicaragua. They help to define the broad outlines of this variant of a "mixed economy" and to identify the pressures under which it operates. They provide a picture of the priority sectors, the internal debates, and the policy tools used by the state. The complex and sometimes contradictory goals and methods of the political leadership are more clearly illuminated.

Such carefully wrought analyses can help us to understand the multiple contradictions and apparently anomalous developments in the Nicaraguan revolution. They can explain why many problems that predated the revolution, such as heavy dependence on foreign trade, continue to exist. They clarify the dynamics behind soaring food prices and falling real wages, in a country where the government is formally committed to providing for the citizenry's basic needs. They help disentangle the relationship between the internal and external pressures on the revolution.

In the process, we see how the interplay between choice and constraint shapes a revolutionary economic "model." These lessons from the Nicaraguan experience can be combined with the theoretical insights drawn from observing revolutions in Mexico, Bolivia, Cuba, and Peru (or perhaps several African states) to construct a broader theory of economic development and revolutionary change. Such careful analysis helps us to understand revolution, not as an apocalyptic event directed by omnipotent ideologues, but as an ongoing human struggle.

REFERENCES

Marx, Karl. *The Eighteenth Brumaire of Louis Bonaparte*. In Karl Marx and Frederick Engels, *Collected Works*, Vol. 11. New York: International Publishers, 1979.

Skocpol, Theda. *States and Social Revolutions*. Cambridge: Cambridge University Press, 1979.

PART I

OVERVIEW OF THE NEW ECONOMIC MODEL

Chapter 1

A Structural Overview of the Nicaraguan Economy

BILL GIBSON

When a column of 1000 Sandinista troops marched victoriously into Managua on July 19, 1979, it seemed to all that this small Central American nation was on the brink of an historic transformation. The 34-year dictatorship of the Somoza family was at last broken, and the hated National Guard was disbanded. The very conception of what Nicaragua was—a "banana republic"[1] subservient to U.S. political and economic interests—was shattered. Gone was Somoza's "crony capitalism" that had served to enrich his friends and associates while impoverishing the large majority of the people. It was now within the power of the architects of the Sandinista revolution to change the basic structures of the society. Three principles illuminated the path forward: popular participation, political nonalignment, and a mixed economy.

Now 7 years after the insurrection, the euphoria of victory has given way to the labor of reconstruction and renewed struggle for self-determination. The Sandinistas have found it much easier to make a revolution than to manage a war economy, especially at time in which the prices of Nicaragua's principal exports have collapsed and a third of export earnings goes to service the foreign debt.[2] The fear is that the revolution will stumble under the weight of external pressure and the Sandinistas will renege on their promise to erect a just, equitable, and democratic society. In the years since the revolution, the Sandinistas have clearly tested the limits of the possible within the framework

---

1. Nicaragua was never literally a "banana republic." A combination of bad weather, labor unrest, and disease forced foreign banana plantation owners to abandon their operations until after World War II. Since then, banana export earnings have been only about 1–2% of the total. The term is nevertheless appropriate for its political connotation.
2. For more details, see the chapter in this collection by Stahler-Sholk.

defined by their three guiding principles. Although it is true that Nicaragua has undergone a profound transformation, there are many basic features of the economy that the Sandinistas are powerless to change. Nicaragua remains a poor, underdeveloped country in which policymakers struggle with many of the same dilemmas of economic development which plagued their predecessors.

This chapter is concerned with questions of basic economic structure and how it has evolved under the leadership of the Frente Sandinista. The chapter provides an overview of the changing structure, problems, and policies of the Nicaraguan economy, beginning with the Somocista period. The following section focuses on the nature of the agroexport model, how it was managed under Somoza, and the impact of the model on the people of Nicaragua. By diverting resources to a small class of wealthy landowners (which included the family itself), the Somoza dictatorship intensified the social contradictions that ultimately led to the insurrection of 1979. The third section broadly outlines the nature of the structural change brought about by the Sandinistas. It is argued that the secret of the relative autonomy enjoyed since the revolution lies in the Sandinistas' ability to control Nicaragua's participation in the world economy. Through the nationalization of the banking system and foreign trade, Nicaragua has so far escaped the grip of the international financial system. The conclusion of the chapter argues that it is ironically the successes of the Sandinistas that pose the ultimate threat to their existence. Indeed, whether Nicaraguans remain in control of their country now largely depends on the international reaction to the Sandinistas' challenge to the traditional means of North–South domination.

THE SOMOZA ERA: COMPARATIVE ADVANTAGE AND PASSIVE MACROPOLICY

A Conceptual Model

It is appropriate to conceptualize the Nicaraguan economy in three broad sectors—agriculture, manufacturing, and commerce—though special caveats apply to each. Agriculture is the engine of growth of the economy in that it is responsible for the lion's share of vital export earnings. This sector consists of a modern, capital-intensive agroexport subsector and a backward, traditional domestic subsector that produces basic wage goods. The agroexport sector depends upon imported intermediate and capital goods and absorbs a disproportionate share of domestic resources, with the exception of labor. Traditionally, export agriculture has been technically advanced; productivity in the food sector, on the other hand, has been by and large at a standstill. Because of productivity differences, total agricultural supply depends not only upon the quantity of land brought under cultivation but also on the mix between the export and domestic market crops. Value added is also influenced by the degree to which agricultural raw materials are processed. The degree of processing increases as the economy matures.

The market price for the agricultural sector does not freely fluctuate to balance supply and demand, but it does vary with the international terms of trade, the exchange rate as well as explicit terms-of-trade policy. Because output in this sector is a weighted average of domestic and export production, exports may be thought of as the equilibrating variable after domestic demand is subtracted from agricultural production. It follows that exports may be increased through a variety of means, ranging from more favorable international terms of trade, to a devaluation to a "cheap food" policy that provides an incentive to shift land from the domestic to the export sector. Note that a fall in employment or a regressive redistribution of income achieves the same effect of increasing exports.

Agriculture provides hard currency earnings for a relatively smaller manufacturing sector, a sector devoted to home-good production and limited nontraditional exports. Nicaraguan manufacturing, as in many Third World countries, consists largely of assembly and mixing processes with extremely high import content. Supply in this sector therefore depends upon the foreign exchange allocated to it and the efficiency with which foreign and domestic inputs are utilized. A substantial fraction of the manufacturing sector may be considered "formal" in that firms hire labor, keep books, pay taxes and duties, and generally operate according to the principles of rational capitalist management. Operating alongside the formal sector is the larger "informal" component of the economy, which consists mostly of commerce, petty commodity production, and services.[3] The objective of the informal sector is less to maximize profits on invested capital than to simply survive in the context of limited formal sector employment opportunities and the miserable conditions of traditional agriculture in the countryside.[4] Productivity in the informal sector is low, and there is little access to capital or imported inputs. Wage labor is not as prevalent as are independent proprietors. Labor in the informal sector acts as an industrial reserve army, satisfying the needs of the formal sector when called upon.

The dynamics of the Somoza economy were guided by the classical theory of comparative advantage, a theory that points out that a country can grow richer if it devotes more of its national resources to what it does best. Even in

---

3. Of course, not all manufacturing is formal nor are all of services and commerce informal, but the distinction is nevertheless useful in constructing an overview of how the economy functions.
4. See data on rural income distribution.

the abstract, the rewards of trade along the lines of comparative advantage need not accrue to all social classes equally. Comparative advantage only guarantees that winners can afford to bribe losers into accepting the arrangement. As in all struggles over income distribution, however, these bribes will not be forthcoming unless the losers are sufficiently powerful to enforce the agreement. In the Third World, where comparative advantage most often rules, the pattern of trade specialization works in favor of owners of scarce capital or land. It works against workers and peasants without access to the jobs and markets of the export sector. Due to the capital-intensive, enclave nature of the export sector, specialization is often itself the cause of unemployment, which undermines the ability of the displaced to press claims for a share in the gains from trade.

Economic Structure

With the exception of its brief experience in the Central American Common Market (CACM), Nicaragua serves as a textbook example of how comparative advantage plays itself out in practice. From the nineteenth century to the Great Depression, Nicaragua's principal exports were indigo, cocoa, and especially coffee from the rich north-central highlands. When demand for primary goods collapsed in the 1930s, Nicaragua exported gold, which in 1940 accounted for 60% of total exports.[5] Through the interwar period to the mid-1950s, Nicaragua's exports essentially consisted of two crops—coffee and bananas. With the cotton boom of the early 1950s, however, the economy underwent a profound transformation. First Luis Somoza, then his younger brother Anastasio Somoza directed the transition from an isolated, backward, and stagnant economy to a more dynamic capitalist economy, that was fully integrated into the world market. Exports diversified somewhat into sugar and beef (and later tobacco and shellfish) as the government took an active role in promoting agroindustrialization and import substitution industrialization. Producers became more price responsive and capitalist in their outlook. In 1950–1951, the area sown to cotton tripled when its world price doubled; cotton passed coffee as the leading dollar crop in 1955.[6] Cotton and coffee accounted for more than half of Nicaragua's export earnings until 1969, as can be seen from Figure 1.

Throughout the 1950s and the decades to follow, large-scale agroexporters displaced small basic grain producers from the fertile volcanic soil of the

5. See Jaime Wheelock, *Entre la crisis y la agresión: La reforma agraria sandinista* (Managua: Communicaciones, MIDINRA, 1984), 119.
6. See Jaime Biderman, *Class Structure, The State and Capitalist Development in Nicaraguan Agriculture* (Ph.D. dissertation, University of California, Berkeley, 1982), 62.

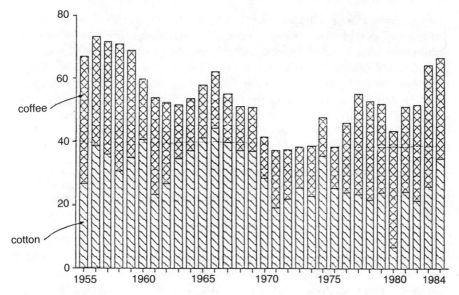

Figure 1. Cotton and coffee exports (percent of total). *Sources*: 1954–59, Dirección General de Estadísticas (DGE); 1961, *Resumen estadística* (Managua: DGE, 2nd. ed., 1961), p. 90; 1960–79, Banco Central de Nicaragua *Indicadores económicos* 1, no. 2 (December, 1979): 75, 82; 1980–83, Wheelock, *Entre la crisis y la agresión*, p. 144; 1984, CIERA *Informe anual de 1984* (Managua: CIERA, 1985), p. 83. Note: cotton seed and instant coffee excluded.

Pacific Plain to the Central Highlands and to the thin, leached lands of the agricultural frontier in the Atlantic coastal region. The growth in cotton cultivation repeated the pattern established by the rise of coffee, except that the highly capitalist nature of Pacific Coast farming reduced peasant participation in export earnings.[7] Small- and medium-sized producers accounted for more than two-thirds of coffee production but only a third of cotton.[8]

Land holdings concentrated rapidly. Between 1952 and 1978, the total area cultivated increased by 162%, whereas the number of farms increased by only 62%.[9] The proportion of land held by large commercial farmers (holdings greater than 500 manzanas) increased from 40% in 1952 to 48% in 1978. Holdings from 10 to 99.9 manzanas declined by 14% and the propor-

7. The class structure in coffee production is still highly diverse in comparison to cotton. For details, see Michael Zalkin, *Peasant Response to State Grain Policy in Post-Revolutionary Nicaragua* (Ph.D. dissertation, University of Massachusetts, Amherst, 1986).
8. Solon Barraclough, *A Preliminary Analysis of the Nicaraguan Food System* (Geneva: United Nations Research Institute for Social Development, 1982), 52.
9. *Ibid.*, 22.

tion in *minifundia* (less than 10 manzanas) decreased by nearly half.[10] In the three provinces of Chinandega, León, and Managua, the area planted to cotton rose from 14% to 62% of the total between 1952 and 1964.[11] Peasants were bought out and sometimes forcibly evicted by the emerging landed aristocracy with the assistance of the National Guard and local police. Much of the land fell into the hands of the Somoza family itself. Leopoldo Salazar, one of the original officers of the National Guard, explains how it was done:

> [Somoza] never stole any properties. The properties were sold to him, some-times for nothing. For instance, when he bought Montelimar, this old German gentleman came to him and he said, "Look, here, I own Montelimar—several thousand acres, beautiful. But I have a thousand squatters there and if I try to take them out they will kill me, so here, you take the place," and he sold it for a song. Of course, Somoza, with his National Guardsmen, he got everybody out and he became owner of Montelimar.[12]

The best and most accessible land went to the biggest growers who sold their crops on the world market rather than producing food for home con-sumption. The total area sown to food rose, but per capita food production declined to the point that rural Nicaraguans were the most underfed in the region.[13] Because the demand for labor was limited to the three harvest months of the year, the dispossesed peasantry was forced to migrate either to the agricultural frontier provinces or to Managua to become part of the urban informal sector. Those that stayed tried to eke out a living on small, marginal plots and looked for temporary work on the large estates. By 1978, 37% of the rural economically active population was landless, almost half of which could not find full-time employment.[14]

As a whole, acreage devoted to export agriculture increased from about 25% of total land in production in 1950 to 50% in 1977.[15] Agricultural production increased by 250%, but agroexports rose ninefold with cotton exports increasing from an 1948–1952 average of 3.6 thousand tons to 131.7 thousand tons in 1978.[16] In the same period, coffee exports more than tripled, and sugar exports rose from 6.3 to 104.9 thousand tons. At least for

10. *Ibid.*
11. Biderman, *Class Structure*, 64.
12. Shirley Christian, *Revolution in the Family* (New York: Random House, 1985), 22.
13. The results of a survey taken by INCAP (the Central American Nutritional Institute) as cited in Richard W. O. Lethander, *The Economy of Nicaragua* (Ph.D. dissertation, Duke University, 1968), and Biderman, *Class Structure*, 83.
14. Carmen Diana Deere, Peter Marchetti, and Nola Reinhardt, "The Peasantry and the Devel-opment of Sandinista Agrarian Policy, 1979–84," *Latin American Research Review* 20. no. 3 (1985): 78.
15. Barraclough, *A Preliminary Analysis*, 19.
16. *Ibid.*, 19.

the case of cotton, export expansion was land extensive rather than intensive. Indeed, there has been no statistically significant increase in cotton yields since 1960.[17] Coffee, however, has increased intensively as well as extensively: yields rose fairly steadily from 1960 through the revolution, but have declined since 1983 with the shortage of skilled pickers due to the war.

Fiscally pampered and subject to the "hothouse" effect of the protected Central American Common Market, both traditional and nontraditional exports accelerated throughout the postwar period. The domestic agricultural sector, on the other hand, stagnated. Somoza followed a "cheap food" policy designed not only to maintain low urban wages but also to force peasants to provide peak-period harvest labor to supplement their nominal incomes. By means of stopgap imports (up to 25% of corn production and 10% of bean production[18]), Somoza held down the price of basic grains to the point that production stagnated. Terms of trade were consistently turned against domestic agriculture with prices of Nicaraguan basic grains running below those of the world market.[19] Small food producers were systematically denied access to the state resources in the form of agricultural credit, inputs, and technical assistance. Favorable exchange rate policies, tariffs, and terms of trade all encouraged the reallocation of land to serve international rather than domestic markets.

As the capital-intensive agroexport sector encroached upon land previously devoted to food crops, large quantities of labor were released. In theory, this labor can be allocated to other productive activities and should not constitute a drag on economic activity. In the orthodox "export-led-growth" scheme, displaced labor is employed in industry. The foreign ex-

17. Regression run on data from Banco Central de Nicaragua, *Indicadores económicos* 5, 1979, 74. The 1950s showed a dramatic increase in yields from 1400 lbs/manzana in 1950−51 to 3168 lbs/manzana in 1958−59; see Biderman, *Class Structure*, Appendix, Table 6. The stagnation in yields is primarily due to monocultivation with increasing applications of DDT and methyl parathion, up to twenty applications per year. See World Bank, *The Challenge of Reconstruction* (Washington, DC: World Bank, Report No. 3524−Nx1, 1981), p. 39, and Joseph Collins et al., *Nicaragua: What Difference Could a Revolution Make?* 2d. ed. (San Francisco: Food First, 1985), pp. 161−166 for details of the social costs of pesticide-intensive cultivation. Although the source material is not cited, Collins notes that between 1962−72 there were 3,000 reported pesticide poisonings; there were 383 fatalities in 1969−70 harvest season alone. Both Collins and the World Bank agree that cotton's potential as a foreign exchange earner is limited by high foreign exchange production costs. Collins refers to a 1977 UN study that computed the annual environmental and human health damage at $200 million (p. 162), whereas cotton export earnings peaked at $150.6 mn. in 1977−78. See Banco Central de Nicaragua, *Indicadores*, 75. Since the insurrection, the government has eliminated or reduced imports of DDT and other organochlorides and has turned to crop rotation and biological pest management to raise yields.
18. Banco Central, *Indicadores*, 79−80. These maxima were reached in the 1973−74 season due in part to the earthquake of the preceding year.
19. Barraclough, *A Preliminary Analysis*, 38.

change needed to import capital and intermediate goods for industrial growth is supplied by the expanding agroexport sector. With constant or declining capital-labor ratios in the nonagricultural sectors, relatively balanced growth can be achieved. Any surplus population can be temporarily held in traditional agriculture or the urban informal sector. Steadily growing formal-sector employment is then the counterpart of the comparative advantage strategy.

In Nicaragua, this happy scenario has not fully played itself out. The rise of agroexports has certainly displaced labor: The percentage of the labor force employed in agriculture has fallen steadily in the postwar period, even though agricultural activities have consistently generated about a fourth of national income. Table 1 shows the percentage of the agricultural economically active population (EAP) falling 27 percentage points from 1950 to 1980. The percentage change in manufacturing is much smaller, rising from 14.5% in 1950, to just over a fifth of the labor force in 1980. On the other hand, the percentage of the labor force absorbed in the tertiary sectors, commerce, and services has more than doubled.

Manufacturing's limited contribution to employment growth was due to its extreme capital intensity, a problem common to many Third World countries that import capital goods designed for the relatively labor-constrained economies of the North. Measured in terms of value added, however, manufacturing was by far the most "dynamic" sector. In 1960, the share of manufacturing was 16%, but by 1978, it accounted for a fourth of national income.[20] During this same period, real GDP grew by 164%, whereas the manufacturing sector increased more than threefold.[21] Growth was spurred by the

TABLE 1
The Structure of the Economically Active Population (EAP)

	1950	1960	1970	1980
Agriculture	68.8	62.0	51.9	41.8
Manufacturing[a]	14.5	15.9	18.7	20.7
Commerce, Services[b]	16.7	22.1	29.4	37.5
Total	100.0	100.0	100.0	100.0

Source: Based on data from PREALC, "Mercados de trabajo en cifras 1950–1980," as cited in CIERA, Managua es Nicaragua (Managua: CIERA, 1984), 23, and the author's own calculations.
[a]Includes mining, construction, and electricity.
[b]Includes transportation.

20. Banco Central, Indicadores, 16.
21. Ibid., 16.

formation of the CACM in the 1960s. During the period 1960–1978, food processing and agricultural chemicals destined for the CACM made up approximately two-thirds of manufacturing value added. The CACM protection promoted severe excess capacity, with utilization rates rarely exceeding 70%.[22] Although productivity was low, profits were high: In 1968, gross profits were 45.6% of Nicaraguan manufacturing assets, the highest in the CACM.[23]

Table 2 is more revealing of the structural shifts that have occurred in the Nicaraguan economy during the postwar period. In 1950, 62.4% of the agricultural labor force was employed on modern farms but by 1980, the percentage had actually fallen to 43.1%. During the same period, value added in the predominantly modern agroexport sector rose from a quarter to half the total.[24] For the urban sectors, 42.6% of the labor force was employed in the informal sector in 1950. By 1980, the figure had *risen* to 48.6%. Contrary to the expectations of traditional "export-led growth" predictions, Table 2 portrays an economy that increasingly marginalized its labor force. Resources were concentrated in the hands of those most subservient to the world market. As will be seen in the next section, the aggregate data on economic performance were dazzling. The internal dislocations caused by the distorted pattern of growth, however, would ultimately have to be redressed.

TABLE 2
Sectoral Composition: EAP

	1950	1960	1970	1980
Rural				
Modern	62.4	54.0	49.9	43.1
Traditional	37.6	46.0	50.1	56.9
Total	100.0	100.0	100.0	100.0
Urban				
Formal	57.4	60.4	57.0	51.4
Informal	42.6	39.6	43.0	48.6
Total	100.0	100.0	100.0	100.0

Source: Based on data from PREALC, "Mercados de trabajo en cifras 1950–1980," as cited in CIERA, *Managua es Nicaragua* (Managua: CIERA, 1984), 23.

22. James Rudolph, *Nicaragua: A Country Study* (Washington, D.C.: USGPO, 1982), p. 134.
23. *Ibid.*, 134.
24. Barraclough, *A Preliminary Analysis*, 19.

Economywide Performance

Between 1950 and 1977 real economic output tripled. During the 1950s, the economy expanded at an average annual rate of 5.8%. In the 1960s this rose to 8.7%, but slowed in the 1970s to 5.5%.[25] Figure 2 shows per capita GDP (in terms of 1980 prices) for the period 1951 to 1984 and then projections to 1990. This graph is striking in its portrayal of growth in per-capita GDP up until 1977 and then its collapse during the revolution. Between 1950 and 1977, per capita GDP doubled, but since the insurrection, income has yet to regain mid-1960s levels. Figure 2 shows the familiar cyclical swings that characterize a capitalist economy. As the export drive took off, the economy grew rapidly in the immediate postwar period but then slumped in the late 1950s along with rest of the world economy. Per capita growth resumed in the early 1960s but was followed by mild recessions in 1967, 1968, and 1970.

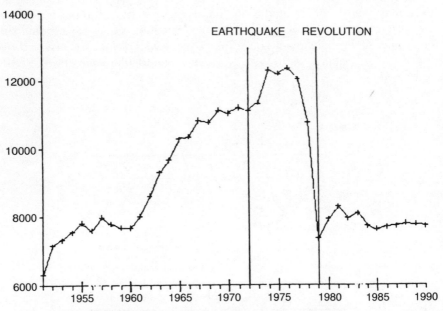

Figure 2. GDP per capita (1980 córdobas). *Sources*: 1951–1977, International Monetary Fund, *International Financial Statistics*, 366–7; 1978–1990, CIERA (internal documents), and World Bank, *The Challenge of Reconstruction*, p. 72.

25. International Monetary Fund, *International Financial Statistics* (Washington, DC: IMF, 1981), 365.

Contributing to the swings in per capita GDP was a pattern of fluctuating investment. For the boom period 1950–1959, the rate of investment was 14.9% of GDP, with 3.8% coming from the public sector. Then in the mid-1960s, with the rise of the CACM, investment accelerated to approximately a fifth of GDP.[26] The public sector component remained small at 5.6% of GDP on average for the same period, roughly comparable to other countries of the region. Real capital spending as a proportion of the total central government budget was stable until the 1972 earthquake at around 2% of GDP and then 4–6% thereafter. But half of public investment from the earthquake until 1977 went to rebuilding government offices and therefore made little contribution to productive capacity.[27] Generally, capital outlays by the central government were devoted to infrastructure and transfers to other governmental organizations.

Investment is decomposed into private, foreign, and government savings in Figure 3, showing that private savings financed the bulk of accumulation in the prerevolutionary period. The share of savings provided by foreigners was small (less than 10%) until after the earthquake. There were few restrictions on foreign investment and from 1960 to 1977, foreigners accounted for 30% of investment in manufacturing and agricultural processing. As a result of the liberalization of trade in the region, foreigners provided more growth capital than did domestic banks between 1962 and 1969.[28] Note that after 1974, foreign savings virtually disappeared—capital flight immediately preceding the insurrection was recently estimated at $518 million.[29] Government savings (calculated as government revenues minus *current* government expenditures) were kept well under 10% through most of the Somoza era. The 1972 earthquake ushered in a period of increasing government deficits, however, that lasted until the revolution.

Monetary and Fiscal Policies

One of the main implications of the structure of the Nicaraguan economy as described in the conceptual model presented in the preceding section is that it offers little scope for the Keynesian demand management policies that are regularly employed in advanced capitalist countries. Instead of seeking to

26. The average for the period between 1960 and 1978 was 19.7% of GDP (Banco Central, *Indicadores*, 15).
27. Banco de América, "Inversión desde 1958," *Actividad económica* (March, 1979):2.
28. Rudolph, *Nicaragua*, 133.
29. INIES, "La economía nicaragüense: Un balance necasario," *Pensamiento propio* 15 (July, 1984): 19.

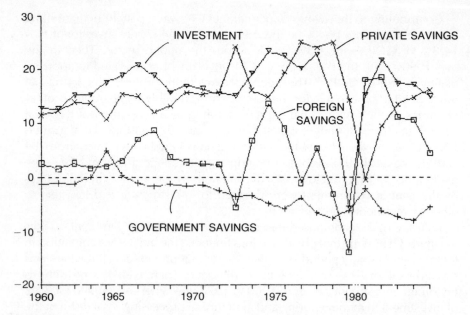

Figure 3. Savings decomposition (percentage of GDP). *Sources:* 1960–78, Banco Central de Nicaragua, *Indicadores económicos,* pp 18, 37; 1978–82, CEPAL, *Notas para el estudio económico de América Latina, 1983, Nicaragua* (México: CEPAL, 1984), p. 42.; 1982–84, MIPLAN, "Plan Económico 1985," (Managua, 1984), p. 87.

counteract the impact of dislocations in the world economy, government policy acts rather as a conduit of instability. The Somozas were well aware of the interconnection between public sector spending and balance of payments crises, which they sought to avoid through careful control of the money supply and the government account. Within its own framework, the government was virtually powerless to resist external shocks (such as the fall in the international terms of trade in the late 1950s and again in the late 1960s) that diminished the economy's foreign exchange earning capacity. Without foreign borrowing or some form of external aid, the formal manufacturing sector contracted with the shortage of foreign inputs. The informal sector would then expand to absorb the surplus population. Were the government to intercede in order to counteract the contraction, matters would only be made worse. Any increase in government spending would accelerate inflation, with consequent appreciation of the real exchange rate (defined as the ratio of domestic to foreign prices). Exports would fall, and the demand for domestic goods increase, causing further balance of payments difficulties. Thus expansionary government policy would stimulate rather than retard the growth of the informal sector and, moreover, exacerbate the fall in the real wage due to the inflation it would provoke.

Consequently, the Somoza regime made little explicit attempt to use monetary and fiscal policy as a means of stabilizing the economy. Except for intervention on behalf of Somoza himself or his associates, state policies were classically liberal. Capital and commodity markets were kept open and free, the currency was convertible at a rate that balanced payments, and government expenditure was limited by tax revenues. Throughout the prerevolutionary period, the money supply was seen as entirely passive, with the quantity of credit determined by the real-sector flows and shifting public demand for liquidity. The Central Bank's objective was to maintain its foreign reserves intact by limiting the creation of domestic assets in periods of low export earnings. A rise in the money supply with convertible currency and inelastically supplied nontradables clearly conflicted with sound balance-of-payments management in the minds of the conservative central bankers.[30] No amount of monetary stimulus could rejuvenate a sluggish economy because emissions would simply be converted into dollars and sent to foreign bank accounts.

Table 3 indicates how conservative state intervention into the economy was under the Somoza regime. First, the government's share of output remained below 10% throughout the entire prerevolutionary period. In the 1950s, the fiscal deficit was never above 2% of GDP and between 1950 and 1965, there was a budget surplus for 11 of the 15 years.[31] In the 1960s and early 1970s, foreign borrowing financed approximately two-thirds of the fiscal deficits shown in Table 3. There was, of course, never any attempt by

TABLE 3
Public Sector (Percentage of GDP)

	1953–1957	1958–1962	1963–1967	1968–1972	1973–1977	1980–1984
Consumption	9.2	8.3	8.2	9.3	8.7	18.1
Fiscal surplus/deficit	+3.2	+2.0	+0.3	−2.1	−5.1	−14.5

Source: 1952–1962: James Nugent, *Economic Integration in Central America* (Baltimore: Johns Hopkins University Press, 1974), 164–165; 1962–1977: Banco Central de Nicaragua, *Indicadores económicos*, 37–38; 1980–1984: INIES, "Trece síntomas de un drama," *Pensamiento propio* 21 (March, 1985): 29.

30. José Luis Medal, *La revolución nicaragüense:Balance económico y alternativas futuras* (Managua: CINASE, Ediciones Nicaragua Hoy, 1985), 36.
31. Dirección General de Estadísticas, *Resumen estadística*, 105; Banco Central *Indicadores*, 38.

the Somoza regime to use the tax system to redistribute income. The ratio of tax revenues to GDP was the lowest in Central America, with two-thirds of tax revenues derived from regressive indirect taxation. Tax evasion was widespread.[32]

Foreign Sector Policies

The management of the foreign sector during the Somoza years was pristine, again a model of liberal capitalist development. In 1929, the currency was devalued from 1 to 5 córdobas per dollar. A system of exchange controls and multiple exchange rates was introduced that lasted until 1959 when a unified rate of 7 córdobas per dollar was pegged.[33] In 1963, the currency was declared freely convertible. Figure 4, which plots exports and imports for the 1956–1985 period, portrays the balance achieved until 1972. The current account deficit as a percentage of GDP was well below the 10% mark from

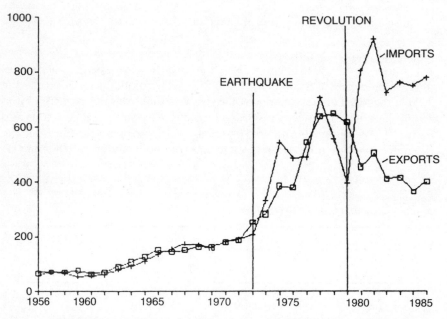

Figure 4. Trade balance (millions of dollars). *Sources*: 1956–78, International Monetary Fund, *International Financial Statistics*, 366–367; 1979–82, CEPAL, *Notas*, p., 42.; 1982–84, MIPLAN, "Plan Económico 1985," p. 86.

32. Biderman, *Class Structure*, 135.
33. Medal, *La revolución nicaragüense*, 1.

1960 until the revolution, with exceptions of the postearthquake years of 1974 (16.9%) and 1975 (11.6%).[34]

Throughout the postwar period until the earthquake, the conservative policies of the Nicaraguan Central Bank insured that the córdoba was not overvalued. There was little attempt to control imports, other than through conservative management of the money supply and the government deficit. Domestic prices were kept in line with international prices. Between 1958 and 1972, the implicit GDP deflator rose by only 22%; consequently, there was little overvaluation of the real exchange rate to stimulate imports.[35] Capital flight was not a problem, and the debt-service ratio was kept in a comfortable 5−17% range between 1958 and 1972.[36] Prior to the revolution, the only year in which there was a deficit on the private capital account was 1972, the year of the earthquake. After 1972 private capital movement plagued the regime and the debt-service ratio increased rapidly. The massive capital flight accompanying the revolution forced the Somoza government to reinstitute exchange controls and eventually devalue the currency to 10 córdobas per dollar.

Economic Development

State-sponsored development projects in the 1960s were largely limited to road building, irrigation, and subsidies for storage, processing, and marketing facilities. Long-term official capital from development agencies was used strictly according to official directives and prerogatives, that is, for infrastructure and institutional development rather than social programs. In the 1950s, the government was criticized by the World Bank for its utterly passive role in promoting economic development. Thereafter, the policies and programs of the Somocista state served to reinforce the inherent tendencies of the agroexport model toward rapid concentration of resources in hands of those who benefited from Nicaragua's comparative advantage. The state subsidized the import of labor-saving agricultural machinery and set up a system of subsidized cotton gins, processing plants for coffee, cottonseed, sugar, and beef. Much of the high value-added processing was controlled by Somoza or his associates in what were effectively state-supported monopolies.

No unified or serious effort was ever made to promote balanced economic development under the Somoza regime. By the 1960s, tension in the countryside advanced to such a point that Somoza felt compelled to introduce a

34. Banco Central, *Indicadores*, 15, 44.
35. *Ibid.*, 20.
36. *Ibid.*, 18, 42.

number of rural development projects and even a nominal agrarian reform in 1963. The land reform amounted to little more than a colonization project for the frontier provinces, benefiting only 16,500 families by the late 1970s.[37] Generally Somoza's development policies were palliative, with limited coverage; they were cynically designed to undermine insurgent activity in the countryside. Nevertheless, rural unrest was mounting. Between 1964 and 1973, there were 240 land invasions reported in the León and Chinandega provinces alone.[38] Behind the facade of INVIERNO and other rural development projects, lurked the fear that the repressive agroexport model would unleash forces even the National Guard could not control.

The Impact of the Somoza Model on the Rich and Poor

Although, from 1950 through the early 1970s, Nicaragua was able to sustain aggregate growth rates among the highest in Latin America, its success was based on concentrating income in the hands of a minority of agroexporters. High growth rates in export agriculture were the product of a policies that allocated most of the best agricultural land to export crops rather than domestic foodstuffs. The process marginalized the great bulk of the rural population and eventually led to the creation of a popular base for the FSLN in the countryside. Though agricultural output was rising at a rapid rate, from 1965 to 1975, the incidence of malnutrition doubled, affecting 60% of children under 4 years of age.[39] In the early 1970s, more than three-fifths of the rural population had deficient food intake.[40] Two-thirds did not consume meat or fish of any kind, though Nicaragua boasted the highest per capita supply of calories and proteins in Central America. Half did not consume any milk, and 57% did not eat any vegetables.[41] Nicaragua's illiteracy rate was among the highest in the region; only 40% of rural schools offered more than three grades and only 2% of children who enrolled in the first grade completed the sixth grade.[42] Although the illiteracy rate was officially reported at 57% in 1978, virtually no one in rural Nicaragua could actually read. Only 20% of the rural population had access to health services, and the death rate due to contagious disease was among the highest in Latin America.[43] Table 4

37. Biderman, *Class Structure*, 116.
38. *Ibid.*, 114.
39. CEPAL, *Informe sobre Nicaragua* (México: CEPAL, 1980), p. 6. See also World Bank, *The Challenge*, 32, and Biderman, *Class Structure*, 113.
40. World Bank, *The Challenge*, 32.
41. *Ibid.*
42. Biderman, *Class Structure*, 114.
43. *Ibid.*, 114. See also Rudolph, *Nicaragua* for a general description of life in rural Nicaragua.

TABLE 4
Distribution of Income in 1977 and Caloric Intake in 1970

PERCENTAGE OF EAP		PERCENTAGE OF INCOME	INCOME PER CAPITA[a]	CALORIES	PROTEIN[b]	FAT[b]
Top	5	28	5,409	3931.2	111.9	114.7
	15	32	2,062	3255.1	90.3	77.9
	30	25	805	2703.5	72.5	54.2
Bottom	50	15	289	1767.2	46.6	31.7
Total	100	100	966			

Source: Data for 1977: Fondo Internacional de Desarrollo Agrícola, *Informe de la Misión Especial de Programación a Nicaragua* (Managua: FIDA, October, 1980), 54; for 1970, CIERA, *Informe de Nicaragua a la FAO*. (Managua: CIERA, 1983), 41.
[a]U.S. dollars.
[b]Grams per capita.

provides nationwide data on resource distribution for 1977. Observe that the very rich (top 5% of the EAP) captured 28% of total income compared to 15% for the bottom 50%. The rich also consumed more than twice as many calories, protein, and fat as the poorest 50% of the population. The distribution of rural income was even more badly skewed than the national average, due to distortions in the access to land, credit, inputs, and other resources.[44]

The failure to share the fruits of the rapid expansion in output during the period of export-led growth explains much of why a militant student movement, outraged by the plight of a desperately poor and increasingly disposessed rural population, was able to catch fire across broad segments of Nicaraguan society. In the minds of urban organizers, the shantytowns that had sprung up in the beltways around Managua as the rich agroexporters drove peasants from their land served notice on an inherently defective system. "Comparative advantage" in Nicaragua meant specialization in export agriculture at the expense of nutritional requirements of the majority of the population. When domestic terms of trade improved for foodstuffs, dollar earnings from exports were used to import cheap food to keep the price of wage goods low and to ensure that the big growers' seasonal demand for labor would be met. As more marginal land of the agricultural frontier was brought into cultivation, lower per capita incomes drove peasants from the land into the cities. The pattern of trade specialization ultimately provided the FSLN with the highly visible urban base from which the regime could be challenged.

44. In the agricultural sector, the ratio of per capita income of owners to workers was 123 to 1 in 1971. See the study by the Comité Nacional Agropecuario, Unidad de Análisis Sectorial (UNASEC) as cited in Orlando Núñez, *El somocismo y el modelo capitalista agroexportador* (Managua: Departamento de Ciencias Sociales de la UNAN, 1981), 50.

STRUCTURE, POLICIES, AND PERFORMANCE UNDER THE SANDINISTAS

A Conceptual Model

There is, unfortunately, a typical pattern that has come to characterize the rise and fall of progressive or popular front governments in the Third World. Consider the following scenario: As the regime comes to power, the political opposition is often successful in blocking revenue generating legislation for social programs the regime intends to implement. Cut off from the (perhaps already overburdened) tax system, the new government turns to the printing press to finance its redistributive policies. The resulting monetization of the economy puts upward pressure on the flexible prices of nontraded intermediate and consumer goods, and the real exchange rate appreciates. The overvalued exchange rate stimulates imports to substitute for domestic production, and exporters find domestic markets more profitable than foreign. The area sown to food rises and that to agroexports falls. Frightened by the prospect of a maxidevaluation, domestic savers transfer their holdings to dollar-denominated foreign accounts. The combination of capital flight, cheap imports, and no incentive to export puts increasing pressure on the balance of payments. Commercial sources of credit disappear, especially for clients pursuing "unsound" economic policies. In theory, devaluation would help; in practice real devaluation is, or is seen as, impossible. Nominal devaluation only stimulates capital flight, further worsening the slide in the balance of payments. Eventually, the Central Bank runs out of dollars and applies to the IMF standby facility. The conditions imposed usually involve dismantling many of the social programs that, in the view of the IMF are the "cause" of the problem.

So far, the Sandinistas have been successful in avoiding this common sequence of events. Although they have not grounded their development policies in an attack on private property,[45] the Sandinistas have taken a basic step in reestablishing national control over the economy, which had been lost to the world market under the Somoza government. Immediately after the revolution, the banking system was nationalized, and the Ministry of Foreign Trade established virtual monopoly control over exports by creating a system

---

45. As had been observed elsewhere, Somoza's immense wealth was widely regarded as "stolen" and thus the nationalization of his property was considered legitimate. See James Austin, Jonathan Fox, and Walter Kruger, "The Role of the Revolutionary State in the Nicaraguan Food System," *World Development* 13, no. 1 (January, 1985). Nor have the Sandinistas incorporated large segments of the economy into the state apparatus. The percentage of GDP controlled by the government is comparable to that of many countries of Latin American and Western Europe.

of state enterprises for the marketing of major exports. Although there is some private sector participation, imports are also by-and-large controlled. Each week the government decides, based on currently available earnings from exports, loans, and donations, what is to be imported. Though the Sandinistas have permitted repatriation of a limited quantity of profits by multinationals, capital flight has effectively been stopped with the strict controls over domestic dollar accounts.[46]

Internally, much of the basic economic structure of the Somoza era remains intact: The economy is still highly constrained by the availability of foreign exchange, and its activity is still dependent upon a limited number of agroexports for survival. In addition to the destruction during the 1978–1979 insurrection, the Sandinistas have been saddled with a counterrevolution financed and directed by the CIA, a trade embargo, highly unfavorable terms of trade, and a concerted effort by the United States to block multilateral foreign assistance. The result is that Nicaragua has been able to pay for only approximately a third of its imports with exports and consequently is weighted down by debt far out of historical proportion. Although the Sandinistas have undertaken appropriate measures to insulate the economy from unfavorable movements in the world market, the U.S. destabilization effort has succeeded in making the economy more vulnerable to the foreign sector than ever.

Figure 2 shows that real per capita GDP has not yet recovered to the prerevolutionary levels of approximately $800. The substantial real growth that occurred in the first 2 years after the revolution (10% in 1980 and 8.5% in 1981) was interrupted in 1982 by "100-year" floods, which according to UN estimates, caused $349 million dollars worth of damage, almost as much as the revolution itself.[47] In 1983, the economy grew at approximately 5%, whereas Latin American GDP as a whole contracted at 3.1%.[48] With the effects of the war starting to make themselves felt, the economy again contracted by 1.4% in 1984. In 1985, the Latin American GDP grew at 2.8% as a

46. There is, undoubtedly, a significant amount of leakage through the black market and remittances, but savers who would otherwise hold dollar denominated accounts in foreign banks are now required to keep their capital in the country. Recently adopted policies such as selling dollars to the public through a limited number of exchange houses and permitting exporters to earn dollars through export promotion schemes have put more foreign exchange in the hands of the private sector but not to an extent that would contribute to significant decapitalization of the econmy.
47. CEPAL, Nicaragua: Las inundaciones de mayo de 1982 y sus repercusiones sobre el desarrollo económico y social del país (México: CEPAL, 1982), p. 44. For comparison, physical damage attributed to the revolution was $481 million. See INIES, "La economía nicaragüense," 18.
48. CIERA, "Informe anual de 1984," 7.

whole, whereas the Nicaraguan GDP contracted by 5.9%.[49] Overall, the economy has contracted by 11.6% since 1980.[50] This rather dismal macroperformance is the product of a series of internal and external factors that will be briefly surveyed here and considered in much greater detail in subsequent chapters.

External Barriers to Recovery

Since the insurrection, the primary objective of government policy has been the reactivation of the economy in the face of seemingly insurmountable obstacles. More than $2.5 billion in foregone income, direct destruction, and indirect damage resulted from the struggle to overthrow Somoza.[51] Now approximately 50% of the government budget is devoted to the Contra war and as of 1984, the total cost of the direct military aggression amounted to 25% of GDP.[52] The war has left 12,000 dead, 50,000 wounded, 300,000 refugees, and 5000 kidnapped. The enormous quantity of resources the government must channel to the war explains in large part why the recovery effort has not yet been successful. Each year Nicaragua subsists on a thinner diet of imported goods: An index of the dollar value of imports to constant-dollar GDP has fallen steadily from its postwar high of 131 to 86 in 1983.[53] The cumulative 1980−1984 trade deficit was more than $2 billion dollars, approximately equivalent to the current annual GDP.[54]

Much of the reduction in the import coefficient can be attributed to the steady deterioration in the terms of trade, which can be seen in Figure 5. In 1981, the prices of all four major export products dropped simultaneously for the first time in Nicaragua's history.[55] Figure 5 shows that on balance, the terms of trade declined almost 30% between 1977 and 1984; the total loss between 1980 and 1984 was $1071 million, $274 million from falling export prices and $787 million from higher import prices.

Although it had no access to the World Bank, the Inter-American Development Bank (IDB), or bilateral U.S. aid, Nicaragua nevertheless managed to

---

49. CEPAL data as cited in Edwin Croes, "CEPAL '85: Crisis para pato," *Pensamiento propio* 31 (March, 1986): 31−32. This data point is not represented in Figure 2.
50. *Ibid.*, 32.
51. World Bank, *The Challenge*, 2.
52. For details, see the chapter by FitzGerald.
53. The index is constructed from data from World Bank, *The Challenge*, 15; and CEPAL, "Notas para el estudio económico de América Latina, 1983: Nicaragua" (México: CEPAL, 1984), 42. and MIPLAN, "Plan Económico 1985" (Managua, 1984), 87.
54. CEPAL, "Notas," 2; INIES, "Trece síntomas de un drama," 28.
55. Francisco Mayorga, "The Economic Trajectory of Nicaragua: 1980−84; An Overview," *Occasional Paper* #14, Latin American and Caribbean Center, Florida International University, 1985, 46.

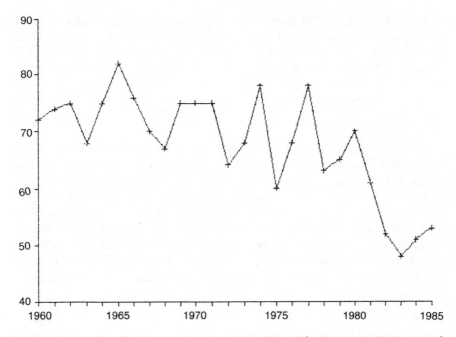

Figure 5. Terms of trade. *Source*: Francisco Mayorga, "The Economic Trajectory of Nicaragua: 1980–84," 47. Note: computed as a ratio of export to import prices, both with base 1980 = 100.

run current account deficits of more than $500 million a year between 1980 and 1984. In 1984, the Economic Commission for Latin America (ECLA) observed that the rate at which capital was entering Nicaragua was seven times its current interest payments and "this puts Nicaragua in a different situation than that which confronts the majority of other Latin American countries."[56] This extraordinary access to foreign sources of finance has been squandered, however, primarily to pay for deteriorating terms of trade and service of old debt. The result is a staggering per capita debt with little increase in productive capacity to show for it. In 1979, Nicaragua inherited a debt of $1.6 billion from the Somoza family, but by 1985 the figure stood above $4 billion.[57] This translated to a per capita debt of $1,347 in 1984, second in Central America only to Costa Rica.[58] The average debt-service

56. CEPAL, "Notas," 32. Author's translation.
57. For details on the current debt structure, see the chapter in this collection by Stahler-Sholk.
58. INIES, "Trece síntomas," 28. Costa Rica's 1984 per capita debt was $1598.

ratio for the 1980–1984 period was approximately 37%.[59] Table 5 shows that the sum of interest payments between 1980 and 1984 was $818 million; in other words, Nicaragua has paid, in interest alone, a sum approximately equal to a third of its debt contracted since 1980. Adjusted for the terms of trade and debt service, real credit absorption has steadily declined through the postrevolutionary period and is now almost negligible. Since 1980, credit has increased Nicaragua's real purchasing power by only 25% of the change in foreign debt.

What is most remarkable about Nicaragua's foreign debt is the complete absence of the IMF or any IMF-styled conditions imposed by its creditors. Because Nicaragua has instituted exchange and direct import controls, it has not had to face the prospect of a debilitating "run" on Central Bank reserves. Foreign exchange speculation has effectively been curtailed (although a flourishing black market in illegal dollars has had a destabilizing impact on production and the inducement to invest). Unlike the Somoza regime, in which the Central Bank was obliged to provide dollars for whatever purpose, the Sandinista government has been able to allocate foreign exchange according to social rather than private criteria.

Internal Policy Issues: The Role of the State

The main internal structural reform undertaken by the Sandinistas was the expansion of the public sector in terms of ownership, planning, and control over investment. In the first year after the revolution, the public sector share in

TABLE 5
Foreign Credit Absorption (millions of 1980 dollars)

	1980	1981	1982	1983	1984	Total
Increase in external debt	408	504	491	584	520	2507
Less interest payments	−108	−121	−149	−210	−230	−818
Effective use of foreign credit	300	383	342	374	290	1689
Less losses through:						
Export prices	—	−9	−88	−122	−55	−274
Import prices	—	−156	−173	−228	−230	−787
Real Credit Absorption	300	218	81	24	5	628

Source: Francisco Mayorga, "The Economic Trajectory of Nicaragua: 1980–84," 52.

59. Banco Central, Indicadores, 15, 42. For recent data, see the chapter by Stahler-Sholk, Table 2. The average reported in the text is actually paid rather than contracted.

output increased from 15 to 37% of the GDP.[60] Partially in response to a private sector capital strike, the share of investment in GDP has fallen in comparison with the prerevolutionary period. During the initial period of capitalization, 18.8% of GDP was invested compared to 23% in the 1973– 1977 period, 18% in the downswing from 1968–1972, and 20.8% in the period 1963–1967.[61] By the end of 1983, much of the capital base of the ministries was in place, and the war began to exact larger toll on state accumulation. Investment fell to 15% of GDP[62] in 1984. Prior to the revolution, private investment accounted for two-thirds of the total, but after 1979, it declined to 21% in 1980 and 19% in 1983.[63]

Since the revolution, rising government deficits and the inflation they create have plagued the regime. Indeed, only the first 3 months of 1980 could be characterized as maintaining anything near fiscal equilibrium.[64] Generally, fiscal deficits were not financed out of tax revenues; the government resorted to the printing press and credit creation to support its social initiatives.[65] Immediately after the revolution, formal reserve requirements were virtually abolished, and domestic credit more than doubled between 1978 and 1980.[66] Most of this credit creation was absorbed by the government; government borrowing was well in excess of its fixed capital needs and was used to finance current expenditures.

The excessive liquidity injected into the economy by government deficit spending did not immediately cause an increase in prices due to the rapid rise in imports, which, in 1980, were virtually equal to the real level of 1978. But by midyear, it was recognized that the growth in credit was untenable due to the pressure on the balance of payments. An official policy of credit containment was adopted.[67] Since then, the inflation rate has increased in step with the expansion in the money supply and reduction in imports. In 1979, the consumer price index increased by 70%, but for the next 3 years, a combination of imports and price controls on key consumer goods kept the rate low

60. *Ibid.*
61. Banco Central, *Indicadores*, 16 and Carlos M. Vilas, "Unidad nacional y contradicciones sociales en una economía mixta: Nicaragua, 1979–84," in Richard Harris and Carlos M. Vilas, eds., *La revolución en Nicaragua* (México:Ediciones Era, 1985), 28.
62. INIES, "Trece síntomas," 27.
63. Vilas, "Unidad Nacional," 28.
64. The revolutionary government instituted a new flat tax and a one-time patriotic tax on capital assets, and the effective tax rate increased dramatically as corrupt tax collectors of the old regime left for Miami. In real terms, current revenues increased by 50% from the 1978 level. See World Bank, *The Challenge*, 13.
65. For details on government financing since the revolution, see the chapter in this volume by Ruccio.
66. World Bank, *The Challenge*, 9.
67. *Ibid.*, 11.

(approximately 22–25% per year) until 1983 when inflation accelerated to 37%. In 1984, inflation surged to 60%, and estimates for 1985 put the inflation rate at approximately 320%, by far the worst in the region.[68] Real minimum wages have steadily declined: By 1984 real wages had slipped to 39% of their 1980 level.[69]

Supply Side Policies: Land and Labor

In the early years of the revolution, fiscal debt was incurred to consolidate the revolution and establish a social base for the FSLN. Now the deficits are regarded as undermining that same social base. Government expenditure is increasingly devoted to the war, ultimately financed by inflating away the real incomes of workers earning "sticky" nominal wages. Policies and programs that have attempted to redistribute real income through increasing the social wage (the literacy and health campaigns for example) have clearly contributed to the growth in liquidity and, consequently, the decline in real wages. The government attempted to protect real incomes through direct consumer subsidies of consumer "basics."[70] The exorbitant cost of these programs, however, led to a dramatic 50% reduction in these subsidies in May 1984, a cut that marked the end of an era under the Sandinistas.

Supply side initiatives to stimulate production and exports have become the focus of recent policies.[71] "Popular participation" is increasingly interpreted not as a safety net but as support for small- and medium-sized agricultural producers who have shown in recent years that they can make a substantial contribution to both domestic supply and export earnings. Of course the mainstay of Sandinista policy to promote agricultural production and development is the agrarian reform. By the end of 1985, land redistribution had affected more than 4 million manzanas of land, benefiting more than 86,500 families as farm owners, state farm workers, or members of farm cooperatives.[72] In total, the agrarian reform had affected 50% of Nicaragua's farmland, although there were an estimated 50,000 families still in need of land.[73] Through the agrarian reform, coupled with an across-the-board reduction in land rent by 85%, the FSLN has made a serious attempt to

68. *Latin American Weekly Report* 7 (Feb. 14, 1986):10.
69. INIES, "Trece síntomas," 30.
70. The prices of sugar, salt, cooking oil, milk, soap, corn, rice, and beans were controlled, and gasoline for private use was rationed. See the chapter by Utting for details.
71. For details, see the chapter by Pizarro.
72. INIES "Talar los grandes árboles" *Pensamiento Propio* 30 (Jan.–Feb., 1986): 35.
73. *Ibid.* See Deere et al., "The Peasantry" for information on the redistribution of land by social sector.

rechannel resources to small and medium producers, implicitly rejecting the basic format of the Somoza-era agroexport model.

By 1981, agriculture as a whole regained 70% of the 1980 loss due to the interrupted cycle in 1979.[74] Exports recovered in an uneven way. The volume of cotton exports in 1983 was only 62% of the 1978 level, whereas coffee exports were 20% higher than in 1978, and sugar was up 12%.[75] Beef exports were down to 41% of the 1978 level, but this reflects an estimated 25 to 35% reduction in herds as cattle were prematurely slaughtered or rustled across the borders during the insurrection. In terms of total area, the export sector still had not recovered the 1970–1977 mean of 408,000 manzanas in 1983–1984, yet the domestic sector surpassed its earlier average in the 1983–1984 crop cycle.[76] It is clear that Sandinista agricultural policy resulted in substitution of domestic agricultural crops for agroexports, at least through the 1983–1984 cycle. In 1981, the Ministry of Agriculture shifted some highly productive land from export to food grains, and corn was sown on irrigated land for the first time in the history of the country.[77] For the 1984–1985 cycle, ten export and domestic market crops were sown to 830,000 manzanas—a postrevolutionary record. The total was nevertheless 260,000 manzanas short of the 1978 level.[78]

Land has been underutilized in the postrevolutionary period in large part due to the shortage of rural labor. Although labor shortage is common throughout Central America (15–20% of coffee crops are not harvested for lack of labor)[79], the problem is especially severe in postrevolutionary Nicaragua. Several factors contribute: the people's militias have given permanent employment to 50,000–70,000 people, in addition to the regular armed forces of perhaps 50,000 troops. The war has caused labor shortages in many parts of the northern coffee-growing regions. Government employees have been mobilized to pick cotton and coffee in the war zone when traditional *cortadores* either joined the urban marginal informal sector or were simply afraid to enter the war zone for the salaries they could earn. In 1983 alone, 811 farmworkers and peasants were killed by Contra forces.[80] In the past, harvest labor shortfalls were filled by migratory workers from Honduras and El

74. Estimates drawn from data in MIDINRA, "Estadísticas agropecuarias de Nicaragua 1980–1984", Managua, May 1984.
75. *Ibid.*, 18. Banco Central, *Indicadores*, 74.
76. MIDINRA, "Estadísticas" 39; CIERA, "Informe," 18.
77. For details, see Austin et al., "The Role of the Revolutionary State" and the chapter by Utting.
78. Mayorga, "The Economic," 33.
79. CIERA, *Managua es Nicaragua*, iii.
80. Collins, *Nicaragua: What Difference*, 145.

Salvador. However, the war in El Salvador and the fact that migrants must cross or even work in a free-fire zone has slowed the flow down to a trickle.

Moreover, explicit government policies have indirectly contributed to the shortage. First, the agrarian reform means that for thousands of Nicaraguan peasants, it is no longer necessary to sell their labor for agroexport harvests. In the cities, policies that award land to squatters and the government policy of supplying drinking water and electricity to marginal neighborhoods has undoubtedly accelerated the flow of labor from the countryside. Foreign exchange controls have also meant that guest workers are no longer able to convert their córdoba wages into dollars. But above all, it is the deficit financing and resulting inflation that has reduced labor supply in the agricultural sector. The excessive monetization of the economy has increased the economic rent accruing the scarce foreign exchange. Workers now find they can earn more in an afternoon's work in the informal sector than an entire week of formal sector activity. High urban prices coupled with price controls on some basic commodities have also sharply reduced the availability of wage goods in the countryside. Given that the budget deficit is partially attributable to the defense expenditure, the war indirectly causes labor shortages by distorting the system of economic incentives.

By 1982, the Sandinistas were aware of the increasingly untenable urban situation created by the scarcity of foreign exchange. One obvious solution was to allow wage increases in the formal sector in order to attract labor. This option was initially rejected on the grounds that it would set in motion a wage-price inflationary spiral that would further erode the incomes of the popular classes. Initially, the Sandinistas embraced a "low-wage" "low-price" approach to macromanagement with subsidies to protect real incomes. Now the underlying philosophy has changed. The government now argues that it can no longer afford to underwrite basic consumption of the entire popular sector and that greater incentives should be provided to the productive sectors of the economy. The system of wage adjustments recently adopted, ostensibly designed to end "wage and salary anarchy," has had a Brazilian-style effect of transferring income to capital and the state. Labor is quick to perceive the inequity of flexible consumer prices and fixed nominal incomes and has continually agitated to squeeze speculators in the informal sector and the few remaining patriotic capitalists.

CONCLUSIONS

Under the Somoza dynasty, Nicaragua had a highly dependent, open economy subject to the dictates of the international division of labor. Macropolicy amounted to abdicating control over the domestic economy to the world market. But however legendary the Somoza dictatorship was as a model of corruption and brutality, it must be said that its policy options were limited as long as Nicaragua retained its basic economic structure. In the face of external shocks, the only viable set of Somocista policies was, as José Luis Medal points out, a "mixture of contractionary and expansionary measures," the former aimed at unproductive, political and other "nonbasic" consumption and the latter at the export sector.[81] Even if a redistributive monetary/fiscal intervention had been tried, it would have likely failed, as it has elsewhere in the Third World, simply due to the lack of an adequate tax base and the extreme openness of the economy. Of course balanced economic development was never part of the Somoza agenda; the regime was little more than a "kleptocracy," a system designed to maximize the wealth of its dictator and his cronies.

In contrast to the Somocista model, which was based on a free-market open economy and comparative advantage, the Sandinistas have sought to erect political-economic structure free of foreign domination. Through selective nationalization of key sectors of the economy, they have to an extent achieved the economic equivalent of the political principles Sandino fought for more than 50 years ago—national sovereignty and self-determination. In a peacetime economy, the system of import and exchange controls adopted by the Sandinistas might have provided an adequate foundation for a program of growth with redistribution. There is no assurance of this, however, inasmuch as the internal structure of the economy has proved so difficult to transform. Many of the structural constraints inherited from the Somoza regime are still in full play, and the number of uniquely domestic barriers to progress has multiplied.

It is the counterrevolution, however, that might tip the scales. What obstacles the international financial system cannot impose in its traditional ways have been left to the violence and the terror of Contra mercenaries, a trade embargo, and a multilateral lending blockade. Through its eclectic development strategies, Nicaragua confirms that it does indeed constitute a threat, not to the military, but to the political and ideological hegemony of the United States. This explains in part why the United States, in Chomsky's words, "typically demonstrates what looks like fanatic opposition to constructive developments in marginal countries."[82] Although the Sandinistas have been successful in confronting the institutional legacies of the past, as yet they remain the victims of the reactionary patterns of the present-day international politics.

81. Medal, La revolución, 22.
82. Noam Chomsky, "Intervention in Vietnam and Central America: Parallels and Differences," Monthly Review 37, no. 4 (September, 1984): 9.

Chapter 2

The Mixed Economy in Nicaragua: The Economic Battlefield

JOHN WEEKS

Revolutions herald the prospect of great possibilities. They also bring forth turmoil. Nicaragua has been a society in turmoil since the overthrow of the last Somoza in July 1979. The purpose of this chapter is to analyze one aspect of that turmoil—the economic organization of post-Somoza Nicaragua. To refer to the economic organization of Nicaragua after the revolution, the term *mixed economy* will be used, which is defined as a situation in which both state property and private property relations play an important role in the productive sectors of the economy. Insofar as a mixed economy can be considered as a conscious strategy pursued in Nicaragua (an issue dealt with later), the goal of this strategy was to secure the cooperation of the domestic and foreign propertied interests in the task of reconstructing a society devastated by war.[1] It will be argued that this goal was not achieved, not even in the early days of the Nicaraguan Revolution.

The issue of primary interest here is why that cooperation proved unattainable. Explaining why is difficult because the forces undermining the cooperation of the large-scale private sector with the revolutionary government fall into three categories—the issues of (a) capital's reaction to a loss of political power, a general question for which Nicaragua provides only an example; (b) the conscious intervention of the government of the United States to undermine any accommodation among antagonistic groups in Nicaragua that

---

1. For an impartial estimate of the war damages of 1978–79, see United Nations, Economic Commission for Latin America, *Nicaragua: Economic Repercussions of Recent Political Events* (Santiago de Chile: ECLA, 1979); and World Bank, *Nicaragua: The Challenge of Reconstruction* (Washington:World Bank, 1981).

might have facilitated cooperation; (c) and the particular character of the Nicaraguan propertied classes themselves. Sorting out these influences is rather like trying to orient oneself in a hall of mirrors—each factor is seen superimposed and reflected upon the other as well as distorted almost beyond recognition.

Common to almost all branches of revolutionary thought is the vision that the process of modernization and struggle for national independence from foreign dominance can at some stage involve a broad alliance of classes, whether it is called a "united front against imperialism" or the "new democracy" (the latter is Mao Tse-tung's phrase). In Nicaragua, a broad alliance was forged in the struggle to overthrow Somoza, including both propertied and nonpropertied classes. The first post-Somoza government included revolutionaries of the FSLN, one of Nicaragua's biggest capitalists (Alfonso Robelo), and a former National Guardsman as Minister of Defense. The alliance did not long survive the day of triumph. Inevitably, the question presents itself: Was the alliance inherently doomed, or did the force of circumstance conspire against it? Although this chapter cannot give a definitive answer to that question, it will argue that although the war initiated by the counterrevolutionary bands from Honduras and Costa Rica was largely the inspiration of Washington, the collapse of the uneasy alliance between the FSLN and the propertied classes lay in the contradictions of the mixed economy, which quickly became a battlefield of class interests. The goal of this chapter is to assess whether those contradictions were inherent or conjunctural. Due to the complexities of the issue, the conclusions reached cannot claim to be definitive.

Little progress in analyzing the concrete circumstances of Nicaragua can be made until certain general questions are dealt with. The most important of these is the nature of a mixed economy, which is discussed in the following section. There, it is argued that the key to understanding the operation of an economy characterized by both state and private property in productive assets is the relationship between the propertied classes and state power. To some this will seem a simplistic and rigid formulation of the problem. It will, however, allow for clarification of a complex phenomenon, which is the purpose of social theory. Placing the mixed economy within a class context provides no definitive conclusion about the role of the propertied classes during a revolutionary period; it only highlights factors that must be investigated in the concrete.

Subsequent sections analyze the concrete circumstances of Nicaragua. Particular emphasis is placed upon the historical development of the Nicaraguan landlord and capitalist classes and their tendency to turn to influential groups in North America to resolve their internal disputes. The Somoza dynasty was a result of this predilection on the part of the Nicaraguan elite as well as the U.S. government's own geopolitical ambitions.

Even before Somoza fell, the FSLN defined a primary goal of the post-triumph society to be national unity, and this nominally has remained a cornerstone of FSLN policy throughout its years in power. This national unity explicitly included members of the propertied classes, if they proved to be "patriotic." The mixed economy was a vehicle by which this unity would be forged, involving the peaceful coexistence of a large-scale private sector, small-scale producers (particularly in agriculture), and a sector of socialized property.[2]

The mix of private and state property was not so much a strategy of economic organization chosen by the FSLN as a situation presented to it at the time of the triumph due to historical circumstance. Despite the monopolistic control over the economy exercised by the Somoza family, other factions of the propertied classes enjoyed a vigorous existence. Further, elements of the propertied classes had played a significant role in the overthrow of the dictatorship and could, therefore, claim a place for themselves in the new society to be constructed. The state sector, which had been miniscule before the triumph, was not the creation of the FSLN but the result of the confiscation of Somocista property, a punitive confiscation undertaken by consensus of all parties that had opposed the dictatorship. Although the FSLN and the anti-Somoza elite may have had different visions of how the mixed economy would evolve, both participated in its creation. Arguments from observers on the left that the leadership of the FSLN was too slow in moving against the propertied classes ignore the momentary prestige enjoyed by the anti-Somoza elite at the time of the triumph.[3] Similarly ahistorical and conspiratorial are accusations from the right that the mixed economy was a ruse to hide a hidden agenda of Marxism-Leninism.[4] A general consideration of the nature of a mixed economy will place these points in an analytical framework.

2. See República de Nicaragua, Ministerio de Planificación (MIPLAN), *Programa de reactivación económica en beneficio del pueblo* (Managua: MIPLAN, 1980); and República de Nicaragua, Dirección de Divulgación y Prensa de la Junta del Gobierno de Reconstrucción Nacional, *The Philosophy and Policies of the Government of Nicaragua* (Managua, 1982).
3. For an article expressing concern over the course of the revolution, see James Petras, "Whither the Nicaraguan Revolution?" *Monthly Review* (October, 1979).
4. Particularly scurrilous versions of this argument are found in the following: United States Department of State, Office of Public Diplomacy for Latin America and the Caribbean, *Broken Promises: Sandinista Repression of Human Rights in Nicaragua* (Washington: October, 1984); and (same source) *Resource Book: Sandinista Elections in Nicaragua* (Washington, n.d.). The latter document is particularly interesting, for it provides an assessment of the November 1984 presidental and national assembly elections in Nicaragua issued before those elections took place.

THE STATE AND THE MIXED ECONOMY

A combination of state and private property in the productive sectors of the economy has characterized a wide range of regimes in both developed and underdeveloped countries in this century. If we take this as the definition of a mixed economy, it describes the countries of Western Europe as well as most of those of Latin America.[5] The fundamental characteristic of all of these mixed economies is that they operate in a context in which the propertied classes enjoy unrestricted political rights. We argue that unrestricted political rights for the propertied classes imply that they control the state, by virtue of their ownership of both the means of production and the channels of communication. In such circumstances, their political power is hegemonic in that they are able to restrict the political alternatives before the population to those consistent with the reproduction and expansion of their property relations. In the case in which capitalist property relations are the dominant form in the society—wage labor prevails as opposed to some form of servile labor relations—we shall use the phrase *the mixed economy under the control of capital.*

This is the situation in Western Europe. Brief consideration of mixed economies in Western Europe helps to illuminate our subsequent discussion of the tensions that emerged in Nicaragua over economic policy after the triumph. The emergence of mixed economies in Western Europe is frequently associated with the strength of the working class movement and policies of nationalization pursued by social democratic parties, whose electoral base is the trade unions. By this interpretation, nationalizations are presented as progressive reforms, reducing or at least moderating some of the abuses of an economy based upon capitalist relations of property. This view is generally accepted in Latin America by both the political right and the left. There is an element of truth in the interpretation, for it is probably the case that the weakness of the working class largely explains the virtual absence of state-owned enterprises in the United States.

But the mixed economy is considerably more complex than this in the developed capitalist countries, reflecting the development of the capitalist class as well as of the working class.[6] Economic regulations and nationalizations should not be viewed in all cases as being contrary to the interests of private capital, accepted only begrudgingly by the business sector. Further,

5. By the definition we are using, the economy of the United States is not "mixed," for state ownership of productive facilities is of no importance.
6. Ben Fine and Laurence Harris, *Rereading Capital* (London: Macmillan, 1979), Chapters 6 and 7. The authors associate the rise of the mixed economy with what they call "state monopoly capitalism".

indirect and direct state interventions in capitalist economies are not necessarily the consequence of pressure from the left of the political spectrum. Although mainstream economic theory in the West ("neoclassical" economic theory) preaches that competition is a stabilizing force, the experience of capitalist economies indicates the opposite. The consolidation of economic power into few hands makes competition a powerful cause of disruption, and over the last 100 years governments throughout the capitalist world have taken a wide variety of steps to temper the competitive struggle. Nationalizations represent one such measure and in part protect capitalists from the destructive tendencies inherent in their own interaction.

On a more concrete level, nationalizations in Western Europe have been explicitly undertaken to protect or reinforce the expansion of capital. Many nationalized industries are ones that are strategic to the operation of the economy but have proved themselves unprofitable when operated in the private sector. The coal industry, steel, and railroads are obvious examples. Here nationalization has allowed a reorganization and rationalization of production that private capital could not afford to undertake. Closely related to such nationalizations are those effected to increase the general competitive position of national capital. Nationalizations have been combined with state financing of ventures that are too long-term or uncertain with regard to outcome to attract sufficient private funds.

Because nationalizations undertaken by governments in a mixed economy under the control of capital are not usually motivated by considerations of short-run profitability, it is frequently the case that the enterprises involved run losses or enjoy quite low rates of return. This provides ammunition for the ideologues of the far right who hark back to an earlier epoch of capitalism when accumulation was based upon a weaker working class and more overtly exploitative behavior on the part of capitalists. The ideology of the Reagan administration in the United States and the Thatcher government in Great Britain are cases in point. The essence of such ideologies is anti-working class with a latent fascist content, for they advocate the destruction of working class power without changing the monopoly character of capital that concentrates economic control in the hands of a few. In consequence, though the original motivation of nationalizations may have been to facilitate capitalist accumulation, denationalization ("privatization") becomes the rallying cry of the political right, and, thus, defense of nationalized industries the program of the left.

Notwithstanding this, under the control of capital, mixed economies are consistent with a wide variety of political regimes, from fascism (Italy and Germany in the interwar period) to the relatively benign welfare states of Scandinavia. The defining characteristic of all of these is that the system of property ownership is an expression of the domination of capital over the economy. Therefore, the practice of the mixed economy in advanced capitalist countries is characterized by a degree of harmony and beneficial interaction between private and state enterprises. The relationship is not without its tensions. In times of economic crisis, the ideologues of the far right find their message particularly attractive to the various factions of capital because one enters into a period when losses must be shared out and each capitalist seeks to minimize his or her portion. During such moments, nationalized industries are vulnerable candidates for absorbing the lion's share of losses because their difficulties will fall directly upon no individual private capitalist. Periods when much of the capitalist class is attracted to far right ideology should not obscure the fact that at other periods state property plays a supportive role of private capital.

With some qualifications, the role of state property in Latin America has been similar to that in Western Europe. Here it is even clearer that the state's role in production need have no origin in progressive reforms demanded by the political left. The clearest case is Brazil, where state ownership of productive enterprises played a major role in economic strategy after the right-wing coup in 1964. This role facilitated turning the country into an exporter of manufactured products. In cooperation with foreign capital, state enterprises led the way in technical innovations that made Brazilian industry competitive on the world market. At the same time, it could be argued that the expansion of the state sector made the Brazilian capitalists more powerful vis-à-vis the working class than previously had been the case. A more complex case is that of Peru during the Velasco regime. Although the "Peruvian Revolution" of 1968— 1975 coincided with considerable militancy by the peasantry and working class, many of the nationalizations were clearly in the interests of the capitalists, even those whose property was nationalized.[7] This was particularly true for the nationalization of the fishmeal industry, which was in total collapse due to overfishing and environmental changes.

The essential point from this discussion is that the mixed economy should be seen as a form in which the social character of capitalist production is expressed, implying in itself little about the balance of class power that provoked it or that results from it. Under the control of capital, the mixed economy differs in operation only in degree from a private enterprise economy without significant state ownership. The tensions within a mixed economy with capital in control are basically the same as those operating in an economy in which private enterprise alone owns productive assets. In other

7. This position is argued in Elizabeth Dore and John Weeks, "The Intensification of the Attack against the Working Class in 'Revolutionary' Peru," Latin American Perspectives III: 2 (Spring, 1976); and in the same journal, Elizabeth Dore, "Accumulation and Crisis in the Peruvian Mining Industry: 1968—1974" IV: 3 (Summer 1977).

words, the mixed economy provides a general form in which a resolution is sought for the conflict between capital and labor and among factions of capital.

THE MIXED ECONOMY FURTHER CONSIDERED

The mixed economy in Nicaragua after the triumph operated in a totally different context from that treated in the previous section. However one might characterize the post-triumph state, it was one in which the propertied classes were excluded from power. This is what makes the Nicaraguan revolution virtually unique. It is difficult to produce any other example of a country in which private capital remained the dominant form of property, while in the political realm capital had been disenfranchised (or at least, where such an arrangement persisted more than momentarily). The typical outcomes are either a counterrevolution by which propertied interests regain the political power commensurate with their economic importance, or a rapid move by the revolutionary government to confiscation of large-scale property (in part to prevent the former outcome).

Thus the leaders of the FSLN are quite justified in claiming that the Sandinista Revolution has been unique: Capital is out of power, but capitalist property continues on a large scale. Although, to a great extent the mixed economy was thrust upon the FSLN, the policy of the government was and remains that the economy of Nicaragua can incorporate capitalist property. Explicit in this policy is the assumption that the cooperation of the domestic capitalist class could be obtained by guaranteeing the limited fulfillment of this class's narrow economic goals.[8] The analytical issue is whether this hypothesis is valid and, therefore, whether a mixed economy of the Nicaraguan type is sustainable. With little relevant historical experience to guide the analysis of this question, it is necessary to pursue further our general discussion of the nature of the mixed economy, or it will quickly revert to a rather fruitless argument over motivations, actions, and conspiracies of the actors on the Nicaraguan scene.

It is useful to begin by setting up a strawman. It might be argued that the situation in Nicaragua after the triumph was the mirror image of the mixed

8. See Anthony Winson, "Nicaragua's Private Sector and the Sandinista Revolution," *Studies in Political Economy* 17 (Summer, 1985), where this strategy is discussed with quotations from FSLN leaders. A discussion of the mixed economy in Nicaragua is also found in Elizabeth Dore, "Nicaragua: The Experience of the Mixed Economy and Political Pluralism," in S. A. Morely and J. Hartlyn (eds.), *Latin American Political Economy: Essays on Financial Crisis and Political Change* (Boulder: Westview Press, 1986).

economy of a social democratic type. One could characterize the latter as a situation in which the working class has little real political power, but its cooperation with the capitalists is achieved through the welfare state in which economic benefits are distributed to the mass of the population. Such political arrangements have proved quite stable in their ability to contain the class struggle in advanced capitalist countries. On a formal level, the two situations—capital in power and permitting the limited fulfillment of working class economic demands and capital out of power but having its economic goals achieved—would seem symmetrical.

The two situations are not symmetrical, however, and the narrow economic goals of capital cannot be separated from the general role of capital in society. Capitalist production is based upon the exploitation of labor in the technical meaning of that term: Profits are the result of wage earners working in excess of the time it takes to produce their consumption bundle. In other words, profit derives from unpaid labor time. This aspect of capitalist accumulation—generally accepted by economists 100 years ago—is one that modern economic theory has successfully sought to obscure. Its political implications are obviously threatening to capitalist society.

One aspect of the reproduction of the conditions for accumulation is for the state to provide an ideology that obfuscates the exploitative nature of capitalist society, just as the church provided such an ideology during the Middle Ages for feudalism. Once capital no longer controls the state, justification of exploitation becomes problematical. A revolutionary leadership is unlikely to supply the working class with obfuscating ideology—certainly the FSLN did not. However, in order for capital to be profitable, exploitation must continue. Merely guaranteeing capitalists a market is not sufficient to guarantee profits. Faced with this difficulty, the FSLN leadership sought to obtain the working class's cooperation with private sector capitalists by stressing the overriding need to reconstruct the economy after the devasting war against the Somoza dictatorship. At times, coercion was required. On a number of occasions, militant trade union leaders were jailed and strikes outlawed.[9] It is a mistake to interpret these, as some observers on the Left have, as a turn against the working class by the FSLN. Rather, these coercive steps represent the inevitable response of a state that is holding the capitalists at bay politically while seeking their cooperation in the economic sphere.

The capitalists are unlikely to find satisfactory a situation in which its opponents provide for the conditions of accumulation. A political leadership

9. The repression of non-Sandinista trade unionists should not be blown out of proportion. In early 1985, a delegation of AFL-CIO leaders visited Nicaragua and subsequently issued a report on trade union rights that was only mildly critical. National Labor Committee in Support of Deomcracy and Human Rights in El Salvador, *Report* (May 1985), pp. 17–24.

whose popular base is in the working class, peasantry, and parts of the middle class, as is the case of the FSLN, is unlikely to enforce the conditions of exploitation with a vigor sufficient to please the capitalists. The difficulties encountered by a revolutionary state in facilitating private accumulation highlight the asymmetry of a mixed economy under capital's control and one in which capital has lost power: The existence of the capitalist class requires exploitation; the existence of the working class does not. Once capital loses its political power, exploitation becomes increasingly difficult to justify, something Nicaraguan capitalists discovered daily on the shop floor after the fall of Somoza.

A second problem arises for the capitalists in this context. Although a revolutionary government may guarantee private property and stand resolutely by that guarantee, this may do little to facilitate the aggregate reproduction of capital. To take but one example, accumulation is dependent upon the credit system. When the credit system is no longer being managed by the capitalists but by a state over which the capitalists have little direct influence, accumulation becomes extremely problematical. Even a liberal credit policy, such as the Nicaraguan government pursued immediately after the revolution, is not satisfactory for accumulation. What is required is a credit policy that reflects the changing needs of capital. At some points this implies tight credit, as in periods of economic crisis when the agenda is for the redistribution of capital toward the more profitable enterprises, not for expansion.

In summary, consideration of the mixed economy in the abstract suggests that it is unlikely to represent a stable compromise in a postrevolutionary situation with capital excluded from political power. A very basic contradiction is involved—capitalists have lost political power but are allowed to retain considerable economic power. Whether this is an inherently unstable and inevitably volatile arrangement cannot be answered in the abstract. In the following sections, we apply some of the insights from the general discussion to the experience of Nicaragua.

THE MIXED ECONOMY IN NICARAGUA

Before treating the specifics of the mixed economy in Nicaragua, it is necessary to consider the relationship between the state and the economy during the late Somoza period. On a formal level of legislation, this period can be described as one characterized by few regulations upon the operation of capital. In practice, however, the economy was highly regulated and far removed from the ideal of a competitive, private enterprise system. The Somoza family held tremendous control over the economy and severely restricted their competitors, particularly other domestic capitalists but also foreign capital. This control took many forms. For example, to be an exporter of beef, one had to sell one's cattle to officially approved slaughter houses, which were controlled by the Somoza clique. Further, any productive undertaking required building permits, licenses, and the like that could only be obtained (if at all) by liberal application of bribery.

The reform of the economy sought by the Nicaraguan capitalists opposed to the Somoza dynasty was the elimination of the dictator's grip over a formally unregulated system. This implied little change in the system of labor relations, which left workers largely unorganized and weak. Thus the anti-Somoza capitalists sought an arrangement by which their domination of the working class would continue but the pursuit of profit making would be free to all with money to invest. The Sandinistas, in contrast, foresaw a process in which the overthrow of the dictatorship would be a vehicle for a fundamental reduction in the control of the propertied classes over Nicaraguan society. For the capitalist opposition, then, the overthrow of Somoza would be the sum of the Nicaraguan revolution; for the Sandinistas, it would only be the beginning of the revolution.

Immediately after the fall of the dictator, the FSLN-dominated government took a number of steps that fundamentally altered the conditions of accumula-tion in Nicaragua. When the revolutionary government took control of the banks and established a state monopoly over external trade, Nicaraguan capitalists faced a situation for which they were unprepared. In effect, the córdoba was rendered nonconvertible,[10] and exporters could no longer receive their earnings in foreign exchange. The fierce opposition of Nicaraguan capitalists to these measures reflected both general and historically specific factors. As a rule, private capitalists are never pleased with restrictions upon their operations. Yet the measures taken by the revolutionary government were not dissimilar to policies applied by other governments in Latin America. Import controls, restrictions on convertibility, and the like have been tolerated elsewhere by capitalists as measures necessary to deal with the particular problems of industrialization in the context of underdevelopment. It is possible, for example, that a Sandinista-type regime in Peru would have faced less virulent opposition to such controls, where they are more familiar and have been instituted by a variety of governments.

But the ferociousness of the opposition to these familiar controls also had a

10. From July 1979 until early 1982, there was a functioning and legal parallel market for foreign exchange in which the córdoba was allowed to float without restriction. However, given that exports were remunerated through the Central Bank at the official exchange rate, trading in this market was extremely unattractive to capitalists if it was their intention to use the foreign exchange to buy inputs. Once the government fixed the rate in the parallel market in early 1982, it fell dormant.

cause that would be relevant in any country. With propertied interests denied significant political power in Nicaragua, the controls were instituted and implemented in a manner over which these interests had little influence. This meant, at the most general level, that the relationship between the private sector and the state sector in Nicaragua was different from that anywhere else in Latin America.[11] The intention of the leadership of the FSLN was that the state sector would be the engine of accumulation, providing direction and priorities in the productive sectors. This vision necessarily implied a state sector that expanded vigorously relative to the private sector. In 1980 and early 1981, when the economy grew rapidly on the basis of excess capacity and foreign loans,[12] the tension between the state and private sectors was subdued, for there seemed to be resources for both. However, once severe balance of payments pressure dictated austerity, the competition between the two sectors became explosive. In both industry and export agriculture, imported inputs were the lifeblood of production, and daily there was less foreign exchange to distribute. In practice, the government distributed the scarce foreign exchange in a manner relatively favorable to the private sector, and state enterprises were among the first to be closed in response to balance of payments pressure.

However, from the point of view of the private sector, the state enterprises that remained were consuming foreign exchange that the capitalists desperately needed. An evenhanded policy (if rather inefficient and excessively bureaucratic) of distribution of foreign exchange implied that the state sector was at least on equal footing with the private sector and not subordinate to the needs of the private sector. Such an arrangement represented a severe constraint upon the accumulation process. In times of economic crisis, capital contains within itself its own form of adjustment, involving bankruptcies, mergers, takeovers, and forced liquidation of assets. These adjustment mechanisms implied the opposite of an evenhanded policy, for they involve the strong destroying the weak in the competitive struggle.

These factors, that capital has lost political power in Nicaragua, had lost the management of the economy at the aggregate level, and was denied control of the mechanisms such as credit by which to reorganize itself, do not in themselves imply that the mixed economy of the Nicaraguan type must necessarily deteriorate rapidly into economic warfare. They do imply that such a mixed economy is a volatile mix indeed, representing a temporary

11. For a discussion of the confiscations carried out against the Somoza clique, see John Weeks, *The Economies of Central America* (New York: Holmes & Meier, 1985), Chapter 7; and John Weeks, "The Industrial Sector," in Thomas Walker (ed.), *Nicaragua: The First Five Years* (New York: Praeger, 1985).
12. See Weeks, *The Economies*, Chapter 7.

arrangement that at some point must revert back to capitalist control or pass on to a system of socialized property. But "temporary" here refers to conceptual time, not chronological time. The actual life span of such a mixed economy is indeterminate. Because a mixed economy out of the control of capital is rent with conflict and instability does not preclude it from being a more-or-less satisfactory ad hoc arrangement for a considerable period of time. In this sense, the leadership of the FSLN did not in its economic program chase a will-o'-the-wisp.

CHARACTER OF THE NICARAGUAN PROPERTIED CLASSES

The period when the mixed economy in Nicaragua operated in a relatively satisfactory manner was quite short, 18 months at the most and perhaps not at all.[13] Despite attempts by the revolutionary government to stimulate private sector cooperation through economic incentives (while tightly containing the political activity of the propertied classes), revolt began almost immediately, first as passive resistance, then turning to active economic sabotage. In great part, the rapid breakdown of the mixed economy reflected the weakness of the Nicaraguan propertied classes. As stated, many wealthy Nicaraguans could claim to have played an important role in the overthrow of Somoza. Despite this, once he had fallen, the propertied classes found themselves virtually without influence and without the means of reconstructing their influence. As a result, they were in no position to negotiate seriously with the FSLN over the economic organization of Nicaragua. Superficially, their weakness could be attributed to the fact that the National Guard had been destroyed and that the FSLN had firm control over the new army. But the weakness of the propertied classes and their total lack of support in the population has a deeper cause, to be found in their history and their repeated tendency to disgrace themselves in the eyes of the Nicaraguan people.

Not until this century was it possible to speak of "Nicaraguan" propertied classes. During the nineteenth century, the dominant classes in Nicaragua were profoundly split along provincial lines, between the Conservatives in Granada and the Liberals in León. These labels stemmed from the two factions of landed property in Central America that struggled over control of

13. Elsewhere I have argued that capitalists in the industrial sector never cooperated with the post-triumph government. To give but one indication, the Nicaraguan government in 1980 and 1981 received loans from the World Bank, part of which were earmarked for the private sector. The conditionality of these loans to private borrowers made them virtually free foreign exchange. Notwithstanding this, it proved impossible to disburse the World Bank money due to lack of applications from the private sector. The issue of private sector cooperation in industry is treated in Weeks, "The Industrial Sector."

the short-lived Central American Federation. The important elements of these two factions resided in Guatemala and El Salvador, and in Nicaragua the labels had little to do with the political philosophy of those who claimed them. After the collapse of the federation, Guatemala became the dominant political power in the region, ruled by the Conservative dictator Rafael Carrera. Carrera's policy of promoting Conservative regimes in the other states of the region brought ascendancy to the Granadan elite in the 1840s and 1850s—an ascendancy over León that it could not have achieved on the basis of its own resources.

To challenge the Granadan position, the elite of León in the mid-1850s also turned to the outside, employing a band of North American mercenaries led by William Walker.[14] The point of mentioning this sordid affair, which left the Liberals discredited for a generation, is to indicate the weakness of the elites in Nicaragua. Given this weakness and lack of national self-identity, they turned to outside forces even to resolve conflicts among themselves. These characteristics persist within the Nicaraguan propertied classes to this day, prompting them to seek latter-day William Walkers for their cause.

The first Nicaraguan leader who could be called "national" was José Santos Zelaya. He asserted his domination over the Nicaraguan elites, expelled the British from the Atlantic Coast, then set out to acquire clients elsewhere in the region. Zelaya has little to recommend him in light of his oppressive and corrupt rule, but until the election of Daniel Ortega in 1984, he held the distinction of being the last and perhaps only Nicaraguan president to achieve his office and to rule without foreign support. When dissatisfied elements of the Nicaraguan propertied classes summoned their courage to overthrow Zelaya in 1909, it was at the prodding of the U.S. government and achieved in no small part by the direct intervention of U.S. troops on the Atlantic Coast.[15]

After the fall of Zelaya, the reliance of Nicaraguan rulers upon an external patron changed from being a tendency to being the foundation upon which state power was maintained. During the occupation of the country by U.S. troops, Nicaraguan presidents ruled at the pleasure of American viceroys. It was by ingratiating himself with the U.S. embassy that the first Somoza came out of petty bourgeois obscurity to rule his country. But it was not merely the

---

14. In virtually all histories of Central America by North Americans, the Walker affair is treated as a minor incident. Booth provides a brief but useful discussion that indicates the impact of the episode upon the consciousness of Central Americans. John A. Booth, *The End and the Beginning: The Nicaraguan Revolution* (Boulder: Westview, 1982), pp. 13–20.
15. On Zelaya, see Mario Rodriquez, *Central America* (Englewood Cliffs, NJ: Prentice-Hall, 1965); and Ralph Lee Woodward, Jr., *Central America: A Nation Divided* (New York: Oxford, 1976).

collaborators and clients that based the fate of Nicaragua upon the largesse and patronage from Washington: Many of Somoza's opponents implicitly accepted that the government of the United States arbitrated Nicaraguan destiny.

For two decades, beginning in 1912, U.S. officials selected Nicaraguan presidents from the rival Liberal and Conservative factions or organized and managed elections to do so. During this period, access to state power was directly through the American embassy, with the ambassador's residence located with appropriate symbolism on the hill overlooking Managua. Somoza's slavish fidelity to the foreign power that had granted his power to rule won him a certain independence. Following a strategy of serving U.S. interests in all things of foreign policy, he gained a free hand in domestic policy.[16] Confident of unqalified U.S. support, the founder of the dynasty and his two sons ruled Nicaragua with little regard for conciliation of the fractious conflicts within the domestic propertied classes. Using the state as a vehicle for family enrichment, the Somozas and their associates established themselves as the most powerful economic group in the country, at the expense of the rest of the wealthy elite. The economic power of the Somozas also, ironically enough, represented a barrier to the penetration of U.S. capital,[17] but this was tolerated by Washington in exchange for the regime's unqualified support for U.S. foreign policy.[18] The basis for the economic power of the Somoza dynasty was in great part the client status of the dictatorship.

Nicaragua under the Somozas was not even a republic of the oligarchy but a despotism of a family. Political parties, even of the elite, existed only as shadow institutions, frequently manipulated by the dictator to provide a facade of democratic opposition. When outcry in the U.S. Congress threatened to undermine the special relationship between the Somozas and Washington, the dormant and morbid "opposition" would be brought out to stage showcase elections. This procedure took place, for example, to comply with the formal requirements of the Alliance for Progress. When genuine opposition elements from the propertied classes formed their own political organizations (such as the Independent Liberal Party and Democratic Conservative Party), these were brutally repressed.

16. For a shameless and unabashed presentation of the argument that Somoza should be supported to the end because he supports the U.S., see Belden Bell (ed.), *Nicaragua: An Ally under Siege* (Washington: Council on American Affairs, 1978).
17. Although reliable figures are hard to obtain, it would appear that in the mid-1970s Nicaragua had less U.S. foreign investment than any other Central American country. See Weeks, *The Economies*, Chapter 4.
18. To take a notorious example, the invasion of Cuba in 1961 disembarked from the Atlantic Coast of Nicaragua, with the second Somoza in attendance as a well-wisher.

In such a context, it is hardly surprising that the elite opposition also turned to Washington. Isolated from the masses of the Nicaraguan population by their class outlook and unable to organize within the propertied classes because of state repression, they sought from Washington the leverage to achieve that which they could not on the basis of domestic politics. Some upper-class opponents of Somoza, such as Pedro Joaquín Chamorro, were outspoken to the point of being imprisoned and were even perhaps willing to consider armed insurrection to overthrow Somoza. But these nationalistic Nicaraguans who preferred that their country be liberated from Somoza by Nicaraguans were few indeed among the wealthy.

The FSLN represented a dramatic contrast: a political movement intent upon removing the dictatorial dynasty on the basis of support within the Nicaraguan population. The FSLN gathered strength and demonstrated the capability of actually achieving its goal. Meanwhile, the elite opposition continued its strategy of petitioning Washington to exercise the traditional viceroyalty powers and remove the dictator. Only when U.S. representatives made it clear that their government had no intention of abandoning Somoza, despite outrages such as the assassination of Chamorro, did a significant portion of the elite enter into uneasy alliance with the FSLN.[19] But it was an uneasy alliance at best, and the bourgeois members probably participated on the hope that the post-Somoza arrangement would involve an army that included a significant portion of the National Guard. Such an arrangement was actually reached just before the dictator fled Managua. At least in the short run, the Nicaraguan political scene might have developed quite differently had the agreement been implemented. However, in a comic gesture that must still leave the Nicaraguan bourgeoise unamused, the caretaker president Somoza had left behind announced his intention to fill out the fallen dictator's term of office. The FSLN, holding effective military control of the chaotic situation and taking this announcement as a betrayal of an agreement never much to its liking, then resolved the matter on its own terms.

At this point the propertied classes of Nicaraguan found themselves disarmed and participants in postwar reconstruction on the terms of the victorious FSLN. In some other country of Latin America with a different history, in which the U.S. government had not played such a colonial role and in which the bourgeoisie had organizational roots in the masses of the population, a temporary and limited cooperation of some duration might have been possible. However, in Nicaragua, where the propertied classes had habitually turned to Washington to resolve their internal disputes, a domestic solution to a conflict over whether they would hold power at all was extremely unlikely.

19. A background and chronology are found in Booth, The Beginning, Chapters 7 and 8.

58   :   John Weeks

ARMED COUNTERREVOLUTION

Following this analysis, one concludes that there was never a "honeymoon" period in the alliance between the propertied classes and the FSLN. In the relatively tranquil months immediately after the triumph, the bourgeois elements merely waited, observing with alarm the consolidation of FSLN support within the population and relying upon the trump card of U.S. intervention, which had been played so often over the previous 80 years. As the conflict between the FSLN and the bourgeois opposition intensified, the reliance of the latter upon foreign patronage became increasingly clear.

This was clearest in the emergence of the Contra as a significant military force. This force, led by ex-National Guardsmen, trained first in Florida and later in Honduras when that country had assumed sufficient client status of the United States. Further, the Contra was funded and directed from the outset by U.S. government agents, with its more spectacular sabotage efforts carried out by U.S. intelligence services. The counterrevolutionary war represented latter-day William Walkerism, again with the Nicaraguan participants playing a client role to American directors.

The right-wing civilian opposition, at first nominally unassociated with the Contra, showed equal need of U.S. patronage. This reliance asserted itself in the Nicaraguan election of 1984. The usual interpretation of the election is that the largest opposition group chose not to participate because of the allegedly heavy-handed behavior of the FSLN. Even granting the claim that the Coordinadora Democrática represented the most important opposition to the FSLN (a questionable claim at best),[20] it is false that the group and its designated presidental candidate, Arturo Cruz, did not campaign. Campaign Cruz did—in the United States, particularly in Washington, the site of his real constituency.

So oblivious to considerations of nationalist feelings was the Nicaraguan bourgeoisie that during the election campaign, Cruz, its designated spokesman, repeatedly presented himself in public in the presence of high American officials, including the president of the United States himself. It is difficult to imagine an opposition leader from any other country of Latin America, no matter how right wing, publically manifesting such a close relationship to a U.S. administration. Such relationships of clientage are hardly rare, but with the exception of the Nicaraguan right-wing opposition, they are practiced discretely. Even Napoleón Duarte kept his public distance from Washington until elected president, in order to cling to some shred of national pride.

20. In an election unharassed by the Reagan administration, the Cruz group might well have finished third in the polling. See John Weeks, "Las elecciones nicaragüenses de 1984," *Foro Internacional* XXVI(1) (Julio–Septiembre, 1985).

Because the propertied classes had such a long and consistent history of U.S. clientage, both for the Somoza group and his opposition, the FSLN had little prospect of developing a successfully functioning mixed economy. It is not too much to say that in Nicaragua there was no nationalist-minded sector of the propertied classes of any significant size. Their participation in the struggle to overthrow Somoza did not reflect the nationalism of the propertied classes but rather the desire to maintain the close relationship with Washington without Somoza. Indeed, there was hope that relations would improve without the notorious dictator as an obstacle. Nationalism, which had briefly flickered in the dominant classes during the rule of Zelaya, was an alien ideology among the wealthy. It was so alien, in fact, that wealthy Nicaraguans commonly arranged for their children to be born In the United States so that they might hold American citizenship.[21]

An irony of the Nicaraguan revolution is that the same phenomenon that made a broad anti-Somoza front possible also made the continuation of that alliance highly unlikely after the dictator fell. The particular character of the Somoza dictatorship created the conditions for the alliance of propertied and nonpropertied classes to overthrow him. U.S. patronage had prompted the Somozas (particulary the last one) to treat the challenges from within the propertied classes with contempt rather than conciliation. But the wealthy opposition, like its powerful adversary, lacked a political base within the country. The mass base of the FSLN prior to the fall of Somoza can also be questioned as to its extent and depth. But when the FSLN through armed struggle broke the dictatorship, it fell legitimate heir to the spontaneous aspirations of the lower classes and to an extent those of the middle class. This left the wealthy opposition to Somoza with nothing, neither political organization nor a credible claim to anything but a supporting role in the dictator's fall. Left by their history with no political base in Nicaragua, the members of the propertied classes turned to U.S. patronage. The move from reliance upon Washington's favor to embracing the Contra and its ex-National Guardsmen proved a short step to take, as shown by the political migration of more than a few erstwhile opponents of the Somoza dynasty.

CONCLUSION

The possibility of a transitory conciliation of a revolutionary state and capital in the economic sphere when capital does not hold political power cannot be

21. To provoke anti-Nicaraguan feeling in the United States, the Reagan administration on a number of occasions claimed that American citizens had been jailed by the Sandinistas. Without exception, these people were permanent residents of Nicaragua, though born in the United States (usually Miami).

excluded by abstract analysis. Theory in this case can point out the contradictory aspects of such arrangement but not pass final judgment. In the concrete case of Nicaragua, such a transitory conciliation proved impossible. From the outset, the propertied classes of Nicaragua chose U.S. patronage rather than attempt to come to terms with the revolution and perhaps turn it along moderate reformist lines. To what extent this was the result of the inherent contradictions of the mixed economy or the consequence of the historic weakness and lack of national identity of the Nicaraguan propertied classes is difficult to judge. For this reason, the rapid degeneration of the private sector in Nicaragua after the triumph can be taken as neither a general indication of the fate of a mixed economy with capital out of power nor as a comment upon the wisdom or folly of Sandinista policies.

Chapter 3

The State and Planning in Nicaragua

DAVID F. RUCCIO

Most theories of transitional or socialist societies make the state the primary feature of such societies. This focus on the state usually means that something called "public" or "state ownership of the means of production" and "state economic planning" are made the defining characteristics of transitional economies. The fundamental theme of these approaches is the rather simple juxtaposition of market-oriented and planned economies.[1]

This emphasis on the essential role of the state is as true in the case of Nicaragua as elsewhere. For example, the transitional project of the FSLN (Sandinista National Liberation Front) is often summarized as the construction of a new state to guarantee the interests of the "majority." In addition, much of the literature on the Nicaraguan economy concentrates on changes in the relative quantitative weight of the state and private sectors since 1979. A standard question in this literature is whether or not the Nicaraguan "mixed economy" is inherently unstable and/or doomed to failure.[2]

The role of the state and planning in Nicaragua since 1979 is also the focus of the present chapter. However, the approach adopted here constitutes a

1. This is as true in orthodox neoclassical theories of the "centrally planned" or "administered" economy as in radical theories of "socialism" or the "transition to socialism." See, for example, the various approaches surveyed in Michael Ellman, *Socialist Planning* (New York: Cambridge University Press, 1979). This market versus planning dichotomy ends up telling us very little about the class-specific nature of different economies.
2. See, for example, the World Bank, *Nicaragua: The Challenge of Reconstruction* (Washington, D.C.: IBRD, 1981); the Inter-American Development Bank (IDB), *Informe económico: Nicaragua* (Washington, D.C.:IDB, 1983); and the Kissinger Commission, *Report of the National Bipartisan Commission on Central America* (Washington, D.C.: U.S. Government Printing Office, 1984).

departure from previous analyses by avoiding two major errors. First, the Nicaraguan transition is not reduced to the mere existence of enhanced state ownership of the means of production. The changes in property ownership since 1979 certainly mark a more or less sharp departure from the period of the Somoza regime; however, such changes are only some of the elements conditioning the existence of a transitional project in Nicaragua. Second, the sterile juxtaposition of the market and planning as alternative allocative mechanisms is rejected in favor of a perspective that emphasizes the existence of different kinds and theories of socialist planning and the contrasting social effects of different approaches to such planning.[3]

In sum, it cannot be merely assumed that a shift toward state property ownership and the existence of economic planning are equivalent to a socialist transition. Such changes may participate in creating some of the necessary transitional conditions; they may, however, have the opposite effect—reproducing the preexisting class structure and even undermining the transitional project. Therefore, the transfer of property ownership and the activity of state planning must be analyzed in terms of the *contradictory* effects they have on the emergence and strengthening of transitional elements in situations such as the Sandinista Revolution in Nicaragua.

The remainder of this chapter examines some of the ways in which the state and planning have participated in shaping the Nicaraguan transition during the 1979–1985 period. The first section analyzes some of the major changes in the role of the state in Nicaraguan political economy under the Sandinistas. The second section focuses on the early attempts at planning in revolutionary Nicaragua. The third section lays out some of the contradictory effects of the Nicaraguan state conceived to be the "center of accumulation." A short concluding section analyzes the most recent planning efforts and presents the specific implications of our analysis of the state and planning in Nicaragua.

STATE AND ECONOMY IN NICARAGUA

It would appear that any far-reaching set of social reforms, such as those called forth by the FSLN-led movement against the Somoza regime, requires an extensive restructuring of the state. No simple change of president or

3. This alternative theoretical approach to planning in transitional economies is elaborated in Ruccio, "Essentialism and Socialist Economic Planning: A Methodological Critique of Optimal Planning Theory," in *Research in the History of Economic Thought and Methodology*, ed. by Warren J. Samuels (Grennwich, CT: JAI Press, forthcoming) and "Planning and Class in Transitional Societies," in *Research in Political Economy*, ed. by Paul Zarembka (Greenwich, CT: JAI Press, forthcoming).

ministers is sufficient in that context. This restructuring is necessary because, on the one hand, the state under Somoza was involved in important ways in providing some of the political, economic, and cultural conditions under which the prevailing class structure was reproduced over time. The National Guard was, of course, the most notorious institution. However, we would also have to include the effects of such diverse entities as the Supreme Court, the public education system, the Central Bank, and the Nicaraguan Coffee Institute. They and the other institutions that comprised the state during the Somoza period had played an important role in creating and maintaining the Nicaraguan class structure through 1979. On the other hand, the Sandinista project of reconstruction and transition implied a different set of social conditions. In this sense, it was necessary both to dismantle many of the economic, political, and cultural aspects or processes that made up the previous state and to create a different state based on a different set of such processes.[4]

In general, any such attempt to restructure the state will probably involve some combination of three different kinds of change: (a) the maintenance and expansion of some processes previously performed in the state; (b) the shifting

4. In this sense, the state can be seen as one "site" within Nicaraguan society at which some historically specific set of social (including class) processes occurs and changes over time. Such an approach must be clearly distinguished from orthodox theories of the state as a class-neutral social wealth enhancer that exists as an expression of the will of its individual subjects. It must also be distinguished from so-called radical accounts of the state as a mere instrument to secure the political rule of one class over another (or, as sometimes in case of analyses of Nicaragua, of one individual over the rest of society). The alternative approach used here views the state as a specific location in society at which a particular set of economic, political, and cultural processes are performed, which in turn define it as a social site. This subset of the range of social processes that make up the wider society is, of course, constantly moved and shaped by the social processes that make up the other social sites (for example, enterprises, families, churches, etc.). At the same time, the state's "relative autonomy" derives precisely from the specific set of component social processes that give the state its particular structure and movement.

   The fact that the state cannot, at least in this view, be reduced to some essential set of underlying political or economic processes means that any particular state comprises a historically contingent set of economic, political, and cultural processes. The state may be the exclusive site of some social processes (for example, as source of legal tender or lawmaking); other social processes may be present in the state as well as in nonstate social sites (as in public and private education and money-lending). In addition, social processes may shift from one social site to another over time.

   For a critical review of alternative theories of the state and a fuller elaboration of the approach underlying the present analysis, see Stephen Resnick and Richard Wolff, "A Marxist Theory of the State," in *Political Economy: Recent Views*, ed. by Larry L. Wade (Boston: Kluwer-Nijhoff, 1983), 121–52.

   The conception of the Somoza state as the dictatorship of one individual over the rest of society is offered by, among others, Jaime Wheelock Román, *Imperialismo y dictadura: Crisis de una formación social*, 3rd ed. (México: Siglo Veintiuno, 1979) and George Black, *Triumph of the People: The Sandinista Revolution in Nicaragua* (London: Zed, 1981).

of other social processes from nonstate "sites" or locations to the state itself; and (c) the transfer of still other social processes from the state to sites outside the state. It also means that tensions and struggles may emerge among and between occupants of positions in the state and occupants of positions in other social sites over exactly what processes will be performed in and through the state. Both of these developments occur from 1979 onward in the course of constructing the new Nicaraguan state.

The downfall of Somoza led to the maintenance and improvement of programs in certain areas in which the state had been involved previously. For example, public expenditures on health and education, although not unknown under the Somoza regime, expanded considerably under the Sandinistas, especially in the early years.[5] The social security system has also been greatly widened, both in terms of its coverage and sponsored programs.[6] In a different vein, the National Guard was disbanded and a new army formed from the original Sandinista forces. Subsequent external aggression has forced the current Nicaraguan state to increase defense spending; in 1985 this reached 40% of total government expenditures.[7]

One of the major themes underlying the early changes in the composition of the Nicaraguan state was, as is well known, its extension into areas previously restricted in large measure to private ownership. Prior to 1979, for example, the Nicaraguan state had only marginal direct participation in the production and distribution of commodities. The role of the so-called public sector was limited to a relatively low level of social services (especially health and education), utilities, internal security, specialized development banks, and the Central Bank. The total state sector (including central government and decentralized entities), in quantitative terms, directly controlled only about 15% of Nicaragua's GDP.

The role of the state changed considerably after the Sandinista victory (see Table 1). Among the first measures of the FSLN was the nationalization of most of the banking and insurance sector (excepting a few foreign banks) and of the commercialization of exports. State corporations were established to administer the financial system (CORFIN, the Nicaraguan Finance Corporation and INISER, the Nicaraguan Insurance and Reinsurance Institute), whereas the control of external trade became the responsibility of the Ministry of External Commerce (and some six exporting enterprises). The government also greatly expanded its participation in the area of construction and trans-

5. These and other "social services" have not only been performed by the state. Nonstate, so-called mass organizations have been an important site where some of these activities have been carried out—the most well known being the 1980 literacy campaign.
6. See, for example, the essays on education, health, and social welfare in Thomas W. Walker, ed., *Nicaragua: The First Five Years* (New York: Praeger, 1985).
7. Comisión Económica para América Latina (CEPAL), *Notas para el estudio económico de América Latina y el Caribe, 1984: Nicaragua* (México: CEPAL, July 1985).

TABLE 1
State Participation in Domestic Production, 1980−1984 (percentage of total)

ACTIVITY/SECTOR	1980 APP[a]	1980 AP[b]	1981 APP	1981 AP	1982 APP	1982 AP	1983 APP	1983 AP	1984[c] APP	1984[c] AP
Gross domestic product	36.2	63.8	37.1	62.9	44.2	55.8	41.2	58.8	42.7	57.3
Primary	16.7	83.3	20.3	79.7	22.2	77.8	22.0	78.0	24.4	75.6
Agriculture	17.9	82.1	20.0	80.0	21.9	78.1	20.2	79.8	24.0	76.0
Livestock	10.4	89.6	13.0	87.0	21.0	79.0	24.0	76.0	22.3	77.7
Forestry	48.6	51.4	74.4	25.6	34.9	65.1	45.8	54.2	32.9	67.1
Fishing	59.5	40.5	78.1	21.9	48.7	51.3	68.9	31.1	82.3	17.7
Secondary	38.7	61.3	39.4	60.6	42.3	57.7	43.8	56.2	43.4	56.6
Manufacturing	30.1	69.9	31.5	68.5	36.0	64.0	37.2	62.8	37.2	62.8
Construction	97.2	2.8	87.4	12.6	87.9	12.1	92.9	7.1	92.9	7.1
Mining	100.0	—	100.0	—	100.0	—	100.0	—	100.0	—
Tertiary	43.7	56.3	43.9	56.1	56.6	43.4	51.0	49.0	51.5	48.5
Commerce	30.0	70.0	30.0	70.0	45.7	64.3	32.0	68.0	32.0	68.0
General govt.	100.0	—	100.0	—	100.0	—	100.0	—	100.0	—
Transport & communication	12.1	87.9	14.6	85.4	66.5	43.5	58.8	41.2	58.8	41.2
Banking & insurance	100.0	—	100.0	—	100.0	—	100.0	—	100.0	—
Energy, electricity, & water	100.0	—	100.0	—	100.0	—	100.0	—	100.0	—
Housing property	3.0	97.0	3.0	97.0	3.0	97.0	3.0	97.0	3.0	97.0
Other services	10.0	90.0	10.0	90.0	11.5	88.5	11.5	88.5	11.5	88.5

[a]APP = area of people's property.
[b]AP = private sector.
[c]Preliminary data.
Source: Unpublished data from the Nicaraguan Centro de Investigaciones y Estudios de la Reforma Agraria.

portation. Therefore, within the first 6 months after taking power, the Sandinista state had extended its participation in the "service" sector far beyond the traditional public enterprises that functioned in that sector under Somoza.[8]

Apart from these government services, a number of new entities were formed in the natural resource, agriculture, and industrial sectors. For example, the state significantly increased its presence in the areas of forestry, gold and silver mining, and fishing.[9] In addition, the enterprises and other prop-

8. Including the National Lottery, Telecommunications and Post Office, Nicaraguan Energy Institute, Nicaraguan Water and Sewerage Institute, and National Electrical Energy Institute.
9. The nationalization of primary resource production was one of the few instances in which property owned by foreigners was directly affected by the state.
  The relevant state corporations are the Natural Resources and Environment Institute (IRENA), the People's Forestry Corporation (CORFORP), the Nicaraguan Mines and Hydrocarbons Institute (INMINEH), and the Nicaraguan Institute for Fisheries (INPESCA).

erty directly owned by Somoza and by close associates of the Somoza regime who left the country after December 1977 became state property. Those holdings included some 168 factories (mainly plastics, timber, foodstuffs, building materials, paper, metal and machinery, and pharmaceuticals), making up 25% of the country's industrial plant, and two million acres of agricultural property that encompassed about half of the farms larger than 500 manzanas. These enterprises formed the basis of the Area of People's Property (APP). They were managed for the first 5 months by the National Reconstruction Trust Fund; they then came under the management of the People's Industrial Corporation (COIP) and the Nicaraguan Agrarian Reform Institute (INRA).

By the end of 1980, the state accounted for 18% of total agricultural production, 30% of manufacturing, 44% of services, and 100% of such sectors as mining, banking, and insurance. In all, little more than one-third of the country's GDP in 1980 was generated within state entities. This level of participation of the state in the Nicaraguan economy has been relatively stable since then.

In addition, the last 6 years have seen the state become involved in a wide range of other activities. The state has increased its participation in the storing, transport, and distribution of domestic products (through, for example, the Nicaraguan Enterprise for Basic Food Products, ENABAS). The emerging trade gap has led to strict state control over foreign exchange (with foreign exchange rationing and multiple exchange rates) and import controls. Prices for six basic consumer items are controlled and some fifty other prices are "regulated." In the area of labor relations, the state has established (and enforced) new minimum wages and a scale for all other wages and salaries (through the Labor Ministry's National System of Ordering Work and Salaries, SNOTS), promoted labor unions and collective bargaining agreements, and, under the temporary emergency laws, prohibited strikes.[10]

This quantitative expansion of the scope of Nicaraguan state activities was accompanied by a qualitative transformation of the state. This new state has comprised a different set of political, cultural, and economic processes from those of the state under Somoza. In particular, as far as the Nicaraguan class structure is concerned, the state has expanded its performance of processes that secure the conditions (from marketing and credit to lawmaking and education) under which capitalists and others engage in production. In

10. During the August 1979—August 1980 period, 200 collective bargaining agreements were signed, covering 50,000 employees. During the 46 years of the Somoza regime, only 46 such agreements were signed. For a fuller discussion, see Carlos M. Vilas, *Perfiles de la Revolución Sandinista* (Havana: Casa de las Américas, 1984).

addition, the Nicaraguan state itself has come to occupy the position of capitalist commodity producer—for both domestic and international markets.

The quantitative and qualitative restructuring of the Nicaraguan state also involves a new set of potential tensions and struggles over the range of social processes performed in and by the state. To take a noneconomic example, the cultural process of education involves not only who is taught but also what is taught. Education involves the training of potential workers as well as the dissemination of conceptions of life, work, politics, and so forth. Therefore, given the changed content of the Nicaraguan educational system since 1979, it is not surprising that capitalists and other occupants of positions in sites outside the state have struggled with occupants of positions in the state over the effects of state-sponsored education. Similar tensions and struggles have emerged over a wide range of other state initiatives, including property ownership, marketing, price setting, law enforcement, and defense.

An additional issue concerning this transformation of the Nicaraguan state, one that is especially relevant for the question of transition, is the extent to which these social processes may lead to changes in the Nicaraguan class structure. In particular, because changes in property ownership and the expansion of state activities do not by themselves mean the elimination of capitalism, two further questions become relevant: Are the conditions being created whereby the state can eventually restrict and/or eliminate its own role in reproducing capitalism? Similarly, do the activities of the new state mean that the reproduction of the conditions of existence of capitalism will be restricted and/or eliminated in other, nonstate sites (private enterprises, churches, families, etc.) in Nicaraguan society?

NICARAGUAN PLANNING

Once the initial steps of restructuring the Nicaraguan state were taken, the stage was set for reactivating and transforming the Nicaraguan economy. The fact that the state had become a site where not only commodity production took place (in the APP) but also where such activities as the creation of money and money lending and the internal marketing and distribution of commodities were carried on meant that no sector of the economy could ultimately escape its influence. The Nicaraguan economy was far from being a wholly state-run economy, but the various activities that made up the new state would have far-reaching effects throughout Nicaragua; and consciously or unconsciously, the intervention of the state must be governed or shaped by some broad view of ends to be pursued and of the effects of attempting to pursue those ends—in other words, by a general plan for the economy. State planning in Nicaragua was born out of this de facto situation.

To be clear, however, the existence of state planning does not mean that compulsory production and other targets are formulated in the planning ministry and carried out by lower-level state and nonstate entities. Economic planning in Nicaragua has never corresponded to the textbook description of the "centrally planned economy."[11] Rather, if by planning we mean the exercise of state authority to intervene in and partially regulate the economy, then a commitment to planning in official circles and concrete attempts at planning existed almost from the start.

The Ministry of Planning (MIPLAN) was one of the first ministries organized during the first 6 months of Sandinista power. The conditions facing the new regime and its planners have been well documented by FitzGerald, the World Bank, and ECLA.[12] The destruction and disruption caused by the insurrection, the inherited external debt, and the necessity to reorient the existing model of development all called for immediate measures bound together by a global plan of action. The first meetings in MIPLAN to discuss this situation took place during July and August of 1979. Those meetings led to the first discussions concerning the "Sandinista model of development" and to studies of the various areas of the economy (the APP, the structure of agriculture, the possibility of an agrarian reform, etc.). The first general outlines of an economic program for 1980 were presented to the Junta of the Government of National Reconstruction (JGRN) and the National Directorate of the FSLN (DN-FSLN) and subsequently approved on October 22, 1979. After successive drafts of the more detailed program and after the naming of Sandinista Comandante Henry Ruiz as Minister of Planning in the December 1979 reorganization of the government, the "Program of Economic Reactivation to Benefit the People" was finally approved in mid-January of 1980.[13]

Plan 80, as it came to be known, received widespread diffusion throughout

11. Nor is it clear that any other so-called socialist economy involves economic planning that conforms to the textbook model. Michael Ellman notes the increasing acknowledgment of the diversity of planning systems and the burying of the myth of the single "Soviet-type economy." See his "Changing Views on Central Economic Planning: 1958–1983," *ACES Bulletin* 25 (Spring 1983): 11–34.
12. See E.V.K. FitzGerald, "The Economics of the Revolution," in *Nicaragua in Revolution*, ed. by Thomas W. Walker (New York: Praeger, 1982): 203–221; World Bank, *Nicaragua: The Challenge*; and CEPAL, *Nicaragua: Repercusiones económicas de los acontecimientos políticos recientes* (Santiago, Chile: CEPAL, August 1979).
13. Ministry of Planning (MIPLAN), *Programa de reactivación económica en beneficio del pueblo* (Managua: Secretaría Nacional de Propaganda y Educación Política, F.S.L.N., 1980).

the country—both in its full form and in more popular versions. The general aim of Sandinista economic policy, as announced in the economic program, was the "defense, consolidation, and advance of the revolutionary process" to overcome the combination of conjunctural difficulties (for example, the financial crisis and the drop in agricultural production) and structural problems (primarily, what was considered to be the "dependent" nature of the Nicaraguan economy). The long-run objective was to "initiate the process of transition." The more specific objectives outlined in the program were four: (a) to reactivate production and distribution with the aim of satisfying the "basic needs" of the population; (b) to build and maintain a level of "national unity" among various key social groups (specifically, as the program saw them, wage and salary workers, small producers and artisans, professionals and technicians, and "patriotic entrepreneurs"); (c) to construct the new Sandinista state (discussed in the preceding section); and (d) to establish and maintain macroeconomic and external sector balances.

The institutional context for carrying out the program would be a "mixed economy" (because of the continued existence of domestic and international markets) in which the state would be the "center" of reactivation and transltion. Notwithstanding this emphasis on the role of the state, the program does make reference to the importance of production in nonstate enterprises. For example, of the total of 140,000 manzanas programmed to be devoted to coffee production, only 16% would be under the direct control of INRA.[14] At the same time, private investment was expected to be minimal: Probable investment was expected to reach 2700 million córdobas during 1980, with only 470 million of that total coming from capitalists and other producers in the private sphere.[15]

The full-scale reactivation of the economy was designed to be carried out over 2 years: 1978 levels of economic activity would be reached by the end of 1980, and 1981 would see the achievement of levels of the previous "normal year"—1977. In practice this would mean using existing excess capacity to reach an overall economic growth rate of 23%. In particular, services were programmed to rise to levels about 37% higher than in 1978, but "material production" would still be 9% less than in that year.[16]

The overall model of export-led growth was not to be fundamentally altered at this stage of development in the revolutionary process. The "differ-

14. The expected participation in total production of enterprises under the control of INRA varied, of course, by crop. For example, the corresponding figures for cotton and sugar cane were 12.4 and 40%, respectively.
15. See MIPLAN, *Programa de reactivación*, 68.
16. "Material production," in the sense used by MIPLAN, refers to production in the so-called primary and secondary sectors, that is, all production except the "tertiary" or service sector (see Table 1).

ential rent" captured from the "comparative advantage" of Nicaraguan exports of agricultural goods would continue to serve as the basis of earning foreign exchange to purchase necessary imports. However, the overall balances of the program demonstrated that an "external gap" (consisting of the trade deficit, service payments, and an increase in international reserves) would remain and amount to some $370 million. This was exactly equal to the calculated need for external funds.

The final chapter of Plan 80 presented the planners' expectations of the "dynamic and tensions of reactivation." Fundamentally, it was argued that increasing incomes (especially of the poorest sections of the population) and using existing excess capacity would run up against constraints imposed by supply inelasticities in agriculture, the shortage of foreign exchange, and the fact that changes in the composition of demand generated by a changed distribution of income would not find the corresponding supply, at least in the short term. In addition, it was acknowledged that private producers, given the wide range of political and other changes taking place, might not respond to the levels of production programmed for them.

Plan 80, then, was a document that attempted to lend coherence to the variety of state initiatives during the first full year of the Sandinista government. It was not, as argued before, a set of obligatory goals that were (or could have been) imposed on the various state and nonstate entities involved in the economic reactivation. Rather, the program outlined in Plan 80 was the product of the joint effort of hundreds of state officials, in conjunction with some representatives of mass organizations and large private capitalists, with the aim of providing an overall framework for specific policies and for analyzing the expected effects of those policies.

The implementation of the program was, of course, delayed by its late publication. Additional disruptions were caused by difficulties inside the JGRN (Junta member Alfonso Robelo finally resigned on April 12),[17] the lack of any centralized direction, and the fact that the nine proposed Coordinating Program Commissions (CPCs) never quite got off the ground. MIPLAN held its

17. Alfonso Robelo—a former president of the Nicaraguan Chamber of Industry (1972–1975), the Nicaraguan Development Institute, and the Higher Council of Private Enterprise (COSEP, 1975–1978)—was one of the leaders of the anti-Somoza Nicaraguan Democratic Movement (MDN) and member of the original post-Somoza JGRN. He resigned from the JGRN after it was announced that the FSLN and Sandinista mass organizations would have a working majority on the Council of State. Robelo and Violeta Chamorro (the other conservative member of the JGRN, who resigned a few days earlier than Robelo "for reasons of health") were eventually replaced by Arturo Cruz (director of the Nicaraguan Central Bank) and Rafael Córdoba. This crisis in the FSLN's attempt to maintain "national unity" continued throughout 1980. Robelo and Cruz are now prominent leaders of the major Contra group, the Nicaraguan Democratic Front (FDN).

first public seminar on planning in Nicaragua in May of 1980, to take stock of this first Sandinista experience with planning and to begin the preparations for pulling together an economic program for 1981. Not surprisingly, at least from MIPLAN's perspective, the lessons drawn from the 1980 seminar (and basically repeated in its 1981 counterpart) were that ministerial "feudalism" and the lack of state discipline were at the root of the problems in carrying out the economic program for 1980.[18] These conclusions expressed MIPLAN's concern with the fact that, although entirely devoted to economic planning, it was just one among twenty other ministries and that Plan 80 was not binding on the other state entities.

Therefore, MIPLAN, although the official center for the elaboration of economic programs and other planning documents, has never enjoyed anything like complete monopoly over planning activities, short-term or annual. This is not unlike other experiences of socialist planning.[19] MIPLAN initiated its activity of formulating plans for the year ahead in 1979, but economic policy was made throughout the year by the interministerial "economic council." Emergency economic programs, negotiations with individual capitalist enterprises, and the continual search for foreign markets and sources of external credits and loans tended to supersede the best-laid plans of prior months. In addition, independent decisions by other ministries, especially one with the weight of Agricultural Development and Agrarian Reform (MIDINRA), would change the parameters according to which the original program was drawn up.

Finally, it must be kept in mind that economic planning has never obeyed the relatively simple conception of a one-to-one correspondence between acts stipulated in the plan and the broad economic and social consequences they are so often said, at least in principle, to cause. Economic plans, whether obligatory or not, represent only one set of proposed interventions in the economy and wider society at any point in time. The complex effects of those planned initiatives are always modified and transformed by the effects of changes in other parts of the state and in other, nonstate sites to produce the various paths of movement registered in the remainder of the economy and society. Moreover, the activity of state economic planning is, in turn, affected by those other changes.

To see this, consider the following example. The attempt to centralize the

18. MIPLAN, "Resumen y conclusiones de 1980: El primer año de economía Sandinista," internal report, 1980; and "Conclusiones y recomendaciones del II seminario de planificación en Nicaragua," internal report, May 1981.
19. See, for example, the description of planning in the USSR by Edwin Haflett Carr and R. W. Davies, Foundations of a Planned Economy, 1926–1929, Vol. 1, Part 2 (New York: Macmillan, 1969), 787–808.

activity of economic planning in one ministry and to impose the results of that activity on other state entities may lead to tensions and struggles with those other entities over the nature and scope of that particular approach to state economic planning.[20] At the same time, planned limits on wage increases may lead to a shortage of labor in the "formal" economy. Employers might respond by attempting to pay wages (in the form of money or in kind) *above* the official rates. These unplanned wage payments might, on the one hand, upset the planned macroeconomic balances; on the one other hand, the low official wages might induce the movement of labor out of the formal sector into the "informal" economy. The latter set of activities is even less amenable to state economic planning. The result of these and other factors that change and modify planned initiatives may be that the activity of planning in the state is itself reorganized. State planning may even be dismantled altogether.

In the case of Nicaragua, the tensions and struggles over economic planning within the state do not appear to have been over whether or not there would be some form of economic planning; rather, they seem to have involved the issue of who would hold the power over economic planning within the state. Thus the activity of state economic planning did not disappear. Instead, MIPLAN was eventually replaced (in early 1985) by a Secretariat of Planning and the Budget (SPP). In formal organizational terms, the SPP is no longer a separate ministry charged with the responsibility of drafting annual plans and attempting to induce other ministries and state entities to make decisions consistent with the plans. The SPP is now considered to be a cabinet office—a technical office without ministerial rank—attached to the National Planning Board (CNP). The CNP, in turn, replaced the "economic council" and is made up of the heads of the relevant ministries organized into five basic economic areas: foreign aid, agriculture and marketing, finance, industry, and infrastructure.

The evaluation of the outcomes of the first economic program brought to the fore the difficulties experienced and the wide-ranging nature of the changes that had taken place in the first year and a half under the new Sandinista government. Not surprisingly, fulfillment of the quantitative targets stipulated in Plan 80 was uneven. The overall rate of growth of GDP, although not of the magnitude projected in the program, did reach 10%. Exports behaved more poorly than expected (down 24.7% with respect to the 1979 level) and imports rose more rapidly than projected (some 75.8% over

20. In the case of Nicaragua, MIDINRA Minister Jaime Wheelock expressed his doubts about the feasibility of MIPLAN's approach to economic planning in the following way: The "introduction of a system of overall planning did not work because society, which has strong mercantile tendencies, does not lend itself easily to planning." Jaime Wheelock Román, *El gran desafío* (Managua: Nueva Nicaragua, 1983), 115.

1979), leading to a widening trade gap (24% of GDP) at the end of 1980. Agricultural production in 1980 was based on the area planted in 1979; thus the disrupted 1979—1980 agricultural cycle meant that production levels fell by 11.6% in that year. However, the area planted in 1980 for the 1980—1981 cycle surpassed the programmed area. Industrial production reached 90% of the planned level, growing at a rate of 7.3% during 1980. In terms of traditional national income accounting, the results of 1980 demonstrated that economic reactivation had, in fact, taken place. However, it was also the case that this reactivation had generated widening internal and external "gaps": Domestic inflation reached 27% (down from 1979 but far above historical rates of inflation), and foreign debt and the trade deficit were growing at alarming rates.

An overall assessment of 1980 by MIPLAN was presented in the economic program for 1981:

> Even if the economic reactivation was very dynamic, it was also uneven. In effect, it was more notable in production for domestic consumption than in export production. Similarly, it was more substantial in the countryside than in the city, and more dynamic in the APP and small-scale production than in the capitalist sector.[21]

The evaluation of the first year of the Nicaraguan "planned economy" also revealed that other changes and difficulties, not captured in the national income accounts, characterized the situation through the end of 1980. New forms of property and organization had emerged, especially in agricultural production: State capitalist farms (UPE) had been organized on INRA land, whereas production and credit and service cooperatives had begun to form among relatively small-scale capitalist and noncapitalist producers in the countryside.[22] These new enterprises existed side by side with traditional large-scale private capitalist farms and agroindustrial complexes. It was also noted that the process of "social differentiation" had accelerated among the other agricultural producers. That is, the small-holding "peasantry" was becoming increasingly divided into two groups: at one pole, producers who employed wage labor and had access to additional land by buying or renting land from others, and, at the other pole, producers who were forced to sell their labor power and rent and/or sell their land to that first group. Finally, in

21. MIPLAN, *Programa económico de austeridad y eficiencia 81* (Managua: MIPLAN, January 1981), 154.
22. For a fuller discussion of these and other changes in the agricultural sector, see Carmen Diana Deere, Peter Marchetti, and Nola Reinhardt, "The Peasantry and the Development of Sandinista Agrarian Policy, 1979—1984," *Latin American Research Review* 20 (1985), 75—109.

terms of the organization of production, "labor productivity" (defined and measured as the total value of production divided by total employees) had dropped precipitously within the APP during the course of the year but had remained virtually constant in private enterprises.

Income distribution had also been modified in important ways during the course of 1980. Such measures as the creation of new jobs (112,300 new jobs were generated, bringing down the official unemployment rate to 17.5%), the lowering of rents on agricultural lands, an increase in agricultural producer prices, the extension of credit, an increase in minimum wages (but a decline in average real wages), and state control and subsidies of basic consumer goods all contributed to changing the existing distribution of income. This same modification of key prices also had the effect of widening the town-country price "scissors" that had originally emerged in 1978: The prices offered to the producers of domestic foodstuffs continued to *fall*, through the end of 1980, with respect to the prices at which they purchased manufactured goods. At the same time, the prices paid to the producers of agricultural exports *rose* in comparison to industrial prices. Therefore, although the overall price scissors widened during the course of 1980, the effects on relatively small-scale independent agricultural producers (located primarily in domestic food production) and larger scale capitalist producers (with a high percentage of export production) were uneven.

The experience in drawing up and attempting to carry out Plan 80 laid the basis for the second Sandinista economic program, the *Economic Program of Austerity and Efficiency*.[23] Formal preparations for this Plan 81 began during the month of June with the drafting of the qualitative aims and quantitative sectoral "control figures" for the year ahead. In conjunction with the DN-FSLN and the JGRN, the strategic objectives of the economic program were worked out during September. The joint efforts of MIPLAN and the sectoral ministries during October led to revisions in the original control figures and the first draft of the program as a whole. Work during November involved further revisions, the drafting of the state budget, and the presentation of the plan to the JGRN. Finally, on January 10, Plan 81 was formally published.

The general approach to drafting the economic plans established during 1980 for 1981 appears to have remained the standard approach through 1985. Control figures in the form of "material balances" for the major agroexport, domestic food, and industrial products were drawn up by MIPLAN, and these were then revised in discussions with the various sectoral ministries. Targets for such goals as employment, investment, and necessary

23. MIPLAN, *Programa económico*.

foreign exchange were determined. The impact of projected policy measures such as wage and salary scales and the government budget were estimated. Finally, "global balances" of aggregate supply and demand, external payments, and finance were calculated for the economy as a whole.

When applied to the drafting of Plan 81, the following target growth rates were established: 18.5% for GDP (compared to an actual rate of 10.7% in 1980); for "material production," 22.3% (compared to 3.8% in 1980); and, for services, 14.6% (18.5% in 1980). Thus Plan 81 was seen as the culmination of the economic reactivation begun in 1979 and carried through 1980.

The four problems that received particular emphasis in the economic program for 1981 were the external sector, productivity, consumption, and "surpluses." As mentioned before, 1980 saw a widening trade gap generated by exports and imports that were, respectively, lower and higher than both programmed and historical levels. Part of this gap was determined by continuing declines in Nicaragua's external terms of trade (down 16 and 3.7% in 1979 and 1980, respectively). However, it was also the case that *quantum* export production levels remained relatively low and imports exceeded projected levels (based on the lack of import controls in the context of an overvalued córdoba exchange rate, restricted domestic supply, and the unchanged high import content of domestic production). It was estimated that labor productivity had dropped by more than 50% since 1979, especially in APP firms. In addition, all three areas of consumption had exceeded programmed levels during 1980: private "basic" consumption (up 23% over 1979), primarily due to the increase in employment and minimum wages; private "nonbasic" consumption (up 34%), based on increases in both middle incomes and profits; and government consumption (up 30%), from government consumer subsidies, the expansion of state sector employment, and investments in economic and "social" (especially hospitals and schools) infrastructure.

These three sets of problems combined to create both internal and external disequilibria that would only be solved over the medium term. They eventually became the focus of the JGRN's "Economic Policy Guidelines 1983–1988": Economic development over the next 5 years would be

> based on structural changes that will gradually eliminate internal and external imbalances and lay the foundation for sustained economic growth that make it possible to attain the basic objectives of the country's development policy: satisfaction of the basic needs of the entire population and growing self-sufficiency.[24]

24. National Reconstruction Government of Nicaragua (JGRN), "Economic Policy Guidelines 1983–1988," Internal report, 1983, 1.

The fourth major problem to which attention was directed in Plan 81 was that of the economic "surplus." Although nowhere specifically defined, MIPLAN's notion of the surplus appears to refer to the portion of GDP available for government expenditures and (state and nonstate) investment. In the nonstate sphere, MIPLAN observed that investment had not risen pari passu with enterprise profits.

> Although objectively profits have recovered much faster than wages and salaries, the cooperation of private entrepreneurs has been limited to raising production; their attitude with respect to investment has been ambiguous.[25]

In addition, according to MIPLAN, the investible surplus itself was less available: It had decreased in certain sectors (especially in the APP); it had been lost through capital flight; and it had been absorbed by government expenditures other than investment. This meant that the only remaining source of surplus or investment funds were "external savings" in the form of foreign donations, credits, and loans. The resulting external debt had risen from $1.1 billion at the end of 1979 to $1.6 billion in 1980.[26] Debt service was expected to absorb some 28% of projected 1981 export earnings. According to the Economic Commission for Latin America, the debt-service ratio actually reached 31%, and the outstanding external debt rose to $2.1 billion.[27]

The virtual absence of private investment and the recourse to higher levels of external debt to finance state investment continued to force the issue of the role of the state in the new Sandinista economy.

"THE STATE AS THE CENTER OF ACCUMULATION"

The original conception of the role of the new state in Sandinista political economy was based, in general, on planning and, in particular, on control of the economic surplus.[28] The state was to become the "center of accumula-

---

25. MIPLAN, *Programa económico*, 121.
26. Economic Commission for Latin America (ECLA), *Economic Survey of Latin America, 1981*, (Santiago, Chile: ECLA, 1983), 571.
27. CEPAL, *Notas para el estudio*.
28. This conception was implicit in the various published (MIPLAN, *Programa de reactivación* and *Programa económico*) and unpublished (MIPLAN, "Nicaragua: Programa económico," internal report, 1982; "Programa económico 1984," internal report, February 1984; and "Plan económico 1985," internal report, December 1984) economic plans, explicit in other MIPLAN documents, and theorized by E.V.K. FitzGerald ("Planned Accumulation and Income Distribution in the Small Peripheral Economy," mimeo, June 1982; "The Problem of Balance in the Peripheral Socialist Economy," *World Development* 13 (1985), 5–14; and

tion" by centralizing the so-called surplus within the Nicaraguan economy and planning the use of that surplus in accumulation. The state was conceived to have *direct* access to the surplus generated in the APP and to have *indirect* access to the surplus produced in nonstate (capitalist and noncapitalist) enterprises. Thus this particular form of "primary socialist accumulation" was not to be based on the wholesale confiscation of previously private property. Rather the nationalization of property would be limited to the holdings of the Somoza regime (the Somoza family and its closest allies) and any property that over time was abandoned or otherwise unproductively utilized.[29]

For the state to serve as this center of accumulation, it needed to mobilize sufficient finance. What this meant concretely was that, on the one hand, state enterprises had to achieve high levels of profitability; on the other hand, the state had to realize a surplus on its current account and to use other mechanisms such as its control over credit and marketing to "siphon off" surplus realized in nonstate enterprises. Once the surplus was effectively captured, its planned use could serve as the basis for the reactivation and restructuring of the economy on the basis of state investment.

Obviously this accumulation strategy is not without its own inherent difficulties. It may be stalled and/or undermined by so-called exogenous factors such as declines in the external terms of trade, foreign aggression, and natural disasters.[30] In addition, attempts to increase the size of the surplus in both state and nonstate enterprises and to gain effective state control over that surplus may themselves create problems. They may, and probably will, involve the state in a wide range of political and economic (including class) tensions and struggles. For example, attempts to lower real wages (to increase the amount of surplus extracted) and/or to increase taxes on capitalist enterprises (to direct the surplus into fiscal revenues) may generate conflicts that imperil the central role of the state in accumulation. Such conflicts may also have the effect of undermining the transitional project itself.

In the concrete case of Nicaragua, the attempt to construct a state that serves as the center of accumulation has been subject to precisely such tensions and difficulties. The short-term strategy to overcome these problems

---

"Apuntes para el análisis de la pequeña economía en transición," in *La transición difícil: El desarrollo de las pequeñas economías periféricas,* ed. by José Luis Coraggio and Carmen Diana Deere [México: Siglo Veintiuno, forthcoming]) and George Irvin ("Establishing the State as the Centre of Accumulation," *Cambridge Journal of Economics* 7 (1983), 125–39.

29. This was the logic that ruled the early nationalization decrees (Nos. 3 and 38) and the Agrarian Reform Law of July 1981.

30. The fall in the terms of trade had been noted previously. The impact of foreign aggression has been analyzed by FitzGerald (this volume) and CEPAL, *Notas para el estudio.* The effects of the May 1982 floods are discussed in CEPAL, *Las inundaciones de mayo de 1982 y sus repercusiones sobre el desarrollo económico y social del país* (México: CEPAL, July 1982).

has been an important source of the increased levels of internal and external debt in the last 6 years. The success of the Sandinista transitional project depends crucially on finding additional means of resolving the political and economic contradictions inherent in making the state the center of accumulation.

One way to get at these potential problems and difficulties is to consider the finances of the Nicaraguan state. In general, any state can be expected to have a heterogeneous source of revenues and pattern of expenditures. The revenue of a typical state in a transitional society can be expected to include some combination of the following: current income from the profits of state enterprises; taxes on the profits of, and the exchange of, services with capitalist and noncapitalist enterprises outside the state; and taxes on the incomes of all other individuals as well as state borrowing.[31] At the same time, the state is engaged in making expenditures that secure those sources of revenue: payments such as managers' salaries and interest payments that directly secure enterprise profits; a legal system, infrastructure, and certain types of education that maintain the state's access to some portion of profits appropriated elsewhere; and consumer subsidies, hospitals, and the like to secure all other revenue sources. Thus the state in a transitional society is characterized by a wide variety of class and nonclass revenues and expenditures.

One of the objectives of the Sandinista state may be considered from this perspective as an attempt to open up some political "space" for the new state initiatives or to create a certain "relative autonomy" for the state by lessening its dependence on the tax portion of private sector profits to carry out its projects. One of the dangers of attempting to tax private capitalists and, instead of making expenditures that serve to maintain those particular revenues, to divert them to accumulation within the state sector would be to lose that original source of revenue. For example, private capitalists might compensate for losing the state-provided expenditures by diverting another portion of their gross profits from accumulation to secure those conditions. They might also decide to create new positions for themselves, possibly by deposit-

31. In Marxian terminology, enterprise profits consist of surplus value directly extracted from state workers (SV); the direct transfers of surplus labor extracted in nonstate enterprises are subsumed class revenues (SCR); whereas all other revenues, including debt, include neither the extraction nor the distribution of surplus labor and are therefore understood as nonclass revenues (NCR). State expenditures can be similarly understood in class terms: The state makes ΣSC, ΣX, and ΣY expenditures to secure SV, SCR, and NCR revenues, respectively. Therefore, assuming that state revenues and expenditures are equal, $SV + SCR + NCR = \Sigma SC + \Sigma X + \Sigma Y$. There is no necessary one-to-one quantitative correspondence, however, between the respective revenue and expenditure terms on the left- and right-hand sides of the equation. For a fuller explanation of these categories, see Resnick and Wolff, "Classes in Marxian Theory," in *Review of Radical Political Economics* 13 (Winter 1982), 1–18.

ing those funds in financial institutions and purchasing assets in other countries. In both cases, private domestic capital accumulation and, hence, future sources of such revenus might suffer as a result. This has been one of the dilemmas of the Nicaraguan "mixed economy."

In principle, the surplus of the APP and the revenues from activities such as state credit and marketing were expected to provide sufficient alternative resources to carry out proposed state projects. However, such a strategy also entails political and economic difficulties. On the one hand, increased state enterprise profits generated from, for example, decreases in real wages might generate struggles between state sector enterprise managers and workers. On the other hand, "expensive" state credit and wide price differentials for state-marketed commodities would threaten the participation of nonstate enterprises and poor citizens in the economic reactivation. Hence additional sources of state revenues through such mechanisms have been limited.

Over the last 6 years, both current government revenues and expenditures have risen dramatically in Nicaragua (see Table 2). The current revenue/GDP ratio has grown from approximately 12% during the 1970s to a little more than 36% in 1984. Similarly, the current expenditure/GDP ratio has increased from 8.7 to 37.7% during the same period. Neither APP profits nor state "savings" have turned out to be an adequate source of funds for state accumulation.

TABLE 2
Government Finance (percentage of GDP)

YEAR	1970–1978[a]	1979	1980	1981	1982	1983	1984[b]
Current revenues	12.1	13.1	20.6	21.7	24.6	29.9	36.2
Current expenditures[c]	8.7	15.0	19.6	22.3	26.3	34.2	37.7
State "savings"	3.3	−1.9	1.0	−0.6	−1.6	−4.3	−1.5
Capital expenditures[d]	6.2	1.7	5.6	5.0	4.0	20.5	15.6
Debt service[e]	1.7	3.1	4.4	4.7	6.5	4.2	4.2
Fiscal balance	−4.5	−6.8	−9.0	−10.4	−12.1	−28.9	−21.2
Financing (as percentage of total financed)							
Internal	22.6	85.8	52.1	66.4	80.5	83.2 ·	74.1
External	77.4	14.2	47.9	33.6	19.5	16.8	25.9

[a]Yearly average.
[b]Preliminary.
[c]Excluding interest payments, internal and external.
[d]Excluding amortization payments, internal and external.
[e]Interest plus amortization payments, internal and external.
Sources: Author's calculations based on: 1970–1982, IDB *Informe económico Nicaragua* (Washington, D.C.: IDB, 1983); 1983–1984, ECLA *Notas para el estudio económico de América Latina y el Caribe, 1984. Nicaragua* (Mexico City: United Nations, 1985).

However, state accumulation (measured here as officially classified "capital expenditures" minus amortization payments) has expanded from 6.2% of GDP during the 1970s to 20.4 and 15.6% in 1983 and 1984, respectively.[32] With state "savings" being negative and debt service payments averaging 4.8% of GDP during the 1980–1984 period, the only short-run alternative was in the form of internal and external borrowing.[33] Thus the Nicaraguan fiscal deficit to be financed rose from 9% of GDP in 1980 to 21.2% in 1984. The mix of internal and external borrowing has also changed during that period. Although external loans available to Nicaragua for government deficit financing more than doubled between 1980 and 1984, their participation in financing the deficit fell from 48 to 26%. The increased importance of internal borrowing, mostly from the Central Bank, has become, in turn, an important factor in creating a highly monetized and inflationary economy.

This "fiscal crisis" means that one of the conditions whereby the Nicaraguan state has become the center of accumulation has been on the basis of internal and external debts. The external debt situation is, of course, critical. Recent "austerity" programs in Latin America provide graphic examples of the tensions created by attempts to service the outstanding debt. At the same time, recourse to this particular set of state income, instead of other revenues—such as further increasing taxes on income and services, increasing profits produced by state employees, or "squeezing" capitalists, agricultural cooperatives, or independent agricultural producers—has been an important factor in building and maintaining the complex alliances upon which the Sandinista project rests and with which the current foreign aggression may be successfully fought.

CONCLUSIONS

The economic program for 1985 included a specific set of "austerity" measures designed, in part, to deal with the problems and difficulties generated by the state in its multiple roles in the Nicaraguan economy.[34] For example, state subsidies for consumer products would be gradually eliminated; state investments were to be sharply curtailed; central government employment

32. Although no exact current data exist, private investment appears to have been minimal throughout the period since 1979. According to IDB, *Informe económico*, private investment averaged little more than 1.7% of GDP during the years 1980–1982 (compared to 12.8 and 9.0% in 1977 and 1978, respectively).
33. An alternative, more long-range policy that has been pursued with the aim of increasing the amount of surplus available has been to attempt to increase the productivity of state employees (within the APP) and of nonstate producers of basic foodstuffs.
34. MIPLAN, "Plan económico 1985."

would be frozen; and new taxes would be applied.[35] The measures publicly announced and put into place on February 8, 1985 also included a devaluation of the córdoba, wage increases, and improved distribution of consumer products for "formal" sector employees.[36]

It is, of course, too early to formulate a final analysis of the consequences of these new policies; their effects would continue to develop over the course of 1985, into 1986. However, the SPP's analysis of the results of the first trimester led to a revision of the initial estimates contained in the economic program.[37] Overall economic growth, instead of rising at a rate of 2%, was projected to fall 1.3%. Industrial production was down 5.3% compared with the first trimester of 1984 (and down 8.8% with respect to the programmed level), and, in agriculture, the actual area planted was only 81.8% of the total initially programmed. Inflation of official consumer prices during the first 6 months of 1985 was calculated at 281.3%, whereas the official average monthly salary increased only 146.2%. Both the fiscal deficit and the deficit on current external account were expected to reach levels at least as high as those in 1984.

The initial control figures for 1986 were based on an extension of the stabilization policies enacted during 1985.[38] The importance of the continuing external "gap" was represented by the fact that all of the targets for production—trade, government finance, and the like—were calculated in three variants, depending on the availability of foreign exchange. Thus, for example, estimates for overall economic growth varied between 4.5 and −0.1%. Similarly, total investment was projected to fall by an amount between −10.5% and −18.7% over projected levels for 1985. Of course, all of the estimates contained in these control figures were highly dependent on the results of the remainder of 1985, any new stabilization measures enacted, the response of state and nonstate producers, and the outcome of the current war. The overall impression is that Nicaraguan economic planning, although never particularly long term and never allowed to escape the influence of external aggression, has been increasingly oriented toward short-term policymaking and putting the economy on a wartime footing.

One of the effects of this "war Sandinismo" is that the role of the state and

---

35. Such subsidies had hovered around 10% of total current government expenditures in preceding years.
36. The austerity measures were published in *Barricada* (February 9, 1985) and are discussed by E.V.K. FitzGerald, "La economía nacional en 1985: La transición como coyuntura," Paper presented at the 1985 Annual Congress of Nicaraguan Social Scientists, Managua, August 1985, and by Pizarro (this volume).
37. Secretariat of Planning and the Budget (SPP), "Evaluación y perspectivas económicas 1985," internal report, June 1985.
38. SPP, "Bosquejo del plan económico 1986," internal report, June 1985.

planning in the Nicaraguan transition has to be reconsidered. If, as some have argued,[39] the tendency is for the Nicaraguan "mixed economy" to become increasingly state run, this does not mean that the state has decreased its involvement in securing the economic, political, and cultural conditions under which capitalism is reproduced in Nicaragua. On the contrary, capitalist production (both outside but especially inside the state) seems to be strengthened, at least in the short term, by the expanded role of the state and planning under the Sandinistas.

However, this short-term movement has been accompanied by other changes (in areas as diverse as cooperative production, foreign policy, the status of women and ethnic minorities, popular education, and forms of mass organization) that may lead to a future situation in which the position of the state in the Nicaraguan political economy can be radically transformed. On the one hand, it may be possible to restrict and eventually eliminate the role of the state in providing some of the conditions of existence of capitalism. On the other hand, it may be possible to revolutionize the state and create for it a new role in securing some of the conditions whereby alternative, perhaps communal, forms of production can emerge and develop.

In this sense, the contradictory roles of the state and planning in the Nicaraguan transition should not obscure the fact that major, epoch-making changes have occurred in that country since 1979.

ACKNOWLEDGMENTS

I would like to express my appreciation for the assistance and support of Valpy FitzGerald, Xabier Gorostiaga, and many other individuals too numerous to list. The research for this chapter would not have been possible without their guidance and cooperation. The comments of Rose Spalding and James Dunkerley on an earlier draft are also greatly appreciated. I am, of course, responsible for the analysis and conclusions presented here.

The research for this chapter was supported in part by grants from the Helen Kellogg Institute for International Studies, the Institute for Scholarship in the Liberal Arts, and the Jesse Jones Faculty Research Travel Fund of the University of Notre Dame.

All translations are by the author.

39. See, for example, Weeks (this volume).

PART II

DEVELOPMENT PRIORITIES AND DILEMMAS

Chapter 4

Industrial Development Strategies in Revolutionary Nicaragua

CLAES BRUNDENIUS

THE NICARAGUAN INDUSTRIAL SECTOR BEFORE 1979

The creation of the Central American Common Market (CACM), or the General Treaty of Central American Integration as it is officially called, proved to be a dynamic, if temporary, incentive to an incipient industrialization of the region. Industrial growth had been sluggish in the 1950s (except in Costa Rica). In 1960, on the eve of the creation of the CACM, the manufacturing share of GDP ranged between only 12 to 15% in the countries of the region (that is, Costa Rica, El Salvador, Guatemala, Honduras, and Nicaragua) or just about the same degree of industrialization as in 1950.[1] By 1970, however, the share of manufacturing value added in the GDP had risen to an average of 17.4% for the CACM members, with the highest ratio in Nicaragua at 21.7%.[2]

This means that quite important structural changes in the economy took place in Nicaragua in the 1960s. The growth of the industrial sector was accompanied by a very drastic decline in the agricultural share of GDP, falling from 45.8% in 1950 to 23.4% in 1960. But in spite of the relatively rapid rate of industrial growth in the period, few new jobs were created in the industrial sector. Employment in industry as a share of total employment increased only from 11.4% in 1950 to 11.7% in 1963 and 12% in 1971. Even as late as 1977, the peak year of prewar economic activity, the ratio was only

1. Claes Brundenius, *Algunos apuntes sobre el desarrollo económico de Centroamérica y del Caribe, 1960–82* (Managua: INIES, 1983).
2. *Ibid.*

15%.[3] With no absorption outlets in urban industry, the growing number of migrants from the rural areas went into "other activities" as self-employed (and underemployed) workers.

In the 1960−1965 period, the industrial sector in Nicaragua expanded at an annual rate of 14%.[4] The industrial sectors that benefited most from the Central American integration in the early 1960s were food, beverages, textiles, chemicals, and metallic products. In the following 5 years, the growth rate slowed down to 8.4%. This was still quite vigorous growth, however, and particularly high in the durable consumer goods sector. Then industrial growth tapered off in the 1970s to an annual rate of 6% during 1970−1975 and dropped down to 4.6% in the 1975−1978 period.[5]

The dynamic effects of Central American integration should not be underestimated. On the other hand, the new regional division of labor was still linked to the inherent logic of capital accumulation in the periphery. As a rule, industrial development was subjected to the interests of minority groups—the landed aristocracy linked to the traditional exports of agricultural products on the world market and a smaller infant industrial bourgeoisie limited to serving the interests of the same groups and those of foreign investors.

In spite of integration, there was paradoxically also a growing dependency in Central American on extraregional imports of both raw materials and manufactured goods during the 1970s. Thus the use of extraregional imported raw materials, components, and other inputs in El Salvador increased from 51.2% to 62.8% between 1972 and 1975 and from 35.3% to 39.9% in Guatemala between 1971 and 1976.[6] The degree of extraregional dependency for the supply of manufactured goods was highest in the durable consumer goods sector (75% in 1978) but was also extremely high in the intermediate goods sector (39% in 1978), as is shown in Table 1.

The high degree of import dependency in the durable consumer goods industries was mainly the result of the type of industrialization embodied in the Free Zone industries established in the area in the 1970s (in Managua such a zone was set up in 1976) based on the principles of assembly plants financed with foreign investment and supplied by foreign-imported components and produced with cheap local labor.[7]

3. MIPLAN, *Programa de Reactivación Economica en Beneficio del Pueblo* (Managua: MIPLAN, 1980), 101, and *Fundamentos para la política industrial nicaragüense* (Managua: 1975).
4. Data from MIPLAN, Industry and Mining Department.
5. *Ibid.*
6. CEPAL, *Características principales del proceso y de la política de industrialización de Centroamérica, 1960 a 1980* (México: CEPAL, 1983), 15.
7. See Mario de Franco and Carlos Chamorro, "Nicaragua: crecimiento industrial y desempleo" in *El fracaso de la integración centroamericana* (San José: EDUCA, 1979).

TABLE 1
Extraregional Imports of Industrial Goods as Percentage of Apparent Consumption of Industrial Goods in the Central American Common Market, Selected Years 1960–1979

SUPPLY COEFFICIENTS	TOTAL	NONDURABLE CONSUMER GOODS	INTERMEDIATE GOODS	DURABLE CONSUMER GOODS AND CAPITAL GOODS
1960				
Extraregional	33.2	8.3	59.0	79.1
Regional	66.8	91.7	41.0	20.9
1970				
Extraregional	28.3	5.3	38.1	73.0
Regional	71.7	94.7	61.9	27.0
1975				
Extraregional	29.0	6.1	32.4	76.7
Regional	71.0	93.9	67.6	23.3
1978				
Extraregional	31.5	6.8	39.3	75.1
Regional	68.5	93.2	60.7	24.9
1979				
Extraregional	30.9	7.1	38.2	74.0
Regional	69.1	92.9	61.8	26.0

Source: CEPAL, Características principales del proceso y de la política de industrialización de Centroamérica, 1960 a 1980 (México,: CEPAL, 26 de noviembre de 1982).

THE DISINTEGRATION OF THE CENTRAL AMERICAN MARKET

Despite impressive intraregional trade, pressures and contradictions growing within the CACM eventually led to its disruption. The treaty establishing the Common Market had not provided for preferential treatment for the relatively less developed countries in the region. By 1968, both Honduras and Nicaragua had expressed dissatisfaction with the way in which the benefits of integration were being distributed. In their view, the other three countries, with more developed industrial sectors, were benefiting most from the intraregional trade. By mid-1969, the situation had rapidly deteriorated, eventually leading to open armed confrontation between El Salvador and Honduras (the so-called "soccer war"). Shortly after, Honduras withdrew from the treaty, and the future of the CACM was at stake. Despite several efforts, Honduras has not returned as a full-scale member of the treaty.[8]

Although growing dissatisfaction with the distribution of benefits of Central American integration no doubt was one important factor in its gradual disinte-

8. Task Force Report on Central America, *Central America in Crisis: A Program for Action* (Washington, D.C.: The Washington Institute, 1983).

gration in the 1970s, there are other factors that were more important. Most important were the structural limitations of economic integration in the region. For some time, there were new markets available for lines of industrial production in the region, especially in intermediate goods as was mentioned earlier. But gradually effective demand for final consumer goods tapered off as a result of the extremely skewed income distribution in the region. Table 2 gives an idea of this dramatic situation.

Thus at the end of the 1970s, the poorest half of the population received only 21% of the income in Costa Rica, 20% in Guatemala, 17% in Honduras, 16% in Nicaragua, and 12% in El Salvador, whereas on the other side the top 20% appropriated between 49% (Costa Rica) and 66% (El Salvador) of the incomes in the region, with Nicaragua falling between with 58%. But these figures do not reveal the extent of extreme poverty in the country concerned. In a recent ECLA report, it has been estimated that of the 20 million people who resided in Central America in 1980, no less than 13.2 million (or 64%) were living in extreme poverty in the sense that their incomes did not cover their basic needs, and about 8.5 million (41%) did not have enough financial resources to cover even the most basic nutritional needs.[9]

It is against this background that the decline of intraregional trade after 1970 should be seen. In the case of Nicaragua, the decline has been dramatic (see Table 3). The Central American share of Nicaraguan exports grew from 4.0% in 1960 to 25.8% in 1970 but then gradually declined, reaching a bottom level for the decade of 15.9% in 1979. The most severely hit have been industrial sectors, decreasing as a percentage of total exports.

The structural economic crisis that started affecting Central American integration at the beginning of the 1970s gradually worsened after 1973 when external shocks, such as rapidly increasing oil prices, severely reduced the

TABLE 2
Income Distribution in Central America around 1980 (1980 U.S. dollars)

| INCOME STRATA | COSTA RICA | | EL SALVADOR | | GUATEMALA | | HONDURAS | | NICARAGUA[a] | |
	(%)	AVERAGE INCOME	(%)	AVERAGE INCOME	(%)	AVERAGE INCOME	(%)	AVERAGE INCOME	(%)	AVERAGE INCOME
Poorest 20%	4.0	309	2.0	81	5.3	194	4.3	141	3.0	108
Next 30%	17.0	876	10.0	271	14.5	355	12.7	245	13.0	312
Next 30%	30.0	1547	22.0	597	26.1	638	23.7	446	26.0	613
Richest 20%	49.0	2039	66.0	2687	54.1	1984	59.3	1394	58.0	2100

[a]1977.
Source: CEPAL, *La crisis en Centroamérica: Orígenes, alcances y consecuencias* (México,: CEPAL, 23 de Febrero de 1983).

9. CEPAL, *Características principales*.

TABLE 3
The Rise and Fall of Central American Integration, 1960−1979

	1960	1970	1976	1979
Nicaragua				
Total exports (million U.S.$)	67.8	178.6	541.9	566.6
Percentage to Central America	4.0	25.8	21.7	15.9
Manufacturing exports (million U.S.$)	2.3	39.3	110.6	80.3
Percentage of total exports	3.7	22.0	20.4	14.2
Percentage to Central America	17.4	94.7	87.6	90.2
Central America				
Total exports (million U.S.$)	443.8	1098.0	3007.7	4484.8
Percentage to Central America	6.8	26.1	21.6	20.2
Manufacturing exports (million U.S.$)	28.2	283.8	747.4	1050.9
Percentage of total exports	6.4	25.8	24.8	23.8
Percentage of Central America	52.8	90.2	79.7	77.8

Source: CEPAL, *Características principales del proceso y de la política de industrialización de Centro-américa, 1960 a 1980*, (Mexico,: CEPAL, 26 de noviembre de 1982).

trade surplus. Up to that point the earnings on traditional extraregional exports (primarily agricultural products exported to the United States and Europe) had served as a pool for covering the deficits of some of the countries in their trade with the other Common Market countries.[10] By 1975, El Salvador had also joined the group of countries with a negative intraregional trade balance; only Guatemala remained as a beneficiary of intraregional trade. By 1979, the trade surplus of Guatemala had increased to $146 million with corresponding deficits for El Salvador ($59 million), Honduras ($42 million), Nicaragua ($2 million), and Costa Rica ($42 million). The relatively low figure for Nicaragua is, however, illusory because of the general decline of economic activity in that year during the final phase of the insurrection. In 1980, when a vigorous attempt was made to rapidly reactivate the economy, the Nicaraguan trade deficit with other CACM countries increased to a record $225 million.

THE INDUSTRIAL STRATEGY AFTER 1979

After the Sandinista government came to power, the first strategy in the industrial sector was simply to reactivate industrial production in all sectors to

10. Edelberto Torres-Rivas, *La crisis económica centroamericana—¿Cuál crisis?* (Managua: INIES-CRIES, 1983).

the prewar peak level (1977) as rapidly as possible. Because of the heavy dependence of most Nicaraguan industries on imported raw materials and inputs, this meant a tremendous increase in imports in 1980 from both the Central American market partners as well as from the United States, leading to a large trade deficit in that year of $353 million. The boost in Nicaraguan industrial imports from Central America was a healthy injection into reactivation of the CACM. The problem, however, was that Nicaragua had little hard currency with which to pay. The neighboring countries, each day having more economic and financial problems, were getting increasingly reluctant to give credits to the Sandinista government, if not entirely for economic reasons, increasingly so for political reasons.

But difficulties in relying on supplies from Central American partners was not the only reason why the government in 1981 started outlining a new industrial strategy. It had become clear that by reactivating indiscriminately all sectors of the economy, one was actually just reviving the old industrial structures inherited from the past. This, it was felt, was not always compatible with the new "logic of the majority" that the government and the planning authorities were advocating. It was thus decided that industrial activities should be planned by order of *priorities*.

Industrial planning, however, cannot rest on desires and wishful thinking. It must be based on realistic assumptions and on the realization that the planners do not make the plans "under circumstances chosen by themselves, but under circumstances directly encountered, given and transmitted from the past," as Marx so well described the problem.[11] This understanding of the heritage of the past and the limitations it places on planning the future was present in the industrial strategy outlined in 1982. The main aspects of the industrial structure inherited from the past were the following:

1. Industrial growth in the 1960s and 1970s was basically induced by the dynamics and logic of the CACM through the insertion of Nicaragua within the international division of labor. Nicaragua was one of the countries benefiting least from Central American integration, as has been mentioned.

2. The development of the industrial sector did not permit an adequate articulation (through linkages) with the agricultural sector, not only in the sense that industry failed to provide the agricultural sector with means of production or means for increasing the standard of living of the rural population but also that export-oriented agriculture did not provide sufficient raw material for the food industry. The import substituting industrialization that

11. Karl Marx, *The Eighteenth Brumaire of Louis Bonaparte*, in *Marx and Engels: Basic Writings on Politics and Philosophy*. Edited by Lewis S. Feuer (New York: Doubleday and Co., 1959).

did take place was primarily aimed at complementing industries serving the agroexport sector, generating hard currency earnings for the landed oligarchy.

3. Relatively large- and medium-sized enterprises coexisted with thousands of small, workshop-type industries representing a great variety of precapitalist relations of production. The latter are important not only because of employment creation and the fact that they are overwhelmingly found in the production of basic consumer goods but also because they are heavily dependent on imported raw materials and other inputs.

The new industrial policies intended to adapt the industrial process in revolutionary Nicaragua to a new logic—"the logic of the majority." This new logic necessitated the *transformation* and *rationalization* of the sector in order to overcome existing structural deformations. Transformation means not only prioritizing between different sectors but also prioritizing between different lines of production *within* a given sector (for instance, bread instead of cookies, simple clothes instead of fashion clothes). Rationalization means making better use of disposable resources, both domestic ones and foreign ones.

The process of transformation in revolutionary Nicaragua was based on the following principles:

1. The promotion of production of inputs for the agricultural sector (such as tools, fertilizers and insecticides) with the aim of increasing productivity and gradually ameliorating the terms of trade between agriculture and industry, and leading to decreasing external dependence in the long run
2. Highest priority given to the accelerated production of basic consumer goods (such as basic foods, clothing and medicines)
3. Better articulation between the industrial sector and the agroindustrial export sector (cotton, coffee, and sugar)
4. The promotion of potential new export industries based on domestic raw materials (such as wood and paper)
5. The promotion of industries producing spare parts and other inputs (e.g., rubber) for the transportation sector
6. The promotion of the construction materials industry (e.g., cement) for the construction of roads, dams, schools, hospitals, factories, and popular housing.
7. The creation of a physical-technical infrastructure (such as smelting, forging, and welding facilities) to promote industries supplying the means of production for the expansion of the industries listed previously.

The problem with this strategy—however appealing it might seem— is, of course, that with serious bottlenecks such as a growing balance of payments deficit ahead, the list of priorities will by necessity have to be reduced. Then the question is, as usual, what comes first? The satisfaction of immediate basic needs, or accumulation (the production of capital and intermediate goods) for considerations of long-term, sustained growth? The Cuban experience in the 1960s with short-term trade-offs between growth and equity is a case in point. A basic needs-oriented strategy is not necessarily a barrier to long-term, sustained economic growth, as the Cuban success story of the 1970s and early 1980s tells us.[12] However, the most difficult time is the transitional phase, which might last as long as 10 to 15 years.

INDUSTRIAL DEVELOPMENT AFTER 1979

Industrial growth started tapering off in 1978, but the real decline came in 1979, the final year of the war of liberation, when industrial output fell by 27%. The sectors most severely affected were the intermediate goods industries and the "engineering goods" sector (consumer durables and capital goods).

In 1980, there was a vigorous recuperation of industrial production in most branches, with overall industrial output rising 18.2%. The momentum was particularly strong in intermediate goods with output increasing by 23.1% (see Table 4), followed by the consumer goods sector (16.8%). The output of consumer durables and capital goods also increased by 16.8%, but then it should be remembered that this was the sector that had declined most between 1977 and 1979.

By the end of 1981, several industries in the consumer goods sector had regained their prewar (1977) levels (see Table 5 for details). The apparel (clothing) industry was 14% above the 1977 level of output; that of beverages 20% above; and the tobacco industry 12% above. The serious matter, however, was that the supply of domestically produced textiles was lagging behind, resulting in an increasing dependency on imported textile fibers. By the end of 1981, the production of the textiles industry was still 20% below the prewar level whereas that of the footwear and apparel industries was 26% above. During the following two years (1982 and 1983) this imbalance was gradually redressed, although it was not entirely eliminated until 1984.

Thus although recovery was relatively rapid and successful in most of the

12. For a discussion of the Cuban experience in this context, see Claes Brundenius, *Revolutionary Cuba: The Challenge of Economic Growth with Equity* (Boulder: Westview Press, 1984).

TABLE 4
Structural Changes and Growth of Nicaraguan Industry by Major Industrial
Branches, 1977–1984

GROUPS	1977[a]	1978[a]	1979[a]	1980[a]	1981[a]	1982[a]	1983[b]	1984[b]
Nondurable consumer goods								
Share	66.5	67.9	73.6	72.7	73.6	75.7	73.0	72.4
Index (1977 = 100)	100.0	102.4	80.5	94.0	97.8	101.6	104.0	104.4
Intermediate goods								
Share	26.3	24.6	21.3	22.2	21.7	19.6	21.7	22.4
Index (1977 = 100)	100.0	93.8	58.9	72.5	72.8	66.7	68.9	72.0
Consumer durables and capital goods								
Share	7.2	7.5	5.2	5.1	4.7	4.7	5.3	5.2
Index (1977 = 100)	100.0	103.5	51.8	60.5	56.9	57.9	72.1	71.4
TOTAL								
Share	100.0	100.0	100.0	100.0	100.0	100.0	100.0	100.0
Index (1977 = 100)	100.0	100.2	72.7	85.9	88.3	89.3	92.5	93.5

Source: Unpublished data provided by the Industry and Mining Department, MIPLAN.
[a]Value added of industrial output.
[b]Based on trend of gross value of production.

basic consumer goods industries, the price was sometimes excessive in terms of increasing imports of raw materials and other inputs without a matching increase in exports. The reason for this disappointing performance of the external trade sector was partly the decline of the Central American Common Market as an outlet for Nicaraguan industrial exports (notably chemicals) but also the decline in world market demand for Nicaragua's traditional agro-industrial exports.

As a result, the "import capacity" of the country has been falling steadily since 1977.[13] In relation to 1977, the import capacity in 1979 was down by 19%; in 1981, it was 25% below 1977 levels. In 1982, it was down by 30%, and by 1983 it is estimated that the import capacity level was 37% lower than in 1977.

In 1982, an attempt was made to curtail imports drastically, and import licenses were curbed for consumer goods that were considered luxury items. But still imports were excessive, and further cuts were made in 1983. The problem, however, was that even when imports of luxury goods were elimi-

13. "Import capacity" or the purchasing power of exports, is defined by $I = X_{vol} \cdot PX/PM$, where I is the import capacity index, X_{vol} stands for the export volume index, and PX/PM for the terms of trade.

TABLE 5

Nicaragua: Indexes of Gross Value of Industrial Production—1960–1983 (1977 = 100)

BRANCH	1960	1970	1977	1978	1979	1980	1981	1982	1983	1984[a]
Food	27.2	71.8	100.0	105.3	88.5	88.3	91.2	103.4	99.3	99.0
Beverages	17.3	47.1	100.0	102.0	81.6	120.4	116.9	108.1	117.3	126.6
Tobacco	36.2	58.7	100.0	97.0	75.7	112.1	108.1	93.4	100.0	106.2
Textiles	24.2	67.3	100.0	96.8	60.7	57.7	79.4	82.1	99.3	99.1
Footwear and Apparel	58.7	111.8	100.0	86.9	49.2	114.2	125.6	115.4	117.4	99.4
Wood and Cork	29.7	55.0	100.0	79.9	47.1	49.0	51.3	44.1	39.5	34.0
Furniture	22.0	76.6	100.0	97.8	67.0	60.8	64.1	55.7	51.3	50.6
Paper and Paper Products	3.5	38.7	100.0	110.4	65.9	54.6	60.0	74.2	83.1	85.3
Printing and Graphics Industry	25.9	80.5	100.0	82.6	60.7	91.3	102.0	106.9	116.3	127.9
Leather and Leather Products	55.4	125.5	100.0	112.6	101.3	108.7	87.0	93.9	78.9	72.6
Rubber Products	22.0	84.4	100.0	101.8	76.1	189.9	200.9	206.4	177.1	195.2
Chemicals	11.8	51.4	100.0	101.1	68.5	72.8	70.3	62.5	62.5	69.4
Petroleum and Derivatives	—	55.3	100.0	89.5	63.1	91.6	102.8	87.9	77.1	72.7
Non-Metallic Mineral Products	12.0	49.0	100.0	85.2	37.2	62.4	58.7	55.3	75.4	82.0
Metal Products	8.5	80.9	100.0	102.6	50.4	71.1	69.0	76.8	93.5	97.5
Machinery (Electric and Non-Electric)	1.5	41.9	100.0	102.7	53.9	41.8	33.5	25.7	34.4	29.0
Transport Equipment	2.8	47.7	100.0	103.7	61.7	66.4	74.8	54.2	74.0	65.0
Other Industries	5.3	74.2	100.0	104.9	62.8	39.6	43.3	39.2	42.4	33.2
Gross Value of Production	21.1	64.8	100.0	100.5	73.6	82.6	84.9	87.0	92.5	93.5

[a]Preliminary figures.

Source: Calculations by the author based on information provided by The Industry and Mining Department, MIPLAN, and (for 1983 and 1984) ECLAC, *Economic Survey of Latin America and the Caribbean 1984* (Chapter on Nicaragua), United Nations, 1985.

nated, there still remained a long list of raw materials and inputs that were vital for most of the priority industries. So the task then was to set priorities within the already narrow frame of priorities—and not only priority between sectors but also priority based on ownership and efficiency criteria, for instance between private and state industry and between large-scale and small-scale industry. Such decisions, of course are bound to have an impact on decisions taken earlier—for instance, the decision to maintain a "mixed economy with political pluralism." The specific problems of small-scale industry will be addressed later.

The foreign exchange constraint has become even further exacerbated by the well-known trade-off dilemma of having to choose between increased current consumpton and investment demand in order to satisfy future needs. Thus both intermediate goods production and capital goods production have fallen behind during the last years, in spite of the fact that both sectors are recognized as the pillars on which future industrial growth will have to be sustained.

In 1983, the level of output of the "capital goods" sector was still 37% below that of 1977 and only 22% above the 1979 bottom level of output. There were several reasons for this. First of all, the prerevolutionary "capital goods" industries consisted largely of assembly plants for the production of consumer durables based on foreign investment and imported foreign technology. These assembly plants were among the most severely hit, and many were actually completely destroyed, by the bombing by Somoza's air force during the insurrection in 1979. Second, a decision was taken at an early stage not to rebuild these assembly plants but to reconstruct the capital goods sector based on the production of *real* capital goods, especially machinery and equipment for the agricultural sector. The building up of an indigenous capital goods industry takes time, and Nicaragua was practically starting from scratch.

CHANGES IN RELATIONS OF PRODUCTION IN INDUSTRY AFTER THE REVOLUTION

The Somoza clan had concentrated so much of the economic wealth of the country into their own hands that just by confiscating their property after the triumph of the revolution, the state gained control of approximately 25% of industrial output. Since the revolution there have been relatively few nationalizations in industry. According to a 1981 industrial survey, wholly state-owned (100%) enterprises controlled a mere 19% of manufacturing value added in 1981 (see Table 6). If mixed enterprises, where the state has the majority of the shares, are added, however, the figure of state control over

TABLE 6
Ownership Structure of Nicaraguan Manufacturing Industry[a]—1981 (Percent Shares of Value Added)

| | | | MIXED | | |
BRANCHES	STATE (100%)	PRIVATE (100%)	STATE MAJORITY	PRIVATE MAJORITY	TOTAL[b]
Food	20.8	30.3	17.4	31.3	100.0
Beverages	0.5	9.8	44.8	44.9	100.0
Tobacco	1.3	0.5	—	98.1	100.0
Textiles	60.1	23.0	—	16.9	100.0
Apparel	39.6	60.4	—	—	100.0
Leather	16.9	83.1	—	—	100.0
Footwear	10.4	89.6	—	—	100.0
Wood and cork	22.4	23.2	54.4	—	100.0
Furniture	14.8	55.8	—	29.4	100.0
Paper	20.9	55.8	—	23.3	100.0
Printing	30.9	68.6	—	0.5	100.0
Industrial chemicals	4.2	46.3	—	49.6	100.0
Other chemicals	29.4	64.7	4.1	1.8	100.0
Petroleum refining	—	—	—	100.0	100.0
Rubber	—	—	—	100.0	100.0
Plastics	21.3	38.5	40.3	—	100.0
Nonmetallic minerals	22.6	8.6	65.9	3.0	100.0
Basic metals	56.6	43.4	—	—	100.0
Metal products	70.0	30.0	—	—	100.0
Machinery (exc. electr.)	65.3	34.7	—	—	100.0
Electrical machinery	18.7	80.0	—	1.3	100.0
Transport equipment	12.3	87.7	—	—	100.0
Scientific instruments	—	33.3	66.7	—	100.0
Other Industry, n.e.c.	—	11.4	88.6	—	100.0
Total	19.0	41.7	14.1	25.2	100.0

[a]Based on a survey covering establishments with 5 or more employed.
[b]Total may not add up because of rounding.
Source: Calculations by the author based on information provided by Encuesta anual—industria manufacturera—1981, Managua: INEC, 1983.

industry increases to 33%. As seen in Table 6, the highest shares of state ownership were found textiles and apparel (clothing) and in wood, basic metals, and nonelectrical machinery. The latter, however, was still very small in absolute size.

The approximately one-third share of state participation in industry was problematic for two reasons. First of all, it was too small to constitute a solid and viable base for industrial planning, especially in strategic sectors such as chemicals, paper, and transport equipment. On the other hand, it was sufficiently large to alienate large sectors of the industrial bourgeiosie who looked with growing suspicion at the Sandinista commitment to a mixed economy. This contradiction in the present transitional phase of the Nicaraguan society is by no means easy to solve.

If the industrial bourgeoisie resists accepting the rules of the game and their role as partners in national development plans drawn up within the framework of the ideology of the Sandinista revolution and instead prefer decapitalizing and even taking capital out of the country, there could only be one outcome—increasing confiscation of private property and a subsequent increase in state participation. The figures on ownership in Table 6 are from 1981, and one might suspect that state participation increased during the following years—especially given the announcement of various nationalizations in the speech by Daniel Ortega on July 19, 1983. However, recent preliminary estimates of ownership in industry for 1984 suggest that the state share (including majority ownership in joint enterprises) has not increased very much.[14] Thus the share of state participation in the manufacturing industry as a whole appears to be the same in 1984 as in 1981 (33%), although the state sector has slightly increased its participation in the capital goods sector.

An increase in state participation would lead to a more solid base for socialist planning but would no doubt create a vicious circle with increasing distrust by the industrial bourgeoisie of the long-term objectives of the Sandinista revolution, leading to further confiscations, and so forth. This situation is particularly fragile because the private sector has such an overwhelming control over the intermediate goods sector—perhaps the most strategic industrial sector in Nicaragua in the present phase. In that sector, the state controls only 27% of output, whereas the private sector controls 73% (see Table 7).

Another problematic dimension of the transitional phase is the large extent of small-scale industry in Nicaragua. However, with proper treatment and adequate support, these small-scale industries, often of workshop or "cottage" character, could be of great importance in the future in terms of employment creation. (Unemployment was still running as high as 13% in Managua 4 years after the triumph of the revolution.)

One difficulty in characterizing small-scale industry and identifying its problems is that Nicaragua lacks a comprehensive, all-embracing census of manufacturing activities. There have been annual industrial surveys (published on a regular basis since 1979), but these only cover establishments with more that five persons employed, and in the group with five to twenty-nine employees, the confidence of the sample is rather shaky. Important insights as to the dimensions and problems of small-scale industry were, however,

14. *Barricada Internacional*, (May 30, 1985).

TABLE 7
Ownership Structure of Nicaraguan Industry by Major Use of Output—1981

| | STATE (100%) | | PRIVATE (100%) | | MIXED | | | | TOTAL | |
| | | | | | STATE MAJORITY | | PRIVATE MAJORITY | | | |
MAJOR USE	M. CÓRDOBAS	(%)	M. CÓRDOBAS	(%)	M. CÓRDOBAS	(%)	M. CÓRDOBAS	(%)	M. CÓRDOBAS	(%)
Nondurable consumer goods	600.3	18.5	1051.6	32.3	492.5	15.1	1109.2	34.2	3253.6	100.0
Intermediate goods	177.3	13.6	845.1	64.7	175.8	13.5	107.6	8.2	1305.8	100.0
Consumer durables and capital goods	137.8	50.8	117.7	43.4	14.8	5.5	0.7	0.3	271.0	100.0
Total	915.4	19.0	2014.4	41.7	683.1	14.1	1217.5	25.2	4830.4	100.0

Source: Same as Table 6.

revealed in the Survey of Small-Scale Industry, carried out by the Ministry of Industry in 1980. The survey tried to cover practically all industrial activities employing between one and twenty-nine persons. On the basis of this survey, it can be estimated that small-scale industry, thus defined, accounted for about 24% of the value added of the manufacturing sector and 30% of manufacturing employment in that year.

The small-scale industries are mainly involved in the consumer goods sector, including food, textiles and apparel, leather and footwear, and furniture and wood products. These branches accounted for 84% of the gross value of production of all small-scale industries in 1980 and an equal share of employment.

A serious problem with small-scale industry is that it is highly dependent on imports of raw materials. According to the survey, small-scale industry imported goods worth $40 million in 1980, equal to 16% of all imports to the whole industrial sector in that year. This high degree of import dependency of small-scale industry is a problem because of the serious foreign exchange constraint imposed upon the Nicaraguan economy at present.

Small-scale entrepreneurs in Nicaragua have traditionally been able to exchange local for foreign currency without problems and then simply go over the border to, for instance, Costa Rica, and purchase the goods they need for their activities. Since May 1983, however, the government has imposed severe restrictions on the purchase of foreign exchange, and the small-scale entrepreneur now has to line up in the state bank with the rest of the people soliciting extremely scarce foreign exchange, filling out numerous forms of applications. Although this move by the government is no doubt understandable (one could even say that it was inevitable and long overdue) in view of the necessity to get the black market under control, it is still a fact that this measure hardly increased the popularity of the government among the small-business people.

THE COLLAPSE OF THE CENTRAL AMERICAN MARKET

Ironically, a serious recession started hitting Nicaragua's partners in the CACM just when the ambitious plans for rapid construction were announced in Managua. Thus, although per-capita income increased by 7.5% in Nicaragua in 1980, it went down by 0.6% in Honduras, declined by 1.7% in Costa Rica, and fell drastically in El Salvador by 12.2%.[15] However, this recession

15. CEPAL, *Balance preliminar de la economía latinoamericana en 1984* (Santiago, Chile: CEPAL, 1983).

did not have immediate negative effects on intraregional trade. The total value of Central American intraregional trade even increased by 28% in absolute terms and rose from 19% to 22% of total Central American trade (see Table 8).

This renewed momentum of intraregional trade was only of a temporary character, unfortunately. The revitalization could, to a large extent, be explained by the vigorous industrial recovery in Nicaragua during 1980 after the drop in 1979, with the gross value of industrial output increasing by 12%.

The economic crisis in the region is a serious handicap for Nicaragua's development plans in the future because of the considerable degree of integration of large sectors of industry in Nicaragua with those of the other members of the Central American Common Market. This dependency on industrial linkages or complementarities with other industries in the Central American market is indicated by the trade flows of industrial goods in 1980.

In that year, 44% of Nicaragua's industrial imports (SITC Groups 5–8) came from the CACM, and no less than 88% of its industrial exports went to that same region.[16] Thus in the case of industrial exports, dependency on the CACM was almost total, ranging from 80 to 100%. About two-thirds of the industrial exports went to Costa Rica (45%) and Guatemala (20%). With respect to imports of industrial goods, the dependency on CACM was lower, although still quite important. Imports of industrial goods from the region accounted in 1980 for 12% of the total in the case of machinery and transport

TABLE 8
Intraregional Trade and Nicaragua's Shares of Intraregional Trade, 1976–1982

YEARS	CENTRAL AMERICAN INTRAREGIONAL TRADE[a] (m. U.S.$)	CENTRAL AMERICAN INTRAREGIONAL TRADE AS PERCENTAGE OF TOTAL CENTRAL AMERICAN TRADE[a]	NICARAGUA'S SHARE OF INTRAREGIONAL EXPORTS (%)	NICARAGUA'S SHARE OF INTRAREGIONAL IMPORTS (%)
1976	1264.0	20.0	18.1	23.0
1977	1518.0	17.9	17.0	22.5
1978	1747.3	20.2	16.9	15.7
1979	1852.4	18.8	10.0	11.7
1980	2367.1	21.8	5.9	28.2
1981	1963.7	19.7	6.9	24.0
1982	1595.1	18.4	6.4	22.2

[a]Exports (f.o.b.) and Imports (c.i.f.).
Source: IMF, *Direction of Trade Statistics—Yearbook 1983* (Washington, D.C.,: IMF, 1983).

16. Calculations based on SIECA, *Anuario estadístico centroamericano de comercio exterior— 1980* (Guatemala: SIECA, 1983).

equipment, for 31% in chemicals, for 65% of intermediate goods (other than chemicals), and for 78% in the case of other manufactured goods (mostly consumer durables).

Because of the relatively high degree of integration of the Nicaraguan industries with those of the CACM members, the revitalized industrial growth in Nicaragua in 1980 provided the CACM with a temporary momentum, although just postponing its final collapse. The problem for Nicaragua was, however, that although in 1980 accounting for no less than 28% of total intraregional imports, its corresponding share of intraregional exports fell to 6% in 1982 (see Table 8). The net result was a record intraregional trade deficit for Nicaragua.

The dilemma that Nicaragua is confronted with could be summarized as follows. Nicaragua's CACM trading partners were, and perhaps still are, in spite of growing political differences, very much interested in exporting to a more dynamic Nicaraguan market. However, since industrial activity in all the CACM—except in Nicaragua—has been regularly declining, there is no corresponding interest in buying industrial goods—and least of all from Nicaragua.

Hundreds of industrial plants in the region have been paralyzed or even permanently closed down, and those that remain are operating with an idle capacity of over 50%. Because Nicaragua lacks foreign exchange (hard currency) to pay for its industrial imports from the region, there is now growing resistance of the CACM members to sell on the Nicaraguan market by offering, for instance, extended credit lines. The result has been that the region has plunged into an even worse recession, leading to the virtual collapse of the Central American Common Market. In the last few years there have, however, been attempts to resurrect the market through bilateral barter trade agreements comprising some hundred industrial products, and Nicaragua has also been a partner in such agreements.

TRADE VULNERABILITY—A DILEMMA CONFRONTING LONG-TERM INDUSTRIAL PLANNING

At the beginning of 1984, encouraging news emerged in Managua about an upturn in the Nicaraguan economy during 1983. According to these reports, the economy fared remarkably well in spite of dismal initial predictions in view of bad weather and increases in Contra intrusions into Nicaraguan territory. The final figures released by MIPLAN in 1984 indicated a GDP growth of 5% rather than the 2% earlier estimated.[17] This upsurge of growth

17. *Latin American Regional Reports* (February 17, 1984).

was, according to the same source, mainly the result of a remarkably good performance of the agricultural sector that increased by 14.3%. On the other hand, industrial production apparently went down by 4.8% (compared with an earlier predicted growth of 7%).

The relatively satisfactory performance of the Nicaraguan economy in 1983, in spite of deep recession in the region, led to strong pressure on the government in Managua to abandon plans prepared on an ad hoc annual emergency basis, in favor of long-term (or perhaps they should be called medium-term) centralized plans ranging from 4 to 5 years. One argument in favor of long-term planning was that the country could not take for granted that generous levels of foreign aid would be flowing into the country in the long run and that Nicaragua must plan future projects strictly in terms of the country's actual and potential domestic resources.

The question remained, however, if it made sense to have centralized, long-term planning in a country that had still not fully recovered prewar production levels and where the private sector still maintained a dominant position in many key sectors. In Cuba after the revolution, there was also an enthusiastic and ambitious attempt to launch a 5-year plan in 1960 (to cover the 1961–1965) period. An outline of a plan was sketched by Michal Kalecki, the late Polish economist.[18] It was very appealing and looked very convincing on paper. Soon, however, the harsh realities of the transitional phase (with an increasing isolation of Cuba backed up with a U.S. embargo on trade with the island) made the earlier plans wishful thinking. The plan was never put into serious practice and was soon replaced by annual plans. This is also what happened in Nicaragua. As of 1985, Nicaragua still used only annual plans.

A major dilemma confronting long-term, and medium-term, planning in a small country like Nicaragua is the vulnerability of the economy to external trade. The collapse of the CACM and the difficulties this implies for Nicaragua, as already discussed, are the case in point. But the matter was not only CACM integration. It was also the high degree of dependency on imports of industrial goods from the United States. Although dependency on U.S. imports decreased folowing the revolution, the U.S. share of Nicaraguan industrial imports in 1982 still accounted for over one-third of the total (see Table 9) This illustrates the difficulties to be encountered by Nicaraguan industry after the U.S. embargo of Nicaragua entered into force on May 1, 1985.

The Nicaraguan government planned the construction of a number of new industries, and Cuba played an important part in these plans. Cuba has been

18. Michal Kalecki, "Hypothetical Outline of the Five-Year Plan 1961–65 for the Cuban Economy," in Kalecki, *Essays on Developing Economies* (Hassocks: The Harvester Press, 1976).

TABLE 9
Dependency on Imports of Industrial Goods from the United States 1978, 1980, and 1982 (Percentage of Total Imports by ISTC Groups)

INDUSTRIAL GROUPS	1978	1980	1982
Chemicals	60.9%	51.5%	39.2%
Other intermediate goods	44.4%	44.2%	26.1%
Machinery and transport equipment	46.2%	40.3%	31.1%
Subtotal	51.8%	47.1%	33.6%
TOTAL IMPORTS	31.3%	27.5%	19.0%

Source: MIPLAN, Nicaragua: Comercio exterior 1978, Nicaragua: Comercio exterior 1980, and data elaborated by the author on the basis of information provided by the Ministry of Foreign Trade.

an important partner and supplier of capital goods and construction materials for the building of a new sugar mill in Nicaragua (the Tipitapa-Malacotoya Project). In 1982, no less than 51% of the $30.6 million dollars worth of imports from Cuba were made up of construction materials (the most important was cement), and most of the remainder consisted of various types of capital goods, including tractors and machines. In July 1985, the Cuban government decided to donate the complete sugar mill mentioned previously to Nicaragua. The mill called "Victoria de Julio," is estimated to be worth U.S. $73.8 million, an amount that was initially granted as a loan.[19]

One problem in Cuban/Nicaraguan trade at present is the limited number of industrial goods that Nicaragua has to offer (that are not competitive with Cuban products). In the longer run, however, there should be a large market, for instance, for cotton textiles on the Cuban market. Most of Cuban's textile apparel industry is based on imported synthetic fibers from the Soviet Union, due to the difficulties of cultivating cotton in Cuba for climatic reasons. There would thus seem to be reason to expect a very fruitful industrial cooperation between Nicaragua and Cuba in the future.

CONCLUDING REMARKS

Although the immediate prospects for rapid industrialization look quite gloomy, there should be, in a longer perspective, a good chance for accelerated and sustained industrial growth. One necessary condition, however, is that trade links be diversified and that industrial complementarities with other

19. "Internationalism: Sweet Symbol of Friendship," Cuba International (Havana), 12 (1985). The figure refers to the Cuban grant only. The project also had minor funding from other sources.

countries in the region be strengthened. Another condition is that credits for imports of essential industrial goods in this first, very vulnerable phase of reconstruction and restructuring of industry be given to Nicaragua on soft terms.

But even if new financial arrangements are made, giving some additional relief to the war-torn Nicaraguan economy, the most ominous specter is still, of course, that increasing and intensified warfare against the Sandinista government by the U.S.-supported Contras will undoubtedly force the Sandinistas in the direction of a virtual war economy, thus postponing indefinitely the preparation of long-term planning for sustained industrial growth.

Chapter 5

Banking Systems and Revolutionary Change: The Politics of Agricultural Credit in Nicaragua

LAURA J. ENRIQUEZ
ROSE J. SPALDING

Banking systems play a major role in shaping national economic development.[1] By absorbing the financial surplus and rechanneling it into investment, banks can accelerate the rate of economic growth. Their role, however, is not politically or socially neutral. The form a banking system takes and the projects it makes possible reflect the larger political/economic context in which it is situated. A commercial banking structure in a capitalist system often strengthens the economic position of entrepreneurial elites. Although some small investors may win bank support for particular projects, the prevailing association is between financial centers and established elites. Under these circumstances, bank operations limit economic mobility and reinforce marginality in lower income groups.

Banks may, however, be structured to play a redistributive role. In a sociopolitical context characterized by an emphasis on more equitable distribution, banks can be used to shift the allocation of financial resources and redefine the process of accumulation. This institutional transformation, however, is highly complex. It requires that the structural alliance between the banks and established elites be broken and that the traditional tendency toward concentrated accumulation be reduced. Such transition processes are fraught with difficulties. The elite's withdrawal from the banking system, coupled with increased funding for marginal producers, may easily lead to a decapitalization of the banking system, fueling broader financial disequilibrium.

---

1. For discussion of the relationship between banking and economic growth, see Mario Rietti, *Money and Banking in Latin America* (New York: Praeger, 1979).

In the Nicaraguan case, the financial system has recently undergone a significant change. Following the 1979 overthrow of the Somoza dynasty, domestic financial institutions were nationalized, the system was reorganized, terms of operation were redefined, and new priorities emerged. Central to that process was the change in the bank's agricultural credit policy. This study focuses on that change.

The relationship between the agricultural sector and the banking system is particularly intricate in Nicaragua. Capital generated by the expansion of the agroexport sector was used to found the most important commercial banks. In turn, the financial assistance provided by the banking system was crucial for the continued growth of agroexport production. This mutually reinforcing relationship greatly changed the Nicaraguan economy in the 1950s and 1960s. Evaluation of recent changes in agricultural credit policy, therefore, highlights the shifting structural alliances between the state, the banks, and the agroexport elite. Simultaneously, it provides useful information about the political realignment between the banks, the peasantry, and the newly created state farms.

This chapter opens with an analysis of the agricultural credit system that emerged during the Somoza era (1936–1979). It then explores the policy and organizational changes adopted by the Sandinista government (1979–1985), illustrating how changing priorities modified the allocation of financial resources. This exploration highlights the complexity of an institutional transformation of this magnitude, illuminating the tensions and trade-offs associated with such transitions. The final section focuses on both the achievements and limitations of the structural change, pointing to several central contradictions that arise during revolutionary transitions.

THE FINANCIAL SYSTEM IN PREREVOLUTIONARY NICARAGUA

A national banking system began to emerge in Nicaragua with the inauguration of the Banco Nacional de Nicaragua (BNN) in 1912. This bank was designed to oversee Nicaragua's foreign loan negotiations and monetary conversion.[2] It also functioned as the country's central bank, issuing cur-

2. At its inception, the country's major bank, the Banco Nacional de Nicaragua (BNN), was owned by the Nicaraguan government. Foreign contributors, however, exercised their option to buy 51% of the stock during the second year of the bank's operation. The majority of the members of the board of directors were from the United States. The bank had been incorporated in the United States under the laws of the state of Connecticut, with disputes arbitrated by the State Department. See Roscoe R. Hill, *Fiscal Intervention in Nicaragua* (New York: Paul Maisel, 1933) and Jaime Wheelock Román, *Nicaragua: Imperialismo y Dictadura* (La Habana: Editorial de Ciencias Sociales, 1980).

rency and handling the government's accounts. The BNN became a primary source of agricultural credit, particularly for expanding coffee production.[3] The coffee sector was the first of a series of agroexport sectors to receive preferential treatment from the bank.

This system, however, only partially penetrated even the most dynamic sectors of the economy in its first 40 years of operation. Private commercial banks were slow to develop, in spite of the growing export-generated wealth. According to a 1953 World Bank report, private enterprise was

> unimaginative and unduly cautious . . . too prone to seek either the safe invest-ment or a quick return. It has engaged in land or real estate speculation or has sought profits from importing and exporting or from usury rather than from increased production.[4]

Partly in response to these criticisms, the private sector began to increase investment activities, and the banking system began to expand in the 1950s. The Banco de América was established in 1952 with financial backing from the growing sugar sector. The Banco Nicaragüense (BANIC) was founded a year later with capital from cotton and coffee producers. The cluster of financial institutions composed of the Banco de América, BANIC, and the Somoza-controlled Banco Nacional came to dominate the economic life of the country.[5]

With this expansion, several trends appeared. First, the banks that had been founded on the surplus generated by export agriculture began to shift resources to the emerging urban and industrial sector. In 1960, agriculture received over 40% of all credit issued by the domestic financial system; in 1978 and 1979, only a little more than 20% went to this sector.[6] Industry, housing construction, and commerce received an increasing portion of bank credit.

Second, lending patterns reinforced the alliance between the banks and agroexport capital that had been inherent in the system since its inception. Although the role of the agricultural sector in the credit system on the whole was reduced, large- and medium-sized producers continued to receive ample credit. In addition, access to credit was sharply differentiated by crop. Export crop producers received over 90% of agricultural bank loans during the first half of the 1960s, although they controlled less than 50% of the agricultural

3. See Hill, *Fiscal*, and Rigo Ordóñez Centeno, *La política crediticia algodonera: El caso de Nicaragua.* (Managua: UNAN, 1976).
4. International Bank for Reconstruction and Development, *The Economic Development of Nicaragua.* (Baltimore: The Johns Hopkins Press, 1953), 100.
5. Wheelock, *Nicaragua*, 141–189.
6. Banco Central de Nicaragua, *Indicadores económicos 5* (1 and 2) (December 1979), 29.

TABLE 1
Use of Land and Credit for Export versus Domestic Market Crops (in percentages)[a,b]

| | EXPORT CROPS | | DOMESTIC MARKET CROPS | |
YEAR	CULTIVATED AREA	CREDIT	CULTIVATED AREA	CREDIT
1960−61	41	91	59	9
1961−62	42	93	58	7
1962−63	45	93	55	8
1963−64	46	94	54	7
1964−65	47	94	53	6
1965−66	45	92	56	8
1966−67	46	91	54	9
1967−68	42	86	58	14
1968−69	41	80	59	21
1969−70	44	86	56	14
1970−71	40	86	60	14
1971−72	41	86	59	14
1972−73	49	90	51	11
1973−74	49	87	52	13
1974−75	42	85	58	15
1975−76	44	75	56	25
1976−77	47	85	53	15
1977−78	50	88	50	12
1978−79	46	88	54	12
1979−80	40	81	60	19
1980−81	38	70	62	30
1981−82	38	71	62	29
1982−83	42	75	58	25
1983−84	41	76	59	24
1984−85	47	69	53	31
1985−86[c]	39	76	61	24

[a]*Cultivated area:* The percentage of harvested land used for the most important export crops (cotton, coffee, sugarcane, and sesame) versus the most important domestic market crops (corn, beans, rice, and sorghum).

[b]*Credit:* The percentage of short term bank credit allocated for export crops (see above) vs. domestic market crops (see above).

[c]Preliminary data based on estimates through November 1985 for area cultivated and through December 1985 for credit allocations.

Sources:

Land & Credit:

1960−61 to 1978−79. Banco Central de Nicaragua (BCN), *Indicadores económicos*, 5 (1 and 2) (December 1979).

Land:

1979−80 to 1981−82. *Centro de Investigación y Estudios de la Reforma Agraria* (CIERA)/Programa Alimentario Nicaragüense (PAN)/Canadian International Development Agency (CIDA), *Informe final del*

land (see Table 1). This pattern of overrepresentation continued with only minor changes throughout the 1967–1978 period.

Cotton producers were particularly favored. Bank credits for cotton production jumped from C\$11.4 million in 1950–1951 to C\$108.2 million in 1955–1956.[7] These credits covered the bulk of the steadily rising production costs in this sector. At one point in the mid-1950s, the banking system was covering up to 90% of production costs for cotton producers before stabilizing during the 1960s and 1970s at approximately 70%.[8] Credits for cotton averaged 54% of all bank credit for agriculture in the 1950s and rose to over 75% in the mid-1960s, before beginning a gradual decline.[9] Bank policies favored the larger, better capitalized cotton producers over the rest. Steadily rising yield requirements effectively limited bank credits to the most efficient cotton farms.[10]

For producers of other crops, credit was less accessible. Staple crops produced for the internal market received less than 10% of agricultural credit

7. Pedro Belli, *An Inquiry Concerning the Growth of Cotton Farming in Nicaragua* (Ph.D. Dissertation, University of California, Berkeley, 1968), 111.
8. Ordóñez, *La política*, 54.
9. Jaime Biderman, *Class Structure, the State and Capitalist Development in Nicaraguan Agriculture* (Ph.D. Dissertation, University of California, Berkeley, 1982), Statistical Appendix, 185.
10. Prior to the 1959–1960 cotton cycle, loan size had been contingent on production plans and the provision of certain guarantees by producers. Following several years of low loan recovery rates, however, the bank issued a new set of requirements for loan applicants. Among them was the stipulation that a producer's yield for the prior three cycles be at least 22 quintales per manzana. See Ordóñez, *La política*, 32. This policy effectively limited bank credit to the larger farms, which could employ more advanced technology, thereby producing higher yields. These minimum yield requirements were continually revised upward over the following years. This led to a self-reinforcing cycle, in which the larger, more technologically advanced farms were granted access to credit, which facilitated increased mechanization and ever increasing yields.

TABLE 1 FTNT *(Cont.)*

Proyecto Estrategia Alimentaria, vol. 3, *Directorio de políticas alimentarias* (Managua: CIERA, 1984); Ministerio de Desarrollo Agropecuario y Reforma Agraria (MIDINRA), *Informe de Nicaragua a la FAO* (Managua: CIERA, 1983), Table 27, p. 54 for sesame.

1982–83 to 1983–84. CIERA/PAN/CIDA; Ivan García, "La producción en tiempo de guerra y sus perspectivas 1983–84," *Revolución y Desarrollo*, No. 2 (July, August, September 1984), Table 1, p. 24 for sesame.

1984–85. Secretaría de Planificación y Presupuesto, "Evaluación y perspectivas económicas 1985," (unpublished document, June 1985).

1985–86. Secretaría de Planificación y Presupuesto, unpublished data.

Credit:

1979–80 to 1981–82. Corporación Financiera de Nicaragua, "Informe Estadístico 1977–1982" (unpublished data, n.d.) Table 2.

1982–83 BCN, "Evaluación del sector agropecuario ciclo 1983/84" (unpublished data, n.d.)

1983–84 to 1984–85 BCN, "Breve evaluación del ciclo 1984/85" (unpublished data, n.d.)

1985–86 BCN, unpublished data.

in 1970, in spite of the fact that these crops were grown on well over half of all agricultural land (see Table 1).[11] Partly as a result of this, staples production grew much more slowly. Export production rose sharply between 1960 and 1965, at a rate of 19.5% annually. In contrast, production for the internal market grew 4.4% per year, only marginally faster than the population growth rate.[12] Pushed out of the desirable land on the Pacific Coast into marginal areas in the interior of the country, without access to credit for improved seeds or fertilizer, without legally recognized titles to their land, and without an adequate marketing system, many staples producers were unable to rise above a subsistence level of production.

Banking Reforms, Somoza Style

By the late 1950s, the Somoza alliance came to see the increasing marginalization of the *campesino* sector as a potentially delicate political problem. The opposition Conservative party began to use the call for agrarian reform as an organizational tool, raising the possibility of a rural challenge.[13] Within this context, the BNN launched the Rural Credit Program in 1959.

Prior to the establishment of this special credit program, all agricultural producers competed "as equals" for loans and operated under the same terms. With the creation of the Rural Credit Program, the *campesino* sector no longer had to compete directly with the large agroexport producers. This program earmarked a certain amount of agricultural credit for small- and

11. The portion of credit allocated to staple crops did rise modestly in the latter part of the 1960s, after the collapse of international cotton prices and the spread of "white fly" infestation. See Peter Dorner and Rodolfo Quiros, "Institutional Dualism in Central America's Agricultural Development," *Journal of Latin American Studies* **5**(2) (November 1973): 230—231. Yet most of the increased credit went into the expanding rice sector where the Somoza family and a handful of other large and medium growers dominated. For the bulk of the small producers whose primary crop was corn, credit remained virtually nonexistent. Although over 40% of agricultural land was planted to corn in 1970, less than 3% percent of agricultural bank credit went to that sector. See Banco Central de Nicaragua, *Indicadores económicos*, and Laura J. Enriquez and Rose J. Spalding, "Rural Transformation: Agricultural Credit Policies in Revolutionary Nicaragua," Paper presented at the XII International Congress of the Latin American Studies Association, Albuquerque, N.M., April 1985.
12. Ciencias Sociales de la Confederación Universitaria Centroamericana (CSUCA), *Estructura agraria, dinámica de población y desarrollo capitalista en Centroamérica* (Costa Rica: EDUCA, 1978), 238.
13. See James Robert Taylor, *Agricultural Settlement and Development in Eastern Nicaragua* (Ph.D. Dissertation, University of Wisconsin, Madison, 1968). For more information about the early development of the Rural Credit Program, see Javier Bone P., *El Crédito Rural de Nicaragua: Período 1964—68* (Thesis: Universidad Nacional Autónoma de Nicaragua, 1970).

medium-sized farmers. The terms under which loans were granted also tended to favor the Rural Credit recipients. For example, although the interest rates fixed by the Banco Central in 1970 for short-term agricultural loans ranged from 10 to 12% for regular borrowers, the rate in the Rural Credit Program was held to 9%.[14]

Although nominally designed to allow small producers to tap into the financial system, this program actually benefited very few. It had only 28,000 reported participants at its peak in 1978, representing roughly 11% of small- and medium-sized producers.[15] Somoza's other major "peasant credit" program had a similarly limited reach. This second program was run by the Campesino Welfare Institute (INVIERNO), a development agency set up at the urging of the U.S. Agency for International Development in 1975. In its first year of operation, it provided only 2882 clients with credit.[16] INVIERNO also tended to assume the same clientele as the Rural Credit Program, even though it was supposed to complement existing programs.

Instead of gradually extending access to credit in ever-widening circles, these programs suffered from a narrowness of scope and from duplication. The vast majority of small and medium producers still did not have access to official bank credit at the end of the Somoza era. As a result, these producers were forced to look outside the formal system for credit at the beginning of the agricultural cycle and when unforeseen costs arose. An extensive network of credit intermediaries developed, creating an array of lending arrangements external to the banks. For example, some larger producers secured more credit than they needed at a controlled interest rate and then reloaned it to small producers at a much higher rate.[17] Intermediaries became enmeshed in the production process in complex ways, intervening at multiple points in the production-consumption cycle. By providing productive inputs, buying up the crop at the end of the cycle, and selling an array of consumer goods, intermediaries played a central role in the system of rural commercialization.

14. Banco Central de Nicaragua, *Indicadores económicos*, 32.
15. Banco Nacional de Desarrollo, *Información general: Crédito Rural comparativo 1978 – 1983* (Managua: BND, 1984). There has been considerable discussion in Nicaragua about the numbers of agricultural producers in different categories, and figures vary from source to source. According to Carmen Diana Deere, Peter Marchetti, and Nola Reinhardt, "The Peasantry and the Development of Sandinista Agrarian Policy, 1979 – 1984," *Latin American Research Review* 20(3) (1985):78 there were 93,377 "rich and middle peasants" (10 – 50 mzs) and 157,357 "poor peasants (.1 – 10 mzs) in the economically active population of 1978. Taking this as an approximation of the population eligible for the Rural Credit Program, around 11% of the potential population was enrolled.
16. Banco Nacional de Nicaragua, *Incidencia de INVIERNO en el Programa de Crédito Rural del BNN en 1976* (Managua: BNN, 1977), 2. In INVIERNO's first year, it served 571 clients who had previously received loans through the Rural Credit Program.
17. Dorner and Quiros, "Institutional Dualism," 223.

For many small producers, credit was inaccessible under any terms. Instead, traditional subsistence-oriented production prevailed. Consequently, a substantial segment of Nicaraguan agriculture was marked by notoriously low output levels, leading to deepening rural poverty and a recurring dependence on imported foodstuffs.[18] In order to reverse this process, a fundamental restructuring of Nicaraguan agriculture would have to be carried out. A new regime with revolutionary priorities would be required to initiate this transformation.

AGRICULTURAL CREDIT UNDER THE SANDINISTAS

The nationalization of the banking system was one of the first actions of the Sandinista government. The banks had been largely bankrupt during the war due to heavy borrowing by the Somoza government, massive capital flight, and widespread nonpayment of debts. Nationalization, therefore, was essentially the assumption of bank debts by the new government. It represented the first step toward restoring some stability to Nicaragua's teetering financial structure.

The shift from a largely private banking system to a fully state-run system had significant consequences. Even in a nonrevolutionary setting, there are notable differences in the way public and private sector banks tend to function.[19] No bank can afford to ignore the question of profits without placing a severe strain on long-term operations. Public sector banks, however, can more easily view profit as only one of several goals to be pursued simultaneously. Under state ownership, a banking system can be reoriented to serve a new set of goals, giving greater emphasis to long-term development and the financial needs of lower income groups.

The lending patterns of the Nicaraguan banks began to shift after 1979, reflecting a reduced emphasis on commercial activity and increased concern about production. Following a 20-year slide in its relative access to credit, agriculture received a major infusion of bank resources and rose to a level of prominence it had not had since the 1960s. After receiving only one-third of all bank credit during the second half of the 1970s, the agricultural-livestock sector secured more than half of all credit in the 1982–1984 period.[20] The

18. See Rose J. Spalding, "Food Politics and Agricultural Change in Revolutionary Nicaragua, 1979–1982," in John C. Super and Thomas C. Wright, eds., Food, Politics, and Society in Latin America (Lincoln: University of Nebraska Press, 1985), 199–227.
19. See Carlos Pomareda, Financial Policies and Management of Agricultural Development Banks (Boulder: Westview, 1984), 1–13 for a fuller discussion of these issues.

economic model developing during this period placed renewed emphasis on rural development. As a consequence, the pattern of excluding small growers and staples producers began to change.

The Rural Credit Program

In 1979, the emaciated Rural Credit Program took on new life. Data from the Banco Nacional de Desarrollo indicate the scope of these changes (See Table 2).[21] Whereas only 28,000 families were enrolled in the Rural Credit Program in 1978, over 100,000 participated in 1980. The area financed by this program also expanded dramatically that year. Even after the program's subsequent contraction, it remained much broader than it had been in the prerevolutionary period.

In 1977, only 10% of agricultural-livestock loans had been funneled through the Rural Credit Program, and this dropped further at the outset of the insurrection (see Table 3). A year after Somoza's ouster, this percentage had almost tripled, rising to 27% of the total. Small- and medium-sized individual producers and cooperative members were being rapidly incorporated into the program.[22]

The overall profile of the program shifted notably. The predominance of export crops in the credit system diminished as a larger proportion of the

TABLE 2
Profile of the Rural Credit Program: 1978–1984

	1978	1979	1980	1981	1982	1983	1984	1985
Clients (thousands of families)	28.0	28.2	100.7	87.6	75.0	83.0	80.9	66.4
Area financed (thousand mz.)	88.0	162.3	427.1	245.5	280.1	270.2	332.3	269.3
No. of agency offices	51	51	63	60	60	86	84	89

Source: Banco Nacional de Desarrollo (BDN), *Información general: Crédito Rural comparativo 1978– 1983* (Managua: BND, 1984). BDN, *Informe estadístico 1984* (Managua: BDN, 1985); and unpublished BDN data.

20. Data from the pre-1979 period are from Banco Central de Nicaragua, *Indicadores económicos*, 29; for the 1982–1984 period, the authors used unpublished BCN data. The average for the three years in the 1982–1984 period was 54%.
21. Shortly after coming to power, the new government combined the BNN with several small development funds and renamed the bank the Banco Nacional de Desarrollo (BND).
22. Operational definitions of "small-" and "medium-sized" producers vary. The value of

TABLE 3
Sectoral Distribution of Agricultural-Livestock Credit[a] (dispersals in millions of córdobas)

| | | | REGULAR BANK CREDIT PROGRAM | | | | |
| | RURAL CREDIT | | PRIVATE SECTOR | | APP | | TOTAL |
YEAR	AMOUNT	(%)	AMOUNT	(%)	AMOUNT	(%)	AMOUNT
1977	183	10	1598	90	—	—	1781
1978	90	4	2432	96	—	—	2522
1979	178	13	1215	87[b]	—	—	1393
1980	831	27	2237	73[b]	—	—	3068
1981	972	23	1863	43	1473	34	4308
1982	1129	21	2238	42	2018	37	5385
1983	1555	24	2331	36	2605	40	6491
1984	2353	29	2464	30	3312	41	8129
1985	5771	31	5225	29	7344	40	18340

[a]Includes short and long term credit.
[b]Includes private sector and APP.
Source: 1977–1981 CIERA/PAN/CIDA, 41. 1982–1985, unpublished data from BCN.

credit was funneled to crops produced for the internal market (see Table 1). After averaging only 15% of the credit in the 1970s, the four key domestic market crops secured an average of 27% of the credit between 1980 and 1985. Within the Rural Credit Program, increased attention was given to the interior region of the country, thereby incorporating more corn and beans producers.[23] As Table 4 indicates, this expansion was most striking among very small producers. Although only a third of the more prosperous medium-sized producers and "rich peasants" who received credit in 1980 were receiving credit for the first time that year, over 65% of the poorest peasants receiving credit in 1980 were newly enrolled.

The program was designed to reinforce a growing cooperative movement.

---

holdings has been used by the BND to define this category and, by extension, those eligible for participation in the Rural Credit Program. BND, *Reglamento de Crédito Rural* (Managua: BND, April 1983), 3–4. MIDINRA, however, has used the following definition:

> *Small Producers* are those who possess up to 15 mzs. in basic grains, 10 in coffee or cacao, 3 in vegetables, 20 in cotton, or 10 in other perennial crops. *Medium producers* are those with 15–75 mzs. in basic grains, 10–30 in coffee or cacao, 20–100 in cotton, or 10–20 in other perennial crops. *Large producers* are those with more land in any of these categories. (MIDINRA, *Plan operativo de granos básicos: Ciclo agrícola 1982/83* [Managua: MIDINRA, 1982], 172).

23. Centro de Investigación y Estudios de la Reforma Agraria (CIERA), *Informe final: Impacto del Crédito Rural sobre el nivel de vida del campesinado* (Managua: CIERA, 1982), 32–60.

TABLE 4
Distribution of New Credit by Size of
Producer—Rural Credit Program

SIZE OF LANDHOLDING	PERCENTAGE OF CLIENTS WHO BEGAN RECEIVING CREDIT AFTER APRIL 1980
0–10 mz.	65.5%
10–50 mz.	48.1%
50–200 mz.	33.8%
Total	53.6%

Source: CIERA, *Informe final: Impacto del Crédito Rural sobre el nivel de vida del campesinado* (Managua: CIERA, 1982), 225.

This emphasis on cooperatives allowed the bank to incorporate large numbers of producers without the delay and expense of reviewing each individual application. Cooperatization allowed the bank to disseminate resources more widely, while promoting the collectivist orientation that the new government favored. Of those affiliated with this program in 1983, 78% were members of a cooperative.[24]

The Rural Credit Program continued to give preferential interest rates to its participants. After 1979, however, the degree of concession became much more marked. Whereas standard interest rates were 17% throughout the early 1980s, the rate for small, individual producers in the Rural Credit Program was 13%. Both in access to credit and terms of repayment, the program revealed a growing alliance between the state and the peasantry.

This alliance was most fully developed with the cooperative sector. Members of Credit and Service Cooperatives (CCS), who banned together for the solicitation of credit and for marketing, were charged an even lower interest rate of 10%. Members of the more fully collectivized Sandinista Agricultural Cooperatives (CAS), who held land in common, were further favored with an 8% rate.[25] Within the Rural Credit Program, credit increases were greatest among the CAS. The short-term credits for CAS cooperatives rose from 5.9% of all Rural Credit allocations in 1981 to 28.6% in 1983; the increase in their portion of long-term credits was even more marked.[26]

---

24. BND, *Información*.
25. All CAS and most CCS cooperatives are treated as collective entities in the distribution of credit. For CCS members, however, repayment is handled on an individual basis.
26. The CAS share of long-term BND credit rose from 2% percent in 1981 to 29% in 1983, whereas CCS and individual participation fell from 32 to 22% and 66 to 49%, respectively (unpublished MIDINRA data).

The Piñata and the Saneamiento

In their eagerness to transform Nicaraguan agriculture and address the his- toric problems of the Somoza era, MIDINRA and BND officials embarked on an innovative program of administrative reorganization. Mobile banks (cajas móviles) were brought into isolated rural areas, loans were handed out in cash, and a "banco aéreo" system was created to fly bank officials into villages not connected to the road system. These policies were designed to alter the elitist nature of the banking system and expand the popular base of the revolution. This policy of "spilling credit" allowed the government to transfer resources from the banking system to tens of thousands of the rural poor, quickly distributing financial resources to impoverished areas.[27] From the beginning, the new credit policies helped to establish the redistributive thrust of the revolution.

In its early years, however, the program probably functioned more directly as a social welfare measure than as a production program. Although some of the new clients used these resources to improve production technologies, the majority did not. In general, new clients were less likely to use new technol- ogy than those who had been enrolled in the program before 1979.[28] Production data provide little evidence of a close association between credit increases and expanded output. Indeed, by providing small producers with an alternative source of income, increased access to credit may have actually contributed to labor shortages experienced in the agroexport sector, thereby lowering output in that sector.[29]

Questions about the impact of the credit expansion generated consider- able controversy within the banking system and MIDINRA. BND officials

27. See Joseph Collins with Frances Moore Lappé, Nick Allen and Paul Rice, What Difference Could a Revolution Make? 2d ed. (San Francisco: Institute for Food and Development Policy, 1985), 51–58.
28. For example, only 19% of the new clients producing corn and 6% of those producing beans used improved seed in 1981. For those who had been bank clients for at least 3 years, the figures were 25 and 8%, respectively. CIERA, Informe final, 230–31. The absence of a control group or longitudinal analysis, however, make it difficult to assess precisely the impact of credit on either production practices or output.
29. Laura J. Enriquez argues that agricultural credit policies during the first few years following Somoza's ouster contributed to a process of campesinización in the Nicaraguan country- side. Campesinización is the preference among the campesino sector to stay and work their own small farms throughout the year instead of participating several months of the year in the agroexport harvests, when provided with the option. Credit policies contributed to the creation of this option through the provision of increased funds to this sector. According to Enriquez, this tendency has played a central role in the harvest labor shortages that have affected coffee and cotton production each year since 1980, although the Contra war has surpassed campesinización in importance since 1984. See Enriquez, Social Transformation in Latin America: Tensions between Agro-Export Production and Agrarian Reform in Revolu- tionary Nicaragua (Ph.D. Dissertation, University of California, Santa Cruz, 1985).

came to refer to 1980 as the *piñata*, the year when credit was scattered generously around the countryside. This year was followed with a sharp contraction of the program in 1981 (see Table 2). BND data show that the area financed under the Rural Credit Program rose from 88,000 mz. in 1978 to 427,100 mz. in 1980 but was cut sharply to 245,500 in 1981. As Table 3 indicates, the amount of credit channeled through this program dropped from 27% of the total in 1980 to 21% in 1982, before rising more gradually thereafter.

This caution was informed by a growing concern over the escalating peasant debt. Some of this debt was a carryover from the final years of the Somoza era but much was incurred after 1979. As Table 5 indicates, in the first year after the insurrection, the "recuperation rate" in the Rural Credit Program was only 26%. The array of factors contributing to this situation included *(a)* the poor quality of the land where many small producers were located; *(b)* inexperience and lack of training in improved production techniques; *(c)* low prices for their products, especially in basic grains; *(d)* an uneven marketing structure that did not facilitate the flow of goods between producers and consumers; and *(e)* perennial climatic problems.[30] These

TABLE 5
Agricultural-Livestock Loan "Recuperation Rates"[a] by Sector (millions of córdobas and percentage)

| | | | REGULAR BANK CREDIT PROGRAM | | | |
| | RURAL CREDIT | | PRIVATE SECTOR | | APP | |
YEAR	AMOUNT	(%)	AMOUNT	(%)	AMOUNT	%
1977	65.1	36	1181.3	74	—	—
1978	89.6	100	2366.2	97	—	—
1979	11.8	7	1147.9[b]	94	nd	nd
1980	219.8	26	1183.1[b]	53	nd	nd
1981	532.4	55	1662.6	89	747.5	51
1982	613.2	54	1833.7	82	1044.6	52
1983	851.8	55	2273.6	98	1510.6	58
1984	1444.0	61	2210.6	90	1995.9	60

[a]One operational definition of *recuperation rates* used by the SFN and CIERA is: total repayments in a given year as a percentage of new disbursements. Because the actual repayment of short-term loans may come in the following agricultural cycle, and several years later in the case of long-term loans, this rate should not be read as a precise measure of repayment. The differences in these percentages, however, do capture sectoral variations in loan repayment patterns.
[b]Includes private sector and the APP.
Source: 1977–1984, CIERA/PAN/CIDA, 43 and 50. 1982–1984, unpublished BCN data.

30. See the study on the peasant debt problem in "Lunes socio-económico," *Barricada* (July 4, 1983).

problems were particularly acute in the interior where producers of corn and beans struggled with an array of obstacles simultaneously.

Recognizing these deep-seated problems, Junta leader Daniel Ortega announced a clearing (*saneamiento*) of the peasant debt on the fourth anniversary of the revolution. Relief was targeted to producers of four basic staple crops—corn, beans, sorghum, and rice. This strategy reflected the fear that heavy debts would turn producers away from the bank and impede the adoption of improved technologies, thus keeping production levels low and undermining the quest for food self-sufficiency. As with lending policies, the *saneamiento* illustrated the preferred position of the cooperatives. The debts of individual producers were forgiven through the 1980–1981 agricultural cycle, whereas those of CCS members were cleared through 1981–1982, and CAS members had their debts pardoned through the 1982–1983 cycle.

By 1982, the Rural Credit Program had begun a process of consolidation. The bank's ability to recuperate loans gradually improved as monitoring of credit use tightened, more lucrative crops were planted, and bank officials began to work more closely with the organizers of cooperatives. The average "recuperation rate" rose from 26% in the 1980–1981 cycle to 61% in 1984–1985 (see Table 5). At the same time, the number of participants in the program began to decline (see Table 2). After rising rapidly between 1979 and 1980 to an estimated 100,700 clients, the number of program affiliates contracted in 1981 and declined further to 75,000 families in 1982. In 1984, membership rose again, before dropping to around 66,000 in 1985. The program had begun to consolidate while covering roughly half of all small- and medium-sized producers.[31]

Regular Bank Credit

In terms of the overall credit system, the most significant transformation occurred in the Rural Credit Program. Yet most resources were still concentrated in the regular bank credit system, which served larger private producers and state farms. As Table 3 shows, over 70% of the agriculture-livestock credit still went to this program in 1984.

Most producers enrolled in the regular bank (*crédito bancario*) program had access to credit even during the Somoza years. For this group, the major change was in the terms under which credit was contracted. The new government lowered interest rates in the Rural Credit Program below 1979 levels,

---

31. According to BND officials, there were approximately 150,000 peasant families that were theoretically eligible for inclusion in the Rural Credit Program in 1984. Data from CIERA, "Informe de la FAO sobre el campesino pobre" (Unpublished manuscript, 1985) also support this finding.

but it allowed regular bank rates to rise. In the latter program, interest rates for short-term agricultural loans increased from 14% in 1979 to 17% in the 1981–1983 period. Yet all of these interest rates were far below the inflation rate, which fluctuated between 22 and 50% in the 1980–1984 period.[32] By keeping the interest rate for regular bank loans well below the rate of inflation, the government subsidized production for even the most prosperous producers.

Furthermore, the percentage of production costs covered by the bank actually increased for many established clients, as the government attempted to stimulate increased production by easing access to credit. Until the adoption of the February 1985 stabilization plan, the bank gave credit advances covering 100% of production costs to producers of cotton as well as basic grains.[33] Credit totaling roughly 80% of costs was provided for the production of coffee, sugarcane, and sesame. Recognizing that private producers would be particularly averse to taking financial risks during a period of profound social change, the government tried to compensate and to stimulate investment by making it relatively risk-free. Producers were required to put up little if any of their own capital in this process.

As both the regional economy and the relationship between the state and the private sector began to deteriorate in 1981 and 1982, the government's generous credit policy started to present serious problems. Some producers began using cash advances to buy up dollars in the black or the parallel market instead of purchasing the prescribed amount of agricultural inputs. Others over-invoiced import bills to obtain bank authorization for additional foreign currency. Concern that private producers were absorbing bank resources without proportionate production increases further heightened tensions between the state and the private sector.

Low international prices for export crops, difficulties securing imported equipment, uncertainty about the future, and hostility to the Sandinista leadership prompted an important sector of the medium and large producers to engage in economic withdrawal. Some left the country; some had their farms expropriated. Objectively, the landholdings of the agroexport elite contracted; the land held in large estates (over 355 ha.) declined from 21% of the total in 1981 to 11.5% in 1984.[34] Subjectively, many of those remaining

---

32. Comisión Económica para América Latina y el Caribe (CEPAL), *Notas para el estudio económico de América Latina y el Caribe, 1984: Nicaragua* (México: CEPAL, July 15, 1985), 3.
33. The exception for basic grains was irrigated rice where 80% of costs were financed. There have been continual complaints by private producers that MIDINRA's cost assessments underestimate actual production expenses. As a result, credit allocations are said to regularly fall below the formally authorized percentage of costs.
34. Deere et al., "The Peasantry", 79.

felt beseiged; they responded with a production slowdown and an investment strike.

Under these circumstances, the relative participation of large-and medium-sized producers in the credit system began to decline. As Table 3 indicates, the portion of credit allocated to this sector dropped from 43% in 1981 to 30% in 1984. The economic withdrawal of the bourgeoisie should not be exaggerated; these producers remained an important element in the national economy, especially in the production of export crops, sorghum, and rice. Their role in the overall system, however, tended to decline relative to that of other sectors.

In contrast, the percentage of credit funneled to the state farms was substantially higher than their control over land would suggest. In 1981, the state farm system in the Area Propiedad del Pueblo (APP) controlled 20% of Nicaragua's agricultural land.[35] Yet the APP received 34% of all agricultural credit (see Table 3). This pattern deepened over the years. By 1984, the APP's allocation of agricultural credit had climbed to 41% whereas it controlled only 19.2% of the land. The state farms had rapidly become the bank's major customer.

Unlike the larger private producers, the state farm administrators continued to design new investment projects and to demand heavy infusions of bank capital to cover inventory and regular operating expenses. The political bond between the state farms and the government encouraged the injection of bank resources into this sector. Although the banking system's formal policy eschewed favoritism, the uneasy relationship between many large private producers and the Sandinista state spilled over into their relationship with the bank, contributing to the previously mentioned withdrawal on the part of the private sector. On the other hand, the structural alliance between the bank and state enterprises deepened over the years. This bond came to take the place of the prerevolutionary alliance between the banks and agroexport elites.

This shift in alliances posed economic and political problems. The state farms had enduring difficulties making timely loan repayments. The dislocations surrounding the change in managers and management style, a dramatic decline in labor productivity, and the costs of providing a gamut of social services for the workers all increased the financial burden of the state farms. The "logic" of production in the state sector was not based entirely on concerns about profit. At times, social priorities prevailed, complicating loan repayment. The absence of an adversarial element in the relationship between the APP enterprises and the bank further reduced repayment pressures.

35. *Ibid.*

Finally, as the war escalated, the state farms were frequently targets for Contra attacks, which had devastating consequences for production. As a result, loan recuperation for the APP fell below that for its private sector counterpart (see Table 5). "Recuperation rates" for the private sector fluctuated between 82 and 98% in the 1981−1984 period. Although the rate for the APP improved steadily during this period, it had reached only 60% in 1984.

These problems triggered a saneamiento for the APP similar to that carried out in the peasant credit program. The state farms were reorganized in 1983, and their capital debts were assumed by the Ministry of Finance. Ultimately, this adjustment totaled more than that for the peasant debt.[36] In spite of this reduction in their debt burden, both the APP farms and the participants in the Rural Credit Program continued to have comparatively low recuperation rates in 1984.

CREDIT AND SOCIAL CHANGE: ACHIEVEMENTS AND LIMITATIONS

Since 1979, many previously existing institutions have been restructured to reflect the new priorities characterizing the Nicaraguan revolution. Changes in the country's financial structure were central to this institutional metamorphosis. Contrary to what might be expected in a situation of revolutionary transformation, the banking system was not eliminated as an important center of accumulation and capital allocation. A restructuring of that system was initiated, however, orienting it to a different set of goals.

An emphasis on a "logic of the majority" informed these changes. The shift in patterns of capital allocation that occurred in the 1979−1985 period reflected a conscious policy of favoring sectors previously excluded from the system. Within agriculture, the small- and medium-sized producers received major infusions of new credit. The state farms, which were seen as institutions of national development generating resources for the public good, were also major beneficiaries of the new credit system. As a consequence, the traditional alliance between the banking system and larger private producers was broken.

The process of restructuring the banking system, however, proved to be quite problematic. In spite of a concerted effort, the system was still unable to fully absorb the array of atomized peasant producers disbursed throughout the Nicaraguan countryside. This problem was manifest in the gradual level-

36. CIERA/Programa Alimentario Nicaragüense/Canadian International Development Agency, *Informe final del Proyecto Estrategia Alimentaria*, Vol. 3, *Directorio de políticas alimentarias* (Managua: CIERA, 1984), 49.

ing off of enrollments in the Rural Credit Program. Although the pool of beneficiaries of the new credit policies was much larger in 1985 than it had been in the prerevolutionary period, expansion had stagnated at the inclusion of roughly half of the eligible population. This stabilization suggests the structural limitations encountered by policymakers in their efforts to reorient the system.

Many factors combined to retard the growth of this program. In spite of land redistribution and an improvement in extension services, many small producers still functioned in a traditional manner. A subsistence orientation, low-yield levels, and geographical isolation impeded their inclusion in the national marketing system. They remained, consequently, disconnected from the intrinsic logic of a lending system.

Some producers, who were integrated into the market, were cautious about participating in the banking system. Post-1979 bank policy precluded the confiscation of peasant land, even in the event of nonpayment of loans. The memory of prerevolutionary confiscations, however, was a deterrent to seeking credit. This was especially significant for those producing crops whose low prices regularly jeopardized repayment prospects. Extensive paperwork, the limited number of branch offices and qualified bank personnel, and delays in loan disbursement were also obstacles to more comprehensive incorporation.

Furthermore, the bank was unable to replicate the full range of services traditionally provided by credit intermediaries (timely cash loans, immediate access to productive inputs, an on-site market for the harvest with cash payments, and consumer goods). This made it an unattractive alternative for some producers. Finally, bank officials' increased concern about recuperation probably slowed the rate of expansion. Although officials in the Rural Credit Program remained committed to continued growth, the procedures they developed to monitor credit use may have deterred applications from marginal producers.

In addition, several killings of bank officials and the displacement of small- and medium-sized producers from the areas of heaviest counterrevolutionary activity worked against the continued expansion of the program. Many new services could not be sustained because of the escalating violence in the interior. In sum, although a process of democratization of the previously restrictive banking system was begun in 1979, the continuing structure of rural poverty, low productivity, and inadequate prices, now combined with the disruptions of war, made it difficult to integrate much of the Nicaraguan peasantry into the credit system.

A second tension associated with the reoriented lending policy is seen in the broader structural economic disequilibrium that emerged. The new loans, combined with relatively low recuperation rates, placed heavy pressure on the bank's reserves. Over the course of several years, a financial deficit emerged in the banking system. Expansive credit policies gradually contributed to financial imbalance, eventually fueling inflation and economic dislocations.

In the first flush years following the ouster of Somoza, a surge of foreign loans and donations provided ample resources for credit expansion. The subsequent contraction of external financing, however, made the credit system increasingly dependent on internal sources. Yet the bank's own resources were limited and did not expand rapidly enough to sustain the new credit policy.

In most banking systems, repayment of principal and interest from previous loans is a major source of revenue for new loans. In Nicaragua, however, interest rates were far below the inflation rate; they constituted a subsidy to borrowers instead of a return for the bank. Low recuperation rates in some sectors and the clearing of the peasant and APP debts further limited the return flow of bank resources. This undermined the traditional process through which loanable funds are generated for the next cycle.

New deposits were equally inadequate to sustain the credit increases. Just as interest rates for borrowers were kept below the inflation rate, interest rates for depositors were also consistently lower than the rate of inflation.[37] Under these circumstances, idle investment resources were not attracted to the bank. Instead, they were readily drawn into speculation and the black market for dollars, where the return was substantially higher.

As the Contra war dragged on and inflation soared, the reluctance to hold bank deposits intensified. Data on the money supply indicate the increasing preference for the security of holding cash to the uncertainties of bank deposits, especially for long-term deposits.[38] To reduce this liquidity and draw money back into the system, the bank started a program of gifts and lotteries for depositors in 1984. Yet this strategy seemed unlikely to counter the exodus from the banking system.

Credit disbursements from the Nicaraguan banks, therefore, relied increasingly on emissions from the Central Bank. This continual expansion of

37. For example, the interest rate for 6 to 12 month time deposits ranged from 10% (with raffle and prizes) to 12% (without raffle or prizes) in 1984. BCN, Normas financieras: Período 1984–1985 (Managua: BCN, 1984). Meanwhile, the inflation rate for that year was 50% percent. CEPAL, Notas, 3.
38. In 1984, córdobas held in cash by the public increased over 100%, whereas those in checking, savings, and term accounts increased by only 51, 40, and 30%, respectively. CEPAL, Notas, 59. See also the Secretaría de Planificación y Presupuesto, "Evaluación y perspectivas económicas 1985" (Unpublished document, June 1985), and Rodolfo Delgado C., "Sobre las medidas de ajuste y la crisis económica de Nicaragua," Ediciones Nicaragua Hoy 1 (April 1985):10.

the money supply without a proportionate growth of production contributed to an inflationary spiral that was already being fueled by rising defense spending. In 1985, the inflation rate soared to over 300% and became a defining feature of the Nicaraguan economy.[39] In the context of Nicaragua's multiple domestic and international economic problems, the expansionary credit policy had financially destabilizing effects.

Recognizing the growing structural problems in the Nicaraguan economy, the Sandinista government initiated a major economic adjustment program at the beginning of 1985. Among the changes introduced were several that affected credit policy. Interest rates for both borrowers and depositors were increased, and the policy of financing 100% of costs for the APP and private cotton producers was tightened.[40] These changes were reinforced by an open campaign conducted by high-ranking MIDINRA officials against public sector inefficiency and mismanagment.[41]

Yet problems with insufficient bank resources continued. Policymakers were concerned that higher interest rates would slow the rate of investment, undermine their efforts to catalyze production, and fuel the inflationary spiral. Consequently, interest rates were left far below the rate of inflation. Cutting back credit in areas with relatively low recuperation rates would require the government to abandon its political commitment to the peasantry, cooperatives, and state farms. Because such changes would threaten revolutionary alliances, they were also found unacceptable.

Unwilling to accept a major change in the revolutionary project, the state avoided a conventional adjustment process. But the economic costs of the new alliances during this period of aggression and transition proved formidable. Ultimately, these costs began to call into question the very viability of the revolutionary credit policy. For government planners, these imbalances pointed to a crucial dilemma. The central question became: How could the nation's overall economic viability be maintained at the same time that

39. For the 6-month period ending in May 1985, the prices for selected basic goods rose 126%. Secretaría de Planificación y Presupuesto, "Evaluación". The annual inflation rate for 1985 was 334%. CEPAL, *Notas para el estudio económico de America Latina y el Caribe, 1985: Nicaragua* (México: CEPAL, July 4, 1986), 2.
40. In early 1985, interest rates for depositors were increased 4 to 12 percentage points, depending on the length of time for which the deposit was committed. Interest rates for borrowers were also increased by 3 points for APP and private borrowers in the regular bank program, 2 points for members of cooperatives, and 1 point for individual producers in the Rural Credit Program. For credit beyond 80% of production costs, cotton producers were required to pay a 30% interest rate instead of 20%. BCN, *Normas Monetarias 1985* (Managua: BCN, 1985). Interest rates were raised again in early 1986, but remained far below the inflation rate. *Latin America Weekly Report* 7 (February 14, 1986), 10.
41. See the presentations made by MIDINRA Minister Jaime Wheelock and Vice-Minister Roberto Gutiérrez to an assembly of state farm administrators, *Nuevo Diario*, March 7, 1985.

productive assets were redistributed? This question captures a fundamental dilemma in the process of revolutionary change.

The legacy of rural poverty, the dislocations of profound institutional change, political resistance from traditional elites, and the advent of war set into motion a series of tensions that confounded the process of transition. Such developments reflect the complexity of designing and implementing a program of revolutionary change. They also suggest the complexity of transforming capitalist institutions, which are designed to operate according to the logic of profit, into institutions that pursue noncapitalist, redistributive objectives. By 1985, the Sandinistas faced a series of difficult choices as they grappled with this gap between their resources, their needs, and their capabilities.[42] The contradiction between the broad development objectives of the Sandinista government and the nation's profound resource limitations, and between the government's aspirations and its realm of control, remain central problems of the Nicaraguan revolution.

ACKNOWLEDGMENTS

Rose J. Spalding wishes to acknowledge the financial support provided by the University Research Council of DePaul University. Both authors gratefully acknowledge the assistance provided by numerous Nicaraguan bank officials, policy analysts, and credit recipients. This work also benefited from comments made by Rodolfo Delgado Cáceres, Richard R. Fagen, E. V. K. FitzGerald, and Peter Utting. The opinions expressed here, however, are those of the authors and should not be attributed to those who have commented on the work or to institutions with which the authors have been affiliated.

42. In its draft version of the 1986 Economic Plan, the Secretaría de Planificación y Presupuesto called attention to these continuing imbalances, and recommended further tightening and rationalization of credit distribution. See "Bosquejo del Plan Económico 1986" (unpublished document, June 18, 1985), 37–38.

Chapter 6

Domestic Supply and Food Shortages

PETER UTTING

Why is it that problems relating to scarcity and rapid price inflation for basic goods have become such a prominent feature of the Nicaraguan economy, when the revolutionary government appears so committed to a basic needs approach? This same question could equally apply to a number of socialist experiences in the Third World, given that these problems are common to societies undergoing rapid structural change.[1] The apparent contradiction between the ideology and policies of the revolutionary government on the one hand and the reality of the supply system on the other can easily be misconstrued. Politically it will inevitably be used against the government and the revolution. The main opposition parties, antigovernment guerrilla forces and the U.S. administration alike, use the issue of scarcity and inflation as a key element in their anti-Sandinista discourse. Problems of this nature, they argue, simply manifest the bankruptcy of a system in which the state increasingly intervenes to regulate or control economic activities and redistribute income. Such intervention only serves to dislocate production and marketing systems and thereby reduce domestic supply.

By examining the experience of Nicaragua between 1979 and 1985, this chapter attempts to contribute to a better understanding of why transitional societies are so prone to problems of shortages and inflation. We focus specifically on the relationship between the process of revolutionary change and shortages of basic food products. The analysis identifies a set of tensions and constraints affecting production, marketing, and the adquisition of con-

---

1. Keith Griffin and Jeffrey James, *The Transition to Egalitarian Development* (Hong Kong: Macmillan Press, 1981), 12.

sumer goods that surface as social and economic relations and structures are transformed. In order to highlight more clearly this relationship, we will not deal at length with a range of conditions normally associated with underdevelopment and dependency that affect the less developed countries in general. It should always be borne in mind, however, that conditions such as these, associated, for example, with deteriorating terms of trade, fluctuating interest rates, indebtedness, inadequate technologies, the vagaries of climate, and the like have clearly had an important impact on restricting supply and conditioning the pace and content of redistributive policies in Nicaragua. A number of these issues are in fact dealt with in other chapters of this book.

The tensions we focus on are generated by three processes of change that may be said to constitute the economic hallmark of the Sandinista Revolution. These are:

1. *The Transformation of Social Relations*   A revolutionary process, by definition, implies the transformation of relations of production, exchange, and class that alters conditions in the labor process and transforms structures of production, income, and wealth. From this process of change emerge numerous tensions that affect domestic production and people's access to food, as traditional production and marketing systems are disarticulated and effective demand is increased with income redistribution.

2. *The Development of the Productive Forces*   While investment in other Central American countries has tended to decline during recent years of economic crisis, the Nicaraguan government has commited itself to expanding the economic base and social infrastructure to raise future standards of living. This is reflected in figures for economic growth where, despite the impact of the war, Nicaragua had the fourth highest growth rate for Latin American nations between 1981 and 1984.[2] Such a program of rapid accumulation, however, generates a series of tensions that in the short term affect domestic supply as resources that might be used for immediate production and consumption are diverted towards long-term investment.

3. *The Redefinition of the Dependency Relation*   The principles of nonalignment and autonomous development have led the revolutionary government to strengthen economic and political ties with a broad range of countries. This process of redefining the dependency relation expresses the antiimperialist character of the revolution and the struggle against the economic and geopolitical domination of the United States in Central America. In response to this position, the United States adopted economic and military

2. CEPAL, *Balance preliminar de la economía latinoamericana durante 1984* (Santiago, Chile: CEPAL, 1985).

actions that had serious consequences for Nicaragua's development process in general and domestic food supply in particular.[3]

Tensions generated by these processes of change have resulted in a situation of market disequilibrium, reflected in problems of shortages and inflationary tendencies for wage goods. On the supply side, the preceding processes have imposed a series of constraints on domestic production and the capacity of the economy to import basic goods. On the demand side, large increases in government spending and deficits required to finance redistributive policies, public investment programs, and the war have significantly increased the demand for wage goods. It is these two sets of conditions that are now analyzed in more detail.

CONSTRAINTS ON DOMESTIC SUPPLY

Although the performance of the Nicaraguan economy during the early years of the revolution compares favorably with other postrevolutionary experiences, changing economic and political relations, nevertheless, conditioned the rate of economic recovery and growth of domestic supply. The insurrection period saw the beginning of a process of disarticulation of the traditional production system that has continued until the present. This process, manifested in the behavior of state and capitalist enterprises, peasant, and working-class sectors, constrained the rate of expansion of agricultural and food production. In particular, the transformation of capitalist relations of production and the disarticulation of traditional peasant farming systems restricted growth. As a consequence, production remained stagnant in three of the most important product sectors in the entire food system, namely cattle, cotton, and corn. These processes also contributed to what became one of the major constraints on economic development, namely labor shortages that affected agricultural production, investment programs, and manufacturing in general. While these conditions restrained domestic production, the total supply of basic food products was further affected by restrictions on imports imposed in 1982.

Stagnation in Key Product Sectors

The collapse of the cotton and cattle sectors had serious repercussions for the functioning of the entire food system. As private growers and ranchers aban-

---

3. The effects of these actions are analyzed in more detail by FitzGerald in another chapter of this book and will not be dealt with in detail here.

doned production or engaged in asset-stripping, the cotton area fell from 248 thousand manzanas during the 1978/79 cycle to 64 thousand in 1979/80. The mass slaughter of the national herd set cattle production back more than 10 years. Difficulties in recuperating production levels reflected to a large extent the response of capitalist producers unwilling to expand production and invest when "the climate" was not right. When property relations were perceived to be threatened by the agrarian reform and more real constraints on the production process, surplus appropriation, and accumulation were experienced, the reproduction of capital was affected.[4] Although production levels in most sectors had generally recuperated or substantially exceeded the prerevolution level, those of cotton and cattle were still well below that point 6 years later (see Table 1).

At first sight, the decline in production in what are normally considered traditional agroexport sectors, might not appear to be a central concern for the availability of basic food products. However, these two sectors constitute two of the most important subsystems in the national food system.[5] In addition to being the prime sources for a range of food products such as vegetable oil (produced from cotton seed), milk, meat, and cheese, which constitute significant calorie and protein sources in the local diet, they also generate a series of by-products that are important raw materials used in the fabrication of animal feed, upon which the poultry and pig industries are dependent. From cotton and cattle also come other raw materials crucial for the leather and shoe, and textile and soap industries, producing important consumer items. As two of the four main export sectors, reduced production levels have also contributed significantly to the drop in export earnings that, as we will see later, was a key factor affecting domestic supply in recent years.

The other major product sector affected by changing social relations and patterns of resource allocation was corn.[6] Despite the introduction of extensive credit and technical assistance programs in 1980 that gave thousands of peasant producers access for the first time to these services, corn production did not respond as expected. Production levels continued to remain stagnant even following the creation of the Nicaraguan Food Program (PAN) in 1981 and the enactment of the Agrarian Reform Law that same year. These programs had expressed in a concrete form the government's desire to assign a

4. E. V. K. FitzGerald, "La economía nacional en 1985: La transición como coyuntura," Paper presented at the 1985 Annual Congress of Nicaraguan Social Scientists, Managua, August 1985, 8
5. CIERA, *El funcionamiento del sistema alimentario* (Managua: CIERA, 1984), 6
6. Corn is the main calorie source in the national diet and, along with beans, the main protein source. It is also an important source of animal feed at the level of peasant production, and in urban areas, an estimated 13,000 artesanal processors depend on corn for their livelihood. CIERA, *El funcionamiento*, 9, 92.

TABLE 1

Evolution of Agricultural Production, 1977–1985 (1977/78 = 100)

PRODUCT	1977–1978	1978–1979	1979–1980	1980–1981	1981–1982	1982–1983	1983–1984	1984–1985[a]
Cotton	100	89	15	53	45	55	62	50
Coffee	100	101	98	103	106	125	85	89
Sugar Cane	100	109*	86	98	114	109	114	95
Rice	100	114	132	133	193	204	213	219
Beans	100	209	71	70	101	115	137	160
Corn	100	155	80	101	106	101	119	129
Sorghum	100	146	148	208	225	124	239	262

	1977	1978	1979	1980	1981	1982	1983	1984
Beef[b]	100	112	100	75	59	63	64	80
Milk[c]	100	93	65	97	128	157	153	144
Chicken[d]	100	117	104	131	183	202	214	187
Eggs[d]	100	113	116	121	131	147	152	139

[a]Preliminary.
[b]Does not include "clandestine" slaughter.
[c]Pasteurized milk only.
[d]Does not include peasant production.
Source: MIDINRA.

131

high priority to basic food production and the peasantry in the structure of resource allocation.

The reasons for stagnating corn production were complex. In part, they related to structural conditions associated with the marginal location and dispersed character of peasant production, lack of infrastructure and adequate technologies, poor soils, and the like. However, a set of conditions associated with the transition process, related to limitations at the level of planning and the impact of changing production and exchange relations, were also important.

In practice, the capacity of the major rural development programs to effectively expand corn production was limited. The agrarian reform clearly played an important role in the process of social change. However, the central focus of the agrarian reform was not a program of land redistribution to the poor peasantry and landless laborers. An ongoing subject of debate is whether or not a more radical program of land redistribution would have stimulated agricultural production in general and basic grain production in particular. For a complex set of reasons, the agrarian reform did not resort to large-scale expropriations and mass redistribution to the peasantry. By the end of 1984, only 31,000 families had received access to new land. This redistributed land represented only 9% of the total agricultural area, and the land recipients represented approximately 25% of the total number of poor peasants and seasonal workers whom one assumes needed land.[7]

The PAN, for its part, had difficulty in fulfilling its original role as an agency that would mobilize resources and peasant producers around bean and corn production. It is not until the 1984–1985 cycle that we see a significant change in the productive structure for basic grains, with the implementation of the so-called "Contingency Plan" for expanding basic grain production on large-scale irrigated farms in the Pacific region.[8]

Difficulties associated with policy design and implementation relate in

7. CIERA, *Nicaragua: El campesinado pobre*, Mimeo, 1985. CIERA estimates the number of poor peasants and seasonal workers to total approximately 122,600 families, including members of production cooperatives. During the latter half of 1985, more emphasis was placed on land redistribution and by the beginning of 1986 nearly 52,000 families had received new lands. This acceleration of the land redistribution process can be expected to continue throughout 1986, given the significant modifications of the 1981 agrarian reform law introduced in January 1986. These effectively do away with the limits established in the original law (of 350 ha. in the Pacific coastal region and 700 ha. in the interior) that an inefficient or unproductive owner could possess before being liable to expropriation. An increasing number of state farms have also been handed over to the peasantry.
8. The PAN's main areas of success have been in vegetable production and large-scale irrigated production of basic grains. During the 1985/86 cycle, it is expected that one million quintales of corn and an equivalent amount of sorghum (that is approximately 25 and 50% of normal production respectively) will be grown on state, private, and cooperative farms integrated in the Contingency Plan.

part to problems of conception and coherency of economic policy but also to the objective difficulty of designing and implementing policies to encourage production among such a heterogeneous and dispersed sector. Policy-makers had difficulties in designing policies specifically adapted to the logic of peasant production. Rather, there was a tendency to treat the diverse forms of peasant, capitalist, cooperative, and state production that comprise Nica-raguan agriculture as one. These subsectors, in fact, operate according to very different logics of production and reproduction and confront different sets of objective and subjective circumstances that condition how they will respond to incentives or regulatory policies.[9]

A number of policies had unanticipated effects detrimental to corn production and marketing. Among certain producers, located particularly in the Pacific region of the country, improved access to resources prompted an expansion of cash crop production. Relatively low official producer prices and a subsidy policy acted as a disincentive to production among the rich peasantry and capitalist producers who traditionally had grown corn for their workforce. Although the policy of establishing guaranteed producer prices protected the peasant producer from the traditional price fluctuations and exploitative exchange relations that historically undermined peasant incomes, prices set for corn were unable to keep pace with rural consumer prices. This also acted as a disincentive to increasing the marketed production of corn. Whereas a machete and a pair of working trousers, for example, cost the equivalent of half a quintal of corn in 1978, by the end of 1984 they cost 1.2 and 5.5 quintales, respectively. Rapidly rising transport costs had a similar negative effect on marketed production.

With the elimination of prerevolutionary forms of tenency, exchange, and credit relations, many producers were no longer obliged to produce the quantities of corn previously required to repay debts and services to landlords, merchants, and moneylenders. Improved access to free rural health services also had a similar impact, given that the peasant family had often sold grains in order to acquire necessary income to cover medical expenses.[10]

For a variety of reasons analyzed later, the state had difficulty in effectively substituting marketing functions previously performed by these agents. The displacement of merchants from rural commerce dislocated rural and urban markets, thereby restricting access to the means of production, consumption goods, and outlets in which to sell produce. Because a number of the larger merchants associated with rural trade imported directly from abroad, the

9. Alejandro Schejtman, "Lineamientos para el análisis integral de los problemas alimentarios nacionales," Paper presented at the First Food Strategy Seminar, Managua, February, 1983.
10. Michael Zalkin, Peasant Response to State Intervention in the Production of Basic Grains in Nicaragua: 1979–1984, (Ph.D. Dissertation, University of Massachusetts, 1985).

displacement of these agents dislocated not only rural and urban markets but also links with the international market. The multiplicity of functions exercised by these agents was decentralized among numerous state institutions. In addition to the limited penetration of these agencies in certain areas of the country, there were problems of coordination that affected not only peasant production but also capitalist and state production.[11] This situation reflects a much broader problem associated with the transition process in general—one that the planning process needs to deal with more effectively. A time lag very often arises between the disarticulation of the old structure and the consolidation of the new. Experience has shown that it is much easier to displace agents than it is to replace those necessary functions that they performed.

Problems such as these have been exacerbated since 1983 with the escalation of the war in the interior of the country. This has further dislocated rural and urban markets and the peasant economy in general. Particularly affected by the war was the production of beans, corn, coffee, and livestock. The war has not only disrupted marketing systems and destroyed infrastructure but also reinforced migratory tendencies that have depleted the rural economy of its labor reserves. Under conditions such as these, what remains of a peasant economy reverts to a subsistence economy.

Labor Shortages

Agriculture and industry were seriously affected by shortages of labor, resulting both from the flow of labor from primary and manufacturing sectors into service and trading activities and from the decline in productivity. Specifically, the availability of manpower was reduced by the absorption of a large portion of the population in four main areas: informal urban employment, education, central government employment, and the army.

The growth of the informal urban sector was a prominent feature of the Somocista period. This sector continued to expand rapidly during the revolutionary period but for a very different set of reasons. These related to the rupture of Somocista policies that had restrained the rate of rural-urban migration, the impact of the war, and a series of unanticipated effects of certain economic and social policies introduced during the 1979-84 period. A number of the major causes behind the exodus of the population from rural areas have been identified as follows:[12]

- The elimination of repressive mechanisms used during the Somocista era to control migration and the halting of colonization programs imple-

---

11. FitzGerald, "La economia nacional," 8.
12. MIDINRA, "Problemas y perspectivas de la migración campo-ciudad," *Revolución y Desarrollo* (1985):21−22.

mented by the previous regime to relocate people in the interior and Atlantic regions of the country.

- The highly permissive attitude of the revolutionary government in allowing squatters to invade and settle in vacant urban lots, particularly in the capital—Managua.
- The concentration and rapid expansion in the cities of a social infrastructure and programs related to education, health, public transport, housing, water, and light services as well as easy access to low-priced basic consumer goods.
- The rupture of cultural and historical ties to the land due to the impact of the war, which by October 1984 had forced the relocation of an estimated 150,000 people, many of whom migrated to the cities.[13]
- The increasing income differential between rural and urban workers, particularly given the relatively large profit margins to be earned in petty-trading activities.[14]

In addition to the proliferation of informal employment, we also see the rapid expansion of the student population, the number of central government employees, and the army. The student sector, for example, doubled in 5 years, from 533,000 in 1978 to 1,167,000 in 1984. This represented an increase from 20 to 37% of the total population.[15]

The number of central government employees has also increased considerably. Official figures recorded an increase from 27 thousand in 1978 to 76 thousand employees in 1985.[16] Although the majority of government employees work in important social service sectors such as education and

13. MIDINRA, *Situación de los asentamientos campesinos*, Mimeo, 1984.
14. A clear example of this is the street vender selling on a daily basis four crates of Coca-Cola. In August 1985, it was calculated by the author that once costs for ice and plastic bags were included (Coke bought on the street is always served in plastic bags), the vender earns a net profit in excess of 1500 córdobas a day or what it would take an agricultural worker 13 days of back-breaking work to earn. What is more, the street vender's monthly wage considerably exceeds that of a top professional working in the state sector.
15. Given limited research in this area, it is uncertain what the short-term impact of a rapidly expanding education sector has been on production. However, the age structure of the working population and the importance of youth labor in agriculture would indicate that a large increase in the student population would adversely affect the availability of labor, particularly in basic grain production. This phenomenom has been experienced for example, in countries such as Tanzania. See G. Mutahaba, "The Political Economy of Food Policy and Nutritional Improvements in Tanzania," Paper presented at IFPRI/UNU Workshop on the political economy of nutritional improvements, Berkely Springs, W.Va., June 1985. Concerning agro-export production, the "massification" of education has, however, been used to alleviate the scarcity of labor during the harvest period, given the policy to mobilize students to work in the cotton and coffee harvests during the long vacation period.
16. The former figure partly underestimates the real number of government employees toward the end of the Somoza era because certain employees in the education sector, for example, were not registered in the official figures.

health, they do not directly contribute to production. Also, the state has absorbed a large number of technical and professional staff who would otherwise work in agriculture or industry.

Finally, it has been estimated that the defense effort in 1984 required between 70,000 and 100,000 men, depending on the prevailing military situation.[17] Many integrated in the permanent army are of peasant origin, and those mobilized on a temporary basis in the "reserve batallions" are often drawn from the ranks of workers in the state farms, cooperatives, and factories.

The transfer of workers and peasants into these sectors has considerably undermined the productive capacity of the food system. This phenomenon has meant that a decreasing number of workers and peasants must produce the food and other basic consumer goods required for a population that is growing at an annual rate of 3.4%. It has been calculated that in 1982, just 12% of the national population was directly engaged in the production of basic consumer goods.[18] The rapid process of urbanization and militarization experienced since then would have reduced this figure still further.

The problem of labor shortages is associated not only with an absolute shortage of labor but also with the decline in productivity. This has emerged during the revolutionary period due to the transformation of social relations of production and as a response to an austere wage policy that operated until late 1984.[19] Traditional mechanisms of exploitation based on repressive or paternalistic relations that guaranteed certain levels of labor discipline and efficiency were to a large extent eliminated during the past 6 years. As Deere et al. explain:

> Throughout the country [the workers] took their "historic vacation." Absenteeism, tardiness, three-hour work days, and low productivity became endemic as the old structures of oppression were stripped away by the revolution.[20]

The decline in productivity was reflected both in the number of hours worked and in the intensity of labor. In labor agreements signed by union

17. Jaime Wheelock (Minister of Agricultural Development and Agrarian Reform), May Day Speech, 1984.
18. CIERA, *El funcionamiento*, 49.
19. As a means of easing pressure on wages and bypassing restrictions on wage increases, unions in a number of factories negotiated payment-in-kind benefits. In certain factories, however, these payments reached such proportions that absenteeism became necessary to market these goods on the parallel market. When it was realized that this form of payment had become one of the principal mechanisms for diverting manufactured goods from the official channels to the parallel market, it was abolished in early 1985, once a wage policy had been devised that would attempt to peg wage increases to those of prices.
20. Carmen Diana Deere, Peter Marchetti, and Nola Reinhardt, "The Peasantry and Development of Sandinista Agrarian Policy, 1979–1984," *Latin American Research Review* 20(3) (1985):80.

organizations, the Ministry of Labor, and production enterprises, the traditional norms regarding productivity have gradually been reduced to the extent that in rice and sugar production, for example, the norms fell by 25 and 40%, respectively.[21]

The problem of declining productivity was associated not only with the working class but also with the technical and professional staff working in the state sector. The productive process was affected by low levels of administrative and organizational efficiency due in large part to the limited managerial and planning expertise for what was an enormous task at hand following the revolution. At the level of production, newly formed state enterprises suddenly found themselves controlling a quarter of primary sector activities and 35% of the food, beverage, and tobacco industries; at the level of planning, the state had to develop an apparatus capable of regulating economic activities and patterns of resource allocation.[22]

Restrictions on Imports

Restrictions on supply were also the product of a set of conditions affecting imports of basic consumer goods or key inputs and raw materials required for their domestic production. In order to bridge the gap between demand and national production, the government resorted to large quantities of basic food imports, particularly during the first 2 years of the revolution. Imports of the principal food products and raw materials required by the food industry soared from $23.8 million in 1978 to $131.5 million in 1981. Important changes also took place in the composition of imports, as basic food imports were given strict priority over nonessential food products. As such, in 1981 basic food imports accounted for 84% of total food imports in comparison with 48% in 1978 (see Table 2).

The economy could not, however, sustain these levels of imports. In 1981, an increasing import bill and the continuing drop in export prices had given rise to a trade deficit of $500 million that was the equivalent of that year's export revenue. In addition, the proportion of total export revenue required to service the external debt had risen from 7% in 1977 to 33% in 1982.[23] As a

---

21. Jaime Wheelock, *Entre la crisis y la agresión: La reforma agraria Sandinista* (Managua: Editorial Nueva Nicaragua, 1985), 107.
22. Productivity among state employees was also affected by a policy of reducing or containing income differentials. This has given rise to high levels of rotation of personnel in search of slightly higher salaries within the state sector, the departure of professional staff to the private sector or other countries, and lack of labor discipline. We must also remember that the revolution never disbanded the Somocista state at the level of intermediary personnel. Hence the lack of "revolutionary commitment" noted among certain state employees also relates to attitudes carried over from the past.
23. CEPAL, *Balance preliminar*.

TABLE 2
Evolution of Food Imports, 1978—1984

	1978	1980	1981	1982	1983	1984[b]
	(Volume index: 1980 = 100)					
Corn	33	100	65	47	264	34
Rice	0	100	61	0	13	48
Beans	140	100	216	18	178	88
Eggs	23	100	76	44	19	23
Chicken	9	100	120	10	17	0
Plantains	98	100	101	34	19	12
Potatoes	65	100	164	38	1	12
Cabbage	20	100	113	4	0	0
Vegetable Oil	14	100	96	76	77	55
Oil Seeds	21	100	52	94	149	128
	(Millions of dollars)					
Basic food imports[a]	23.8	88.4	131.5	64.8	72.8	76.2
Total food imports	49.5	125.0	155.8	84.1	80.1	91.5
Total imports	593.9	887.2	999.4	775.5	806.9	826.2
	(Percentages)					
BAS.FOOD/TOT.FOOD IMPTS.	48.1	70.7	84.4	77.1	90.9	83.3
BAS.FOOD/TOTAL IMPTS.	4.0	10.0	13.2	8.4	9.0	9.2
TOTAL FOOD/TOTAL IMPTS.	8.3	14.1	15.6	10.8	9.9	11.1

[a]Includes 19 finished food products or basic raw materials used by the food industry.
[b]Preliminary figures.
Source: Ministry of Foreign Trade.

major investment drive in development projects got underway in 1982, imports of consumer goods had to compete with those of capital goods. This development effort, concentrated in areas related to the social infrastructure, energy, agriculture, and agroindustry, reflected the committment of the revolutionary government to autonomous development and to raising the standard of living of the mass of the population. The extent of this committment is apparent when we realize that during this period of regional economic recession, other Central American countries were reducing investment, particularly in agriculture, whereas in Nicaragua it increased significantly.[24]

Between 1980 and 1984, the composition of imports was to alter as capital goods destined for industry increased from 7 to 18%, whereas nondurable consumer goods dropped from 24 to 13%. The absolute scarcity of foreign exchange and the changing composition of imports restricted domestic sup-

24. Centro de Ingestigación y Estudios de la Reforma Agraria (CIERA)/Programa Alimentario Nicaragüense (PAN)/Canadian International Development Agency (CIDA), *Informe final del Proyecto Estrategia Alimentaria*, vol. 3, *Directorio de políticas alimentarias* (Managua: CIERA, 1984).

ply in a number of ways. First, imports of food products were substantially reduced. The value of a group of basic food imports was cut by half in 1 year, from $132 million in 1981 to $65 million the following year (see Table 2).[25] Basic food imports stabilized at around $75 million in 1983 and 1984.[26]

Second, the volume and timing of imports of certain inputs, raw materials, spare parts, and packaging materials required for domestic food production, particularly in the food industry, were also affected. A government evaluation of the causes behind the shortages of fifteen products during the month of July 1983 revealed that eleven were scarce because of import restrictions on raw materials, packaging materials, or the products themselves.[27]

Third, strict controls exercised by the state to rationalize the allocation of scarce foreign exchange inevitably led to delays in acquiring imports.[28] Bottlenecks in production and distribution arose given difficulties in anticipating and contracting necessary imports on time and because of delays in the arrival of shipments and in distribution from portside. A report published in 1983 identified these types of problems as being behind spot shortages of products such as rice, corn, flour, and vegetable oil.[29]

It is important to emphasize the degree to which the food system is vulnerable to shortages in foreign exchange. From the 1950s onward, Nicaragua experienced the rapid growth of an agro-food industry atypical of the type of industry established in many other Latin American countries, in that it was oriented in large part toward production for the internal market. Moreover, the type of goods produced were not exclusively for higher income groups. The food processing industry also produced a range of consumer goods acquired by low-income sectors, particularly in urban areas. These included, for example, products such as vegetable oil, coffee, flour-based products, processed dairy products, rice, sugar, and beef. This industry was, however,

---

25. The reduction in imports experienced in 1982 particularly affected the availability of products such as chicken, eggs, and plantains. Although domestic production of poultry products was, in fact, increasing rapidly, supply could not keep pace with demand for products such as these, which had become important substitutes for beef, whose production and consumption had declined.
26. In 1985, it was expected that imports of basic food products paid for in hard currency would be reduced even further. Policy statements made at the beginning of the year announced the government's intention of restricting foreign currency allocations for food imports and giving priority instead to imports of inputs and capital goods required to produce food domestically.
27. CIERA, El ABC de abastecmieinto, Mimeo, 1985.
28. The extent of this problem was illustrated in a report evaluating the performance of the agricultural sector during the 1984/85 cycle where the problem of delays in the acquisition of foreign exchange for necessary imports was highlighted as one of the principal factors behind the failure to meet production targets. MIDINRA, "Informe del sector agropecuario, January-March 1985," internal document, 1985.
29. CIERA, La situación del abastecmieinto (Managua: CIERA, 1983), 17.

highly dependent on imports of raw materials, inputs, and capital goods, particularly from the United States.[30] This dependent situation has left the food·system vulnerable to foreign exchange crises, given the relatively large exchange component in food production costs.[31]

REDISTRIBUTIVE POLICIES AND "EXCESS" DEMAND

Problems of market shortages and food lines are a product not only of constraints on production and imports but more precisely of the inability of total supply to meet effective demand. A range of redistributive policies introduced since the revolution served to transform the income structure and increase the demand for wage goods. When coupled with the rapid recovery of production levels in most product sectors plus large-scale imports in 1980 and 1981, this "democratization" of the income structure translated into significant increases in per capita consumption levels.

Table 3 shows the changing levels of consumption for eleven food prod-

TABLE 3
Per Capita Consumption 1972—1984

PRODUCT		PRE REVOLUTION		POST REVOLUTION		
		1972—1975[a]	1976—1978[a]	1980—1982[a]	1983	1984[c]
Corn	Lb.	197	181	174	192	165
Beans	Lb.	35.9	39.7	46.0	38.8	49.1
Rice	Lb.	50.8	40.3	65.1	70.5	80.8
Flour	Lb.	32.8	31.4	39.9	38.4	37.2
Veg. Oil	Lb.	16.0	17.1	23.7	26.6	22.7
Sugar	Lb.	79.6	98.1	91.1	102	104
Eggs	Doz.	2.2	5.0	6.4	6.7	6.3
Chicken	Lb.	2.5	4.6	9.0	8.1	6.7
Pork	Lb.	5.3	5.2	6.9	4.8	4.6
Beef	Lb.	21.7	25.7	20.3	18.2	18.9
Milk[b]	Gal.	4.1	4.7	5.5	6.2	5.6

[a]Yearly average for the period.
[b]Pasteurized milk only.
[c]Preliminary figures.
Source: CIERA.

30. CIERA, *Managua es Nicaragua: El impacto de la capital en el sistema alimentario nacional* (Managua: CIERA, 1984), 56.
31. Many sectors of agriculture are also highly dependent on imported inputs and capital goods, but in practice industry has been more vulnerable than agriculture, due to the strict priority that has been given to agriculture in sectoral allocations of foreign exchange.

ucts since 1972. It is evident that average annual per-capita consumption levels for most of these products increased during the 1980−82 period. However, this advance was curbed in 1983. As the foreign exchange crisis and the war made their impact felt, consumption levels for five products fell. With several notable exceptions, consumption levels continued to fall in 1984. Despite this reversal of trends, however, consumption levels for eight of the eleven products still exceeded prerevolution levels.[32]

The changes that have taken place in the demand for basic food products are a consequence of a series of redistributive policies that improved people's access to a range of basic goods and increased the purchasing power of certain sectors of the population. The main policies are summarized as follows:

1. The growth and consolidation of the cooperative movement integrating approximately half of all rural producers channeled considerable credit, technical assistance, and land toward these producers. Production levels and incomes of much of this sector clearly benefited as a consequence.

2. Pricing policy established subsidies and official retail prices for basic consumer goods. Although price controls in the traditional marketplace have been virtually impossible to implement, these policies nevertheless ensured that products sold in what are locally referred to as the "secure outlets" may be acquired cheaply. The subsidy policy that was in effect from 1980 to mid-1984 also ensured that retail prices for milk, sugar, beans, and rice as well as the prices at which tortilla makers and animal feed plants bought corn and sorghum respectively remained relatively stable (see Table 5) and considerably below producer prices. Subsidies for these products reached 1703 million córdobas in 1984 or 6.3% of government spending.[33]

In the face of pressures on government spending, a large fiscal deficit, and a series of contradictory effects relating to disincentives at the level of production and the resale of subsidized produce on the parallel market, the government began to rethink its subsidy policy. In mid-1984, the policy was modi-

32. Some of these figures, however, should be read with caution. Although pasteurized milk production (based to a large extent on reconstituted imported milk powder) and consumption clearly increased, that of raw milk declined due to problems outlined earlier regarding the reduction of the national herd. Also, figures relating to chicken, eggs, and pork consumption are based on production figures for state and capitalist enterprises. As such, a significant share of total production located on peasant holdings is not included for lack of data. Although this means that these per-capita figures underestimate real consumption, it is also probable that the post-1982 decline is even worse, given the disarticulation of peasant economy referred to earlier. The inverse is true, however, of beef consumption. An increasing quantity of cattle has, in recent years, been slaughtered "informally" outside of the official slaughter houses. This could well mean that the decline in beef consumption recorded during recent years has not been quite so sharp.
33. Calculation based on data from the Secretariat of Planning and the Budget.

fied when the price differential for basic grains was removed. Subsequently, in February 1985, direct food subsidies were drastically reduced, with the announcement of major increases in official consumer prices. Price controls and subsidized prices, nevertheless, contributed to increased demand for a number of basic food products for several years.

3. A planned distribution system established family and/or regional quotas for essential food products such as grains, sugar, vegetable oil, flour, and salt. In 1984, wholesale marketing was nationalized for a group of eighteen food and manufactured products. The criteria for nationalization related to the importance of the product in the popular consumption basket and the ease with which the state could effectively control procurement (i.e., where production was concentrated in a few production units). For other basic products such as corn and beans, where production is dispersed among thousands of peasant producers, the state competed with the private sector, purchasing in 1984 27% and 33% of the corn and bean crops respectively. By exercising a monopoly over grain imports, however, the state-owned Empresa Nicaragüense de Alimentos Básicos (ENABAS) was able to increase its control over the wholesale market.

The distribution of certain basic food products controlled by the state was designed to work on an equitable basis among the different regions of the country, according to population. Such a system attempted to reverse the logic of the marketing system that operated during the Somoza era, which had tended to concentrate distribution of food products in the Pacific region and in particular, in the capital. After 1983, quotas were increased for a number of regions in the interior of the country where the effects of the war were felt most. Through this system, the privileged position of Managua has been slowly eroded. Shortages experienced in the capital in recent years were clearly related to the system of planned distribution.

The regional distribution system, however, was subject to bottlenecks and delays, particularly in the interior regions of the country where spot shortages frequently arose because of insufficient transport to deliver the quota on time. Another important constraint on domestic supply was that the system operated with few or no regional reserves. Hence any delay in getting products out to the regions was immediately reflected in shortages.

At another level, a policy of planned distribution established family quotas for rice, salt, oil, sugar, beans, and certain nonfood products such as laundry soap through the guaranty card system. Although the quota was often insufficient to cover household requirements, it nevertheless ensured that the majority of the population had access to a minimum volume of some of the most important food products in the local diet at low prices.[34] In this sense, it

34. In urban areas, each family member generally received 4 lb. of rice and sugar per month; the

protected many low income consumers from inflationary tendencies and speculation on the open market.

In practice, however, the system's coverage was limited primarily to urban areas. Even the regional distribution system tended to concentrate products in the main provincial towns. This "urban bias" was a consequence of the state's material and administrative limitations,[35] the lack of participation of rural organizations in establishing the new distribution system in the country-side, and the difficulties of establishing a quota system among a highly dispersed and mobile population, particularly in areas affected by the war.

Also, domestic supply policy suffered from a certain urban bias as reflected in the selection of priority products that were more in accordance with urban needs and tastes. In 1985, however, there was a more conscious attempt to resolve the supply problem in rural areas by giving priority to a range of products, including basic manufactured goods, which are essential to the reproduction of the peasant household.

4. For supply policy to be effective in improving people's access to food, it was also important to facilitate physical access to retail outlets selling at the official prices. To achieve this, the state has experimented with a number of alternatives, including state-run stores located in the "barrios" (tiendas populares), workplace commisaries, and small outlets operated by the local neighborhood organizations—the Sandinista Defense Committees (CDS).

By 1982, however, it was apparent that the state could not directly operate a highly decentralized marketing system and that the best alternative would be one based on the traditional neighborhood retail outlet—the pulpería, with the corresponding advantages of existing infrastructure, marketing experience, and integration with the local community. An increasing number of pulperías were transformed into "people's stores" (expendios populares) that sold ENABAS-supplied goods at official prices. Although profit margins on these goods were very low, this system essentially provided the store owner

---

quota of other basics tended to oscillate. Vegetable oil, for example, varied between a half liter to a liter per person per month, depending on the total supply the state controlled at any one time.

35. The state grain marketing agency, ENABAS, still depended on the private transport sector to move up to 48% of its grain volume in 1983, CIERA, El funcionamiento, 77. As spare parts and tires became increasingly scarce with the foreign exchange crisis, many trucks were kept off the road. By the end of 1983, up to a third of the ENABAS fleet was inoperative. See Joseph Collins, et. al What Differences Could a Revolution Make? 2d ed. (San Francisco: Institute for Food and Development Policy, 1985), 218. Also, with the deterioration of the road network and the spread of the war, many transport owners reorientated operations away from areas of the interior. Producers that depended on the private transport sector had to cover rapidly increasing charges. This phenomenon affected not only those producers using motorized transport but also those who had to hire donkeys and mules. The marketing of corn was particularly affected by these conditions, given its relatively low price/weight ratio.

with a large clientele that had to buy at that particular store in order to acquire the products sold on the quota system. To these consumers, the retailer could sell other goods, the prices of which were not regulated. In 1984, this network was rapidly expanded and by the end of the year, some 6000 *expendios* were operating throughout the country.

5. Social programs assisted certain sectors of the population either by providing subsidized meals in the workplace or by actually donating a specific quantity of food products to nutritionally vulnerable groups. By 1984, nearly 2000 workplace cafeterias were providing subsidized meals in state enterprises and institutions as well as in some private establishments.[36] Various state institutions, including the ministries of Health (MINSA) and Education, the Social Welfare Institute, and the Nicaraguan Food Program operated nutritional programs.[37]

The policies we have outlined that improved access to food are part of a broader policy package reflecting the welfare orientation of government policy. The revolutionary government assigned a high priority to economic and social programs associated with basic food production and distribution, health, education, housing, and other areas that directly determined the standard of living of the population. In 1983, for example, approximately one third of the budget was allocated to expenditures in health, education, and subsidies.[38]

Until 1985, redistributive policies and programs and the expansion in government expenditure due to investment and defense costs were financed to a large extent by monetary emission, given the restricted tax base and low profits from state-sector enterprises. The fiscal deficit increased from 1838 million córdobas in 1980 to an estimated 11,148 million in 1984—an increase from 8 to 23% of GDP. Although the fiscal deficit has been one of the main factors behind the increasing money supply, several others associated with the redistributive process also played a role. The expansion of credit for agricultural producers coupled with relatively low levels of recuperation (including the moratorium on peasant debt in 1983) significantly raised the deficit on the government's financial account. Also an overvalued exchange rate led to considerable foreign exchange losses as the córdoba cost (set by guaranteed producer prices) of each dollar's worth of agro-exports considerably exceeded that at which imports were being sold.[39] As a consequence of

36. Collins, *What Difference*, 217.
37. One of the largest of the direct assistance programs was that run by the Ministry of Health that delivered a monthly quota of 8 lb. of flour, 1 liter of vegetable oil, 2.5 lb. of powdered milk and two cans of meat to 60,000 women and children in five regions of the country.
38. Wheelock, *Entre la crisis*, 141.
39. As the financial blockade promoted by the U.S. government took effect, external funding for development projects was restricted. This further increased deficits as the government was obliged to fund ongoing projects.

policies such as these, the money supply increased by 257% between 1980 and 1984.[40]

Although few studies are available that enable us to establish precisely which sectors have benefited most from policies such as these, it is evident that the pattern of incorporation of low-income consumers into the consumption structure has not been uniform. The so-called "popular sectors" constitute a highly heterogeneous social category, and redistributive policies clearly had unequal effects among social groups differentiated by class, income, and geographical location. The restricted coverage of the guaranty card system in rural areas and an austere wage policy implemented until 1984 caused real wages of many workers to fall. This reflects the partial character of the process of income redistribution for certain sectors of the peasantry and the working class. On the other hand, rural producers integrated into the cooperative movement and/or receiving credit and services provided by state agencies as well as urban workers who benefited from improved employment opportunities in construction and the state sector fared better.

The proliferation of petty-trading activities in the cities and the increased economic rents obtained in the urban informal sector point to a possible improvement in consumption levels for this increasingly large sector of the population. The increased volume of money in circulation caused commercial activity to rise in response to the excess demand. The commercial sector responded to this situation and to the state's inability to effectively control distribution and prices by simply increasing prices. This has become particularly apparent since 1983, when the disequilibrium between demand and supply became more acute. Between 1983 and 1984, the rate of inflation on the general retail price index virtually doubled. Although the rate of increase in retail prices had remained relatively stable at around 23% between 1980 and 1982, it increased in 1983, reaching 50% in 1984 (see Table 4). Consumer prices soared during the first few months of 1985 as an immediate response to a range of measures introduced at the beginning of the year, including large wage increases, rising guaranteed producer prices, the elimination of subsidies on a number of products, and the devaluation of the córdoba.

Table 5 compares price tendencies for a group of popular consumer products generally acquired on the open market and another normally purchased at the official prices. For many of these products, price rises tended to exceed those reflected in the general price index. The table also shows that official prices for a range of basic food products remained relatively stable until 1985.

---

40. This calculation is based on data from the Secretariat of Planning and the Budget.

TABLE 4
Annual Percentage Increase in "General" and
"Food, Beverages, and Tobacco" Price Index, 1981−1985[a]

	1981	1982	1983	1984	1985[a]
General price index	23.3	22.2	32.9	50.2	184.8
Food, beverages, and tobacco products	25.9	23.9	45.1	58.6	204.7

[a]1985 figures correspond to first 6 months only.
Source: National Institute of Statistics and Censuses.

TABLE 5
Official and Market Price Index of Selected Basic
Consumer Products May 1981−May 1985[a]

		1981	1982	1983	1984	1985
Market Price	Beans[b]	100	137	139	245	1083
Index for	Eggs	100	120	152	235	1207
selected	Cheese	100	142	204	255	894
consumer	Meat	100	112	158	181	633
products	Soap	100	100	267	222	2116
Official	Beans[b]	100	100	100	140	561
Price Index	Rice	100	104	104	169	357
for selected	Sugar	100	100	100	100	635
food	Veg. Oil	100	108	126	138	471
products	Milk[c]	100	100	100	100	400

[a]Based on prices recorded in the month of May in Managua. 100 = May 1981.
[b]Large quantities of beans are sold on both the parallel and official markets.
[c]Based on prices for pasteurized milk only.
Source: Ministry of Internal Trade.

CONCLUSION

The redistributive policies we have outlined were instrumental in raising per capita consumption levels, particularly during the early years of the revolution when production in numerous sectors recovered rapidly and large quantities of basic food products were imported. Consumption levels for corn and beef, however, fell in response to stagnating levels of production. In 1982, the disequilibrium between demand and supply was reflected in spot shortages for a number of basic goods, culminating in a more generalized supply crisis in mid-1983. With domestic supply unable to keep pace with demand,

advances in per capita consumption levels were restrained or actually reduced for a number of basic foods, whereas excess demand, fueled by
government deficits, was manifested in increasing prices on the parallel
market.

In practice, short-term gains in the standard of living gave way to an
investment program that channeled substantial resources toward future production, to a war that consumed an increasing percentage of government
expenditure, and to a foreign exchange crisis that restricted the possibility of
importing large quantities of consumer goods. At the same time, we have seen
how changing social relations were affecting capitalist production, labor
productivity, and the physical availability of labor for productive activities,
while an inexperienced planning apparatus was having difficulties determin-
ing the right blend of policies needed to regulate certain economic activities
and boost production among very different types of producers. Conditions
such as these, when added to a range of structural conditions reflecting
Nicaragua's status as an underdeveloped and dependent society, imposed
formidable constraints on the production system; domestic production was
unable to keep pace with demand.

These changes have given the Nicaraguan food problem a new character.
Without a doubt, malnutrition used to be the defining characteristic of the
food problem during the Somoza era.[41] High levels of poverty and unemployment served to restrict demand for basic consumer goods. Because
domestic production could generally meet these levels of effective, as opposed to real demand, there was little evidence of chronic market shortages
or excessive dependency on basic food imports. During the revolutionary
period, however, the nature of the food problem changed significantly. On
the one hand, consumption levels of large sectors of the population would
appear to have increased. Although little research has been undertaken to
determine how the nutritional status of the population has changed during the
postrevolutionary period, it is to be expected that improved access to food,
health services, and nutritional programs, particularly in urban areas and in
the Pacific region of the country, had a positive impact, although malnutrition
clearly continued to be a major problem.[42] On the other hand, we have seen

41. In 1976, it was estimated that 57% of the rural population suffered from calorie deficiency,
   and the percentage of children below 6 years of age suffering from malnutrition reached
   68.7% in 1977.
42. Although hard data are lacking on these aspects, we can point to a number of nutrition-
   related indicators such as the marked drop in infant mortality from 122 to 71 per 1000
   children under the age of 1 born between 1978 and 1984 and the drop in the incidence of
   diarrhea as the principal cause of infant mortality. Also, we have seen that a variety of food
   and nutritional programs and policies have been implemented during the revolutionary
   period.

how problems associated with market shortages, inflation, and dependency on food imports intensified.

From the preceding analysis, it would appear that problems of shortages and inflation are unlikely to be resolved in the short term. Until such time as the productive base is sufficiently developed, they will constitute a structural feature of the economy, given that many of the tensions and constraints from which they derive will persist as the process of revolutionary transformation continues. However, previously marginal social groups are increasing their participation in income and consumption structures; traditional exploitative relations of production and exchange are being transformed; the state is investing in social and economic development; and the dependency relation that subordinated Nicaragua historically is being undermined and redefined. These changes all indicate that the major underlying causes of poverty and underdevelopment are being addressed.

ACKNOWLEDGMENTS

The author would like to thank Bill Gibson, Valpy FitzGerald and Rose Spalding for their comments on this paper.

PART III

EXTERNAL PRESSURES AND FOREIGN RELATIONS

Chapter 7

Foreign Debt and Economic Stabilization Policies in Revolutionary Nicaragua

RICHARD STAHLER-SHOLK

When the FSLN overthrew the Somoza dictatorship, the new Nicaraguan government faced the highest foreign debt burden in Latin America in terms of total debt/GDP. The inherited debt was a product not only of the war of liberation but also of the chronic external economic disequilibria that characterized the Nicaraguan variant of dependent capitalist development.

The revolutionary triumph brought an end to the concentration of political power in the hands of the agroexport-based bourgeoisie. However, the underlying economic structures were not immediately transformed; the economy remained heavily dependent on a few primary product exports, and Nicaragua continued to be deeply inserted into international trade and financial markets. As the revolutionary project unfolded, Nicaragua suffered restricted access to traditional sources of external financing. In addition to U.S. economic pressures, military attacks by U.S.-sponsored counterrevolutionary forces disrupted coffee harvests (the No. 1 export earner) and inflicted substantial economic damage. Declining terms of trade and other conjunctural factors aggravated the growing foreign exchange shortage. This combination of economic constraints, reflected in external indebtedness, posed serious challenges for the revolution.

The Sandinista government successfully renegotiated its foreign debt to private banks in 1980 and received significant flows of new external resources from multilateral development banks to finance its economic reconstruction program in the first 2 years after the revolutionary victory. Beginning in late 1981, Nicaragua's access to foreign exchange became problematical for a number of reasons, and these constraints[1] began to appear in the form of

---

1. Sylvia Maxfield and Richard Sholk, "The Economy: External Constraints," in Thomas W. Walker, editor, *Nicaragua: The First Five Years* (New York: Praeger, 1985).

external and internal disequilibria. By mid-1983, Nicaragua was unable to meet the payments due on its foreign debt, and new renegotiations were initiated with private banks. Wage and price policies were reevaluated in the light of rapidly accelerating inflation in 1984. In February 1985, the Sandinista government announced a comprehensive economic adjustment program. The new program, which differed in important respects from traditional IMF-style stabilization programs, aimed for economic adjustment without recessionary and inegalitarian side effects.

PRE-1979 DEBT AND EXTERNAL IMBALANCE

The structural origins of Nicaragua's foreign debt crisis can be seen in the evolution of Nicaragua's entry into the international economy. The introduction of coffee cultivation for export in the late nineteenth century set the stage for the development of the agroexport-based economy in Nicaragua. Agroexport dependence was reinforced in the 1950s by a tremendous boom in cotton production, responding to rising world prices. When cotton prices slumped in the late 1950s and 1960s, the agrarian bourgeoisie invested in beef and sugar production for export, responding to the growth of the U.S. fast-food hamburger industry and the U.S. reapportionment of the Cuban sugar quota.

International loans were an important source of financing for the major expansion of agroexport production and supporting infrastructure in this period. Agricultural modernization implied more capital-intensive production; and cotton, in particular, depended on imported fertilizers, pesticides, small airplanes for pesticide spraying, and tractors.

The export boom was accompanied by an expansion of industrialization, with the formation of the Central American Common Market (CACM) in the early 1960s. The CACM model proved to have a destabilizing effect on the balance of payments. Intra-Central American trade (mainly in light manufactured goods) grew rapidly in the 1960s, but imports of intermediate and capital goods for industrialization rose much faster than exports. The highly unequal distribution of income and the tendency of the elites to imitate foreign consumption patterns also led to increased imports and aggravated balance-of-payments problems. Consequently, Central America's current account balance went from a positive $16 million in 1950 to a deficit of $188 million by 1970, with import coefficients that far exceeded the Latin American average. Nicaragua's imports, for example, rose from 16.6% of GDP in 1950 to 33.3% by 1965.[2] Industrial growth was heavily dependent on

2. CEPAL, "Centroamérica: El financiamiento externo en la evolución económica, 1950–1983" (México: CEPAL, 4 March 1985), 17–19.

external finance: Nicaragua's external public debt grew forty-one-fold between 1960 and 1977, whereas Central America's grew by a factor of 35.[3]

The export-led growth of the 1950s and 1960s was stalled by the 1970s. The CACM model of regional industrialization had reached its limits. Nicaragua's terms of trade began to fluctuate in the 1970s, peaking briefly in 1977 due to good cotton prices, and falling sharply thereafter. Various other conjunctural factors added to the growth of foreign indebtedness in the 1970s. The 1972 Managua earthquake brought an influx of reconstruction financing, much of which was misappropriated by Somoza and his associates. The external public debt more than doubled between 1972 and 1974. At the same time, petrodollar recycling after 1973 opened up new flows of private bank lending. Nicaragua was considered a good risk,[4] in part because of the U.S. backing enjoyed by the regime. Large private bank loans to Nicaragua in the 1970s were arranged through Ultramar Banking Corporation, headed by a Cuban expatriate who also served as a government financial advisor and shared the commissions and bribes with Somoza.[5] Between 1972 and 1976, Ultramar contracted twelve loans for a total of $310 million—nearly half the total public borrowing in that period—before quietly disappearing in the early months of 1977.

By 1978, it was clear that Nicaragua could no longer service its foreign debt. At the same time, the mounting political crisis of the *Somocista* state[6] —marked by the fractionalization of the bourgeoisie and the coalescence of an organized mass opposition movement among the urban and rural popular sectors—meant an acceleration of foreign borrowing for military spending and other costs associated with shoring up a regime in crisis. In December 1978, Somoza's treasury ministry notified international banks that Nicaragua would be unable to meet its debt service payments.

U.S. support for the Somoza dictatorship was crucial for continued flows of external financing in the late 1970s—particularly for $65 million in IMF loans approved only 9 weeks before the collapse of the regime.[7] An earlier

3. Banco Central de Nicaragua, *Indicadores económicos* (1978); Edelberto Torres-Rivas, "Central America Today: A Study in Regional Dependency," in Martin Diskin, editor, *Trouble in our Backyard: Central America and the United States in the Eighties* (New York: Pantheon Books, 1983), 15.
4. Sylvia Maxfield, "Revisitando la trampa de la deuda: El caso de Nicaragua," *Gaceta Internacional* (México, 1984).
5. Oscar Ugarteche, "Pagar o no pagar en Nicaragua," *La Revista* 2 (1980). See also Nicholas Asheshov, "Endgame in Managua," *Institutional Investor* (Sept. 1979).
6. Discussed in Harald Jung, "Behind the Nicaraguan Revolution," *New Left Review*, 117 (Sept.–Oct. 1979); Orlando Núñez Soto, "La tercera fuerza social en los movimientos de liberación nacional," *Estudios Sociales Centroamericanos* 27 (Sept.–Dec. 1980); and Edelberto Torres-Rivas, "Notas para comprender la crisis política centroamericana," in CECADE/CIDE, *Centroamérica: Crisis y política internacional*, 2d ed. (México: Siglo XXI, 1984).
7. Jim Morrell and William Jesse Biddle, "Central America: The Financial War," *International*

IMF team requested by the Somoza government in September 1978, when insurrection was erupting in the major cities, rejected an application for a Standby loan. A new IMF mission in February 1979 imposed an orthodox stabilization package including a 43% devaluation of the *córdoba*, causing price hikes that reinforced popular opposition to the regime.[8] The IMF then approved the $65 million package (Standby and Export Shortfall loans) in May 1979, despite the by-then obvious diversion of loans by Somoza for military purposes and outright theft. One week after that loan, considered to be among the most ill-conceived in IMF history, Nicaragua presented its plan for restructuring its debt to private banks. The restructuring was still under discussion at the time of the Sandinista revolutionary triumph in July 1979.

FINANCIAL STABILITY IN THE REVOLUTIONARY PROCESS

Revolutionary transformations in small, peripheral economies tend to carry high financial costs that are potential threats to the process of transition.[9] The Nicaraguan experience points to some of the reasons, which may be generalizable. Capital flight is one common problem. Economic destruction in the process of overthrowing the *ancien régime* is another. Higher defense costs are likely, particularly if the country is located near the United States and/or is not a candidate for major defense commitments by other socialist countries. Policies that involve expansion of the public deficit may be politically necessary in the transition period. The possibilities of economic blockade, sabotage, and counterrevolution exist. External financial constraints will be worsened if the terms of trade decline before the economy can change the basis of its insertion into international commercial markets. Debt negotiations

---

Policy Report (Washington, D.C.: Center for International Policy, March 1983); and Ugarteche, "Pagar o no pagar."

8. George Black, *Triumph of the People: The Sandinista Revolution in Nicaragua* (London: Zed Press, 1981), Ch. 1–4; John A. Booth, *The End and the Beginning: The Nicaraguan Revolution* (Boulder: Westview, 1982), Ch. 3–4; and Richard Millett, *Guardians of the Dynasty: A History of the U.S.-Created Guardia Nacional de Nicaragua and the Somoza Family* (Maryknoll, N.Y.: Orbis Books, 1977).

9. See: E. V. K. FitzGerald, "Diez problemas para el análisis de la pequeña economía periférica en transición," INIES/CRIES/PACCA Seminar on Problems of Transition in Small Peripheral Economies (Managua: 3–8 Sept. 1984); FitzGerald, "Stabilization and Economic Justice: The Case of Nicaragua," Kellogg Institute *Working Paper* 34 (Notre Dame, IN: Sept. 1984); Barbara Stallings, "El financiamiento externo en la transición al socialismo en pequeños países periféricos," forthcoming in José Luis Coraggio and Carmen Diana Deere, editors, *La transición difícil: La autodeterminación de los pequeños países periféricos* (México); and Stephany Griffith-Jones, *The Role of Finance in the Transition to Socialism* (Totowa, N.J.: Allanheld, Osmun, 1981).

with capitalist creditors may be complicated by the government's economic and political orientation. Where the means of production are not all socialized, there is the problem of economic planning in a mixed economy. And finally, revolutionary transformation implies a reduction in the exploitation of labor, which in the short run poses the problem of declining productivity and the need for material incentives. Nicaragua faced many of these characteristic financial difficulties along with the challenge of constructing new social and political institutions to consolidate the revolution.

When the Sandinista Revolution ousted the Somoza dictatorship in July 1979, Nicaragua's need for financing was already substantial. Foreign debt (public and private, including short-term debt) stood at about $1.6 billion, the highest ratio of debt/GDP In Latin America, and foreign reserves covered only two days' worth of imports (because Somoza had stolen all available dollars before he left for Miami). Table 1 shows the Nicaraguan debt burden in comparative perspective.

Some 75% of the servicing of the medium- and long-term external public debt contracted in 1979 was owed to commercial banks and suppliers, at unfavorable rates of interest; and nearly all the debt of the Nicaraguan private sector and banks (the latter subsequently absorbed by the state) consisted of short-term credits.[10] Total debt service owed in 1979 would have exceeded the value of exports for that year. Capital flight in the last year had amounted to about $1.5 billion. Direct war damage was estimated at $481 million (one-third of 1979 GDP). Real per capita GDP was set back to 1962 levels. Major new inflows of financing would be required to restore economic production to allow Nicaragua to make debt payments.

The Sandinista government accepted its inherited foreign debt obligation—despite the unsavory history of Somoza-era borrowing—in order to remain eligible for international financing and to maintain private sector cooperation. In December 1980, Nicaragua signed an agreement restructuring $582 million in debt to private banks. The renegotiation agreement was relatively favorable for Nicaragua. The refinancing covered a 12-year period, including a 5-year grace period for payments on the principal. During the grace period, the interest rate would rise gradually from 1% over LIBOR (the London Inter-Bank Offer Rate) during the first 3 years to 1¾% over LIBOR in the following 2 years; but an interest ceiling of 7% was set, and difference between the contracted rate and 7% was refinanced. Past-due interest (PDI) was recalculated at below the originally contracted rates. Several features of

---

10. Data in this paragraph are from CEPAL, "Nicaragua: El impacto de la mutación política," (Santiago, Chile: CEPAL, Jan. 1981), 37−44; World Bank, *Nicaragua: The Challenge of Reconstruction* (Washington, D.C.: World Bank, 1981).

TABLE 1
Comparative Debt Indicators, Selected Latin American Countries

	1978	1979	1980	1981	1982	1983	1984	1985[a]
				Total Debt/GDP (%)				
Nicaragua	51	74	86	99	123	143	170	196
Honduras	49	56	59	60	61	68	74	79
Costa Rica	54	59	73	73	78	84	85	87
Mexico	26	25	27	33	34	37	38	37
Latin America	30	31	33	37	39	43	44	44
				Total Debt/Exports (%)				
Nicaragua	133	168	319	397	624	777	992	1181
Honduras	141	153	160	193	235	291	295	298
Costa Rica	186	213	266	286	327	446	441	466
Mexico	316	262	210	249	286	413	402	454
Latin America	246	222	210	242	301	393	370	400

[a]Preliminary figures.

Source: Figures derived from ECLA, *External Debt in Latin America: Adjustment Policies and Renegotiation* (Boulder: Lynne Rienner, 1985), 50; and "Balance preliminar de la economía latinoamericana 1985," *Notas sobre la Economía y el Desarrollo*, CEPAL 424/425 (Dec. 1985).

the agreement—including the interest rate ceiling and the recalculation of PDI at lower rates—were considered unprecedented in banking circles. A similar agreement was subsequently concluded for the $180 million owed to private foreign banks by Nicaraguan commercial banks (which were in a state of bankruptcy after the overthrow of the Somoza government and were nationalized in 1980).

Several factors explain Nicaragua's success in obtaining rather unprecedented terms in the 1980 renegotiation with private creditor banks.[11] The new government initially enjoyed widespread international support. The banks' bargaining position was weakened by the evident bad judgment reflected in their past lending to the Somoza regime. Also, by negotiating with the private banks without waiting to first reach agreement with the IMF or the Club of Paris, Nicaragua (with the assistance of a hired consultant from a U.S. investment firm) was able to skillfully take advantage of divisions among the creditor banks.

The Sandinista government also moved to renegotiate the public debt to official bilateral lenders through a meeting of the Club of Paris in October

11. See Richard S. Weinert, "Nicaragua's Debt Renegotiation," *Cambridge Journal of Economics* 5, (2) (June 1981); Maxfield, "Revisitando la trampa de la deuda,"; and John Dizard, "Why Bankers Fear the Nicaraguan Solution," *Institutional Investor/International Edition* (Nov. 1980).

1980.[12] This debt amounted to $266 million in July 1979 and was owed primarily to the United States, Spain, and West Germany. When the Paris Club meeting failed to produce an agreement, Nicaragua negotiated its debts bilaterally with Spain and West Germany. A settlement with the United States proved impossible as relations deteriorated rapidly with the inauguration of Ronald Reagan in January 1981. Obviously, there was little incentive to repay AID loans when the United States cut off bilateral lending.

Relations with the IMF were initially complicated by the circumstances surrounding that institution's questionable loans to Nicaragua in the last days of the Somoza dictatorship.[13] Part of those loans came from the IMF's Compensatory Financing Facility, which provides balance-of-payments support in cases of temporary shortfalls in export earnings. The rules provide for an "early drawing procedure," by which up to 6 months of exports can be reported on the basis of estimated figures. When the final figures were in, it turned out that Somoza had rigged the estimates in order to pocket the funds as quickly as possible—which meant that Nicaragua was obligated to repay the loan immediately. The Sandinista government repaid the loan and also in 1981 began making payments on the 17 million SDRs that were part of the 1979 IMF Standby loan to the Somoza government (due over a 5-year period, with 2 years' grace). Repayment of the Standby was completed in April 1985. Relations with the IMF remained businesslike, but the Sandinista government received no financing from this source and showed no interest in accepting the kind of "conditionality" required for receiving balance-of payments support from the IMF. By accepting their international debt obligations and clearing up accounts with the IMF, the Sandinistas maintained the international respectability that was a necessary condition for receiving new flows of external resources.

The revolutionary government's strategy of economic reactivation initially envisioned significant flows of external financing, along with high levels of public and private investment to revive production in general and exports in particular. However, it soon became clear that the Nicaraguan bourgeoisie was reluctant to undertake major investments (much less repatriate the capital they had spirited out of the country).[14] An ambitious program of state investment was launched, centered around agroindustry.[15] This reconstruc-

12. World Bank, *Nicaragua: The Challenge of Reconstruction*, 20–21.
13. Interview, former member of Nicaraguan representation to the IMF (Managua: 6 Sept. 1985); and Morrell and Biddle, "Central America: The Financial War," 11.
14. See my article, "The National Bourgeoisie in Post-Revolutionary Nicaragua," *Comparative Politics* 16(3) (Apr. 1984).
15. Jaime Wheelock Román, *Entre la crisis y la agresión: La reforma agraria sandinista* (Managua: Editorial Nueva Nicaragua, 1985), 76–87.

tion program was affected by a sharp decline in the terms of trade, an escalation of external military and economic aggression, and a decline in access to international finance.

The main external financial constraints faced by the Sandinistas stemmed from the conflict between the popular alternative represented by the Nicaraguan revolution on the one hand, and the U.S. project to retain domination of the region on the other hand.[16] The brief attempt by the Carter administration to mold the Nicaraguan revolution into an acceptable form soon gave way to an active destabilization campaign encompassing economic as well as military hostilities.[17] By the close of the 1970s, declining U.S. hegemony had triggered an interventionist U.S. backlash. The resurgent Right came to power vowing to reverse the"Vietnam syndrome" and to "draw the line" in Central America.[18] The creaky machinery of international alliances and institutions formed during the peak years of post-World War II U.S. hegemony was cranked up in support of the U.S. crusade.

The U.S. campaign of economic destabilization directed against Nicaragua[19] bore some similarities to earlier U.S. efforts to reverse transitions to socialism in Cuba, Chile, Jamaica, and Angola. Shortly after taking power in January 1981, the Reagan administration cut off bilateral aid (the last $15 million of the heavily conditioned $75 million loan approved under the Carter administration plus $11.4 million in Rural Development/Education/Health loans); Export-Import Bank credits; and $10 million in PL-480 financing (a credit program for sales of U.S. surplus agricultural production to Third World countries) for imports of U.S. wheat. Trade was also disrupted by an escalating series of hostilities (see Michael Conroy, Chapter 8 of this volume). These precipitous disruptions affected foreign exchange earnings and complicated the problems of financing imports.

16. For analysis of this contradiction, see Xabier Gorostiaga, "Geopolítica de la crisis reigonal," *Estudios Sociales Centroamericanos* 12(35) (May– Aug. 1983); Roger Burbach, "U.S. Policy: Crisis and Conflict," in Roger Burbach and Patricia Flynn, editors, *The Politics of Intervention: The United States in Central America* (New York: Monthly Review Press, 1984); and William M. LeoGrande, "Through the Looking Glass: The Kissinger Report on Central America," *World Policy Journal* 1(2) (Winter 1984).

17. Richard Fagen, "Dateline Nicaragua: The End of the Affair," *Foreign Policy* 36 (Fall 1979); Richard H. Ullman, "At War with Nicaragua," *Foreign Affairs* 62(1) (Fall 1983); and William I. Robinson and Kent Norsworthy, "Nicaragua: The Strategy of Counterrevolution," *Monthly Review* 37(7) (Dec. 1985).

18. William M. LeoGrande, "A Splendid Little War: Drawing the Line in El Salvador," *International Security* 6(1) (Summer 1981).

19. For details, see Richard Sholk and Sylvia Maxfield, "U.S. Economic Aggression Against Nicaragua." Paper presented at XI Congress of the Latin American Studies Association, Mexico City, 29 Sept.–1 Oct. 1983; and Michael E. Conroy, "External Dependence, External Assistance, and Economic Aggression Against Nicaragua,"*Latin American Perspectives* 12(2) (Spring 1985).

The U.S. government also organized a financial blockade that included pressure on private U.S. banks not to lend to Nicaragua—disrupting a $130 million loan organized by a London-based bank syndicate in March 1982 and a $30 million loan being organized by Bank of America in early 1983.[20] Private bank lending was also indirectly influenced by the U.S. government's Inter-Agency Country Exposure Review Committee, which demoted Nicaragua's risk assessment classification from "substandard" to "doubtful" in early 1983, even though Nicaragua was making regular payments on its foreign debt.[21] In addition, evident U.S. hostility and military attacks obviously reduced Nicaragua's attractiveness for commercial lenders.

The United States also maneuvered to cut off Nicaragua's access to official multilateral and bilateral lending, with partial results. In February 1982, U.S. representatives in the World Bank were influential in the drafting of a confidential report calling for reduced lending to Nicaragua on thinly veiled political grounds. The Reagan administration subsequently instructed U.S. representatives to multilateral financial institutions to prepare technical excuses for vetoing Nicaraguan loan applications and in 1983, the Treasury Department confirmed that it was U.S. policy to oppose all multilateral loans to Nicaragua.[22] As of early 1986, Nicaragua had received no new loans from the World Bank since 1982; from the Inter-American Development Bank (IDB) since 1983; and from the Special Operations Fund of the IDB (a soft-loan facility in which the United States has controlling votes) since 1980.

Western European and Latin American opposition to this financial blockade mounted. At a meeting of European Economic Community foreign ministers in Costa Rica in September 1984, the French representative publicly denounced a letter that U.S. Secretary of State Shultz had sent to each of the delegates pressuring them to exclude Nicaragua from their economic assistance programs.[23]

Shultz touched off further protest in January 1985 when he wrote a letter to

20. "Nicaragua Loan Talks Reported: U.S. Policy is Questioned," *New York Times*, 10 Mar. 1982; interviews with U.S. bankers, June 1983; and Richard Karp, "The Nicaraguan Gambit," *Institutional Investor* (Mar. 1983).
21. Mark E. Hansen, "U.S. Banks in the Caribbean Basin: Towards a Strategy for Facilitating Lending to Nations Pursuing Alternative Models of Development," Paper prepared for Policy Alternatives in the Caribbean and Central America (PACCA) Conference, Washington, D.C., Oct. 1983, Part IIA, 7–8.
22. World Bank, *Country Program Paper: Nicaragua* (Washington D.C.: Feb. 1982); "Bank Shock for the Sandinistas: Political Factors Prompt a Secret Call for Slashed Aid," *South* 25 (Nov. 1982); "U.S. Charged with Bias in IMF votes," *Wall Street Journal*, 18 May 1983; Center for International Policy, "U.S. Threatens Bank over Nicaragua Loan" *Aid Memo* (15 Jan. 1985); and "U.S. Will Oppose Loans to Nicaragua," *Washington Post*, 1 July 1983.
23. Robert Armstrong, Marc Edelman, and Robert Matthews, "Sandinista Foreign Policy: Strategies for Survival," *NACLA Report on the Americas* 19(3) (May–June 1985), 32. See also Daniel Siegel, Tom Spaulding, and Peter Kornbluh, "Outcast Among Allies: The Interna-

the president of the IDB, Antonio Ortíz Mena, warning that U.S. contributions to the bank would be jeopardized if a $58 million loan for Nicaraguan small farmers was approved. The loan proposal was subsequently sent back to the bank's technical committee for further review. Growing opposition to the U.S.-organized financial blockade was evident at the March 1985 annual meeting of the IDB in Vienna, where delegates condemned this flagrant example of U.S. political intervention in the bank. An IDB delegation to Nicaragua in September 1985 sharply criticized the U.S. interference, pointing out that "they call themselves champions of support for private enterprise, but this is a position contrary to their own philosophy." The IDB in Washington simultaneously announced a new $100 million package to help the poorest countries of the region—specifically including Nicaragua among the eligible countries. Nevertheless, the tabling of the $58 million proposal effectively killed the loan because the funds were not available for planting for the 1985–1986 agricultural cycle and the economic calculations on which the proposal was based would have to be completely revised.[24]

New private bank lending virtually ceased after the 1980 debt renegotiation. Although the Sandinista government made every scheduled interest payment to private banks twice a year until June 1983, expected flows of new private financing did not materialize. Nicaragua paid over $563 million in debt service between 1979 and 1983 but received only $12 million in new commercial bank financing—on 90-day terms.[25] Although renegotiations helped reduce annual debt service payments to less than the originally contracted level, payments nevertheless ate up a growing proportion of export earnings, as is shown in Table 2.

In June 1983, Nicaragua was unable to meet the interest payments owed to commercial banks, and a new round of renegotiations began. An agreement was reached in May 1984, but Nicaragua soon had to initiate a third round of renegotiations, concluded in July 1985. The terms of the 1985 agreement were sufficiently lenient that the banks asked the Nicaraguans not to divulge the details for fear of setting a precedent. By this point, the renegotiation was something of a formality: The Nicaraguan debt to commercial banks was trading at ten cents on the dollar, and new commercial bank lending was basically limited to a few short-term loans (backed up by export guarantees) from West German and Swiss banks that were not creditors from the earlier

---

tional Costs of Reagan's War Against Nicaragua," Institute for Policy Studies *Issue Paper* (Washington, D.C.: Nov. 1985).
24. *Inforpress Centroamericana* 622 (17 Oct. 1985); and interviews, Ministry of External Cooperation, Jan. 1986.
25. *Cable Centroamericano*, 5 July 1982, 96; and Instituto Histórico Centroamericano, *Envío* 24 (June 1983), 9c.

TABLE 2
Nicaragua: Indicators of External Public Debt, 1980–1984

	1979	1980	1981	1982	1983	1984[a]
	Millions of U.S. Dollars					
External public debt[b]	1136	1588	2200	2730	3324	3918
New disbursements[c]	188	265	424	458	367	334
Debt service						
Contractual obligation	n.d.	201	208	252	313	357
Actually paid[d]	60	80	171	169	83	119
	Percentage					
Debt service/exports of goods and services						
Contractual obligation	n.d.	40.6	37.6	56.4	67.6	83.4
Actually paid[d]	8.9	16.2	30.9	37.8	17.9	27.8

[a]Preliminary figures.
[b]Medium and long term (does not include short-term debt).
[c]Excludes renegotiation debits.
[d]The difference between debt service obligations and actual payments reflects a combination of renegotiations and accumulated arrears.
Sources: CEPAL, "Notas para el estudio económico de América Latina y el Caribe, 1984: Nicaragua" (México: CEPAL, 15 July 1985), 44, 47.

renegotiations.[26] The share of Nicaragua's total foreign debt owed to private banks had dropped to 25% by mid-1985 (see Table 3).

Official flows of external financing to Nicaragua reached a peak in 1981. The Sandinista government received significant quantities of loans and credits from Western Europe, Latin America, and socialist countries, but these did not quite compensate for the U.S.-organized financial blockade, which significantly affected Nicaragua's access to loans from multilateral institutions. The changing composition of Nicaragua's external finance and the decline in the total financial flow since 1981 are reflected in Table 4.

It is worth noting that capitalist countries (principally Western Europe and Latin America) accounted for a substantial portion of Nicaragua's external financing from 1979 to 1984. The U.S.S.R. and Eastern Europe were cautious about making economic commitments to Nicaragua.[27] Libya provided a significant one-shot loan of $100 million in April 1981, after the U.S. sus-

26. Interviews, Ministry of External Cooperation and Central American Bank for Economic Integration (Managua: Sept. 1985).
27. Rubén Berríos, "Economic Relations between Nicaragua and the Socialist Countries," The Wilson Center/Latin American Program, *Working Paper* No. 166 (Washington, D.C.: 1985).

TABLE 3
Composition of Nicaragua's Accumulated Foreign Debt,
by Source, 1979−1985 (in percent)

	OFFICIAL		PRIVATE BANKS	OTHER[a]	TOTAL
	BILATERAL	MULTILATERAL			
1979	23	32	43	2	100
1980	29	34	36	1	100
1981	31	31	38	0	100
1982	35	28	37	0	100
1983	49	22	27	2	100
1984	51	19	27	3	100
1985[b]	55	18	25	2	100

[a]Suppliers' credits, etc.
[b]Based on first semester figures.
Source: Central Bank of Nicaragua.

TABLE 4
Official External Financing[a] Contracted: Distribution by Source, 1979−1985 (%)

	1979	1980	1981	1982	1983	1984	1985[e]	1979−85
Multilateral	78.4	36.4	11.4	18.9	16.3	0.0	0.0	18.0
Bilateral	21.6	63.6	88.6	81.1	83.7	100.0	100.0	82.0
Capitalist countries	21.6	54.0	65.5	36.4	50.8	39.6	15.9	41.4
W. Europe	5.4	13.5	7.9	7.8	21.6	9.8	14.1	11.6
Latin Amer.[b]	16.2	25.2	43.9	27.9	20.8	25.2	0.7	23.1
U.S.A.	0.0	15.4	0.0	0.0	0.0	0.0	0.0	2.1
Canada	0.0	0.0	0.0	0.0	0.0	4.6	1.0	0.7
Africa/Asia[c]	0.0	0.0	13.6	0.6	8.4	0.0	0.0	4.0
Socialist countries[d]	0.0	9.5	23.1	44.8	32.9	60.4	84.1	40.5
Total (%)	100.0	100.0	100.0	100.0	100.0	100.0	100.0	100.0
Total (millions of U.S. $)	271.7	472.0	757.3	495.7	401.9	341.7	756.3	3496.6

[a]Loans and credit lines. Excludes donations. Columns may not add up exactly due to rounding. In addition to the loans and credit lines, foreign donations from 1979−1984 amounted to a total of perhaps $450 million. This figure is only a rough approximation because Nicaragua received some donations in the form of goods of undetermined value as well as donations that were not channeled through the Ministry of External Cooperation.
[b]Excludes Cuba.
[c]Includes Taiwan and Libya.
[d]Includes Cuba.
[e]Preliminary figures.
Source: Ministry of External Cooperation.

pended bilateral aid. Overall, however, the largest single lender in this period was Mexico. Both Mexico and Venezuela began supplying petroleum to Central America in 1980 on concessionary credit terms under the San José accords. However, Venezuela cut off oil credits to Nicaragua in September 1982—ostensibly because of payments arrears, though the suspension was not applied to other Central American countries that were behind on payments. Mexico, reportedly under pressure from the IMF, interrupted oil deliveries in late 1984, and the Soviet Union stepped up its supplies of petroleum to Nicaragua.[28] By 1985, the Soviet Union was the only supplier of oil credits to Nicaragua. This shift contributed to the jump in the socialist countries' loans in 1984–1985, shown in Table 4.

The preliminary figures on loans contracted in 1985 indicate an increase in external financing, for the first time since 1981. President Ortega's and Vice-President Ramírez's trips to Western and Eastern Europe (reported in the U.S press as "Ortega Goes to Moscow") netted some $400 million in credits, divided equally between Western and Eastern sources. Nicaragua also established diplomatic relations with the People's Republic of China in late 1985 and contracted a $10-million credit line, which officials hoped would be expanded as commercial relations between the two countries developed.

Despite the sharp decline in lending by multilateral development banks, Nicaragua was able to obtain new loans (mostly from bilateral sources) on relatively favorable financial terms: 62% of new external resources contracted between 1979 and 1983 were classified as "soft" or "very soft" loans.[29] However, a major share of new bilateral financing came in the form of lines of credit, tied to purchase of goods from the lending country. (For example, only 7% of loans contracted in 1985 were in the form of liquid foreign exchange.) Credit lines rose from 10% of Nicaragua's means of financing imports in 1980 to 19% in 1983 and 25% in 1984, whereas liquid foreign exchange (from export earnings, loans, and other sources) fell from 81% in 1980 to 33% in 1983 and 22% in 1984—complicating the process of matching import needs with possibilities. This meant that Nicaragua had to acquire a hodgepodge of machinery and technologies that were not always compatible or interchangeable, creating inevitable inefficiencies.

The structure of foreign trade became increasingly linked to the availability of credits from potential trade partners. Moreover, an estimated 90% of those credit lines were further restricted to imports of certain types of goods (typi-

28. See Armstrong et al., "Sandinista Foreign Policy," 47.
29. Hugo Mejía Briceño et al., "La deuda externa de Nicaragua, 1979– 1984," Paper presented to IV Congress of the Asociación Nicaragüense de Cientistas Sociales, ANICS, Managua: 30 Aug.–1 Sept. 1985, 20.

cally, for example, a specified percentage must be used to purchase capital goods), or even specific articles.[30] These rigidities were aggravated by the May 1985 U.S. trade embargo, which made it difficult to obtain spare parts for U.S.-made equipment.

The shortage of liquid foreign exchange hampered foreign trade. Expectations of export recovery and sustained flows of external finance had led to a sharp increase in imports from other Central American countries in 1980–1982. Nicaragua's growing intraregional trade deficits quickly exhausted the limits of the Central American Compensation Chamber. These deficits were initially covered by financing from the Central American Bank for Economic Integration (CABEI), but access to these loans was closed when Nicaragua fell into arrears on its payments to the CABEI in November 1982, as the foreign exchange shortage set in. In late 1985, there was discussion of possible significant new loans to the CABEI from Western Europe—in which case Nicaragua let it be known that it would pay up its arrears in order to become eligible for the new financing.[31]

Nicaragua's public foreign debt (excluding short-term borrowing) rose from about $1.1 billion in 1979 to nearly $4 billion in 1984. A substantial portion of that increase in indebtedness, however, was actually composed of renegotiated old debt, because capacity for servicing the debt was severely limited. Of the nearly $3 billion in new debt that accrued to Nicaragua between the beginning of 1980 and the end of 1984, only about $1.2 billion (40%) actually represented new net disbursements available for investment.[32] The remainder was rescheduled debt (which means, in effect, new loans to make payments on old loans), amortization payments, and credits for Mexican oil.

As Table 2 shows, debt service obligations rose steadily, reaching 83% of export earnings in 1984. Actual payments hit a peak of 38% of export earnings in 1982. The gap between debt service obligations and actual payments widened beginning in 1983, reflecting a combination of renegotiation and increasing arrears.

By 1984, Nicaragua was clearly prioritizing debt service payments according to expectations of continued financial flows from each source. For example, debt service payments to West Germany were suspended, because no official bilateral loans had been forthcoming since 1980, but repayment

30. Office of Planning, Ministry of Foreign Trade; CEPAL, "Notas para el estudio económico de América Latina y el Caribe, 1984: Nicaragua" (México: CEPAL, 15 July 1985), 45; and interviews, Ministry of External Cooperation (Managua: Sept. 1985).
31. Interviews, Central Bank of Nicaragua, and Central American Bank for Economic Integration (Managua: Sept. 1985 and Feb. 1986); and Barricada, 23 Jan. 1986.
32. Interview, Nicaraguan Investment Fund (FNI), Nov. 1985.

continued on bilateral obligations to the rest of Western Europe. Also in 1984, an agreement was signed with the socialist countries, postponing debt service payments until 1987 (including over $330 million that would fall due in 1985 and 1986). With respect to multilateral debt, Nicaragua fell behind in payments to the World Bank and the CABEI but showed a readiness to settle up these accounts at the first sign of new financing. This strategy of renegotiating when possible and repaying when necessary was a pragmatic response to immediate constraints.

Total flows of new external resources tapered off after 1981, and an increasing share of the new financing took the form of tied credit lines. While external borrowing became tighter, export earnings suffered from declining terms of trade and from the U.S.-backed counterrevolutionary forces that directed their attacks at coffee harvests and other economic targets. As a result of persistent trade deficits and restricted access to external finance, the Nicaraguan economy faced external imbalances reflected by a growing shortage of foreign exchange.

ECONOMIC POLICY AND STABILIZATION MEASURES

Although about 60% of production remained in private hands after 1979, the state sector accounted for 80% of investment[33]—reflecting not only the sluggish reactivation of private investment but also high coefficients of state investment. An important goal of the state investment strategy was to break out of the traditional agroexport dependence model by investing in the industrial transformation of Nicaragua's agricultural products (e.g., the Chiltepe dairy project, TIMAL sugar refinery, and production of cooking oil from African palm). Jaime Wheelock, Minister of Agriculture, summarized the state investment strategy as follows:

> After the triumph we could not extend the agroexport model based on raw materials, nor the industrialization model requiring imported intermediate goods, because neither of the two would get the country out of the indebtedness which we still have to suffer today . . . Nicaragua must center its development on the industrial transformation of its own natural resources, with the agro/livestock sector as its base. Agroindustry must be the focus of this industrial transformation, which should also include, by extension, forest resources, fishing and mining. In this way it is possible to overcome dependence.[34]

33. Carlos M. Vilas, "Unidad nacional y contradicciones sociales en una economía mixta: Nicaragua, 1979–1984," in Richard Harris and Carlos M. Vilas, editors, La revolución en Nicaragua (México: Ediciones Era, 1985), 28; and Richard Harris, "Transformación económica y desarrollo industrial de Nicaragua," in Harris and Vilas, editors, La revolución en Nicaragua, 90–92.
34. Wheelock, Entre la crisis y la agresión, 45–46.

Many of the major investments were long-term, capital-intensive projects, influenced by the upbeat projections of the first 2 years of the revolution when expectations of foreign exchange availability were still optimistic. For example, some 35% of the financing for projects supervised by the Special Fund for Development (FED), the agency in charge of channeling state investment into productive activities between 1980 and 1982, came from international organisms, principally the IDB and World Bank[35]—two sources that subsequently dried up. In 1982–1983, it was actually felt that there were not enough preinvestment projects ready for projected investment levels, leading to a scramble to put together projects (sometimes without comprehensive feasibility studies).[36] Another problem was that part of the rationale for large-scale, high-technology investment schemes responded to the lender countries' preference for showy projects, rather than to the logic of the Nicaraguan economy. After 1983, investments had to be increasingly curtailed and oriented around available lines of credit. In addition, major investments in fishing, mining, tobacco, and other projects with export potential were affected by increasing military attacks. Reorienting investments proved difficult, however, because the portfolio was full of ongoing long-term projects.

Without sufficient external support to sustain economic expansion, a series of internal bottlenecks emerged, and economic imbalance deepened.[37] In February 1985, a sweeping new economic adjustment package was announced (see Pizarro's chapter for fuller discussion). Key features included the elimination of most price subsidies, substantial salary increases, and expanded distribution of basic goods through workers' commissaries—a combination intended to squeeze the informal sector (particularly commercial intermediaries) while protecting the standard of living of salaried workers. The measures also included a currency devaluation that maintained exchange controls but narrowed the gap between the exchange rates that were fixed for calculating import prices and export earnings. The devaluation was designed to (a) reduce monetary emission; (b) absorb excess money in circulation; and (c) rationalize imports by raising their prices relative to domestically produced goods, without producing a generalized recessionary effect. To reduce the fiscal deficit, new taxes were enacted that aimed at

35. Interview, Nicaraguan Investment Fund (FNI) (Managua: Sept. 1985). The FNI, a dependency of the Central Bank, absorbed the Special Fund for Development (FED) in 1983.
36. Interviews, Nicaraguan Investment Fund (FNI) (Managua: Sept.–Nov. 1985).
37. For more information on the impact of these problems and the effort of organized labor to address these imbalances, see Richard Stahler-Sholk, "Organized Labor in Nicaragua," in Sheldon L. Maram and Gerald Michael Greenfield, editors, *Latin American Labor Organizations* (Westport, CT: Greenwood Press, forthcoming 1986).

capturing the unreported earnings of professionals and the informal sector. Plans were made to freeze social spending and to rationalize the operations of state enterprises. In order to crack down on unproductive speculation while improving the supply of basic goods available for working-class consumption, the government stepped up enforcement of remaining price controls. Also, a legalized free market in dollars was created, through Exchange Houses regulated by the Central Bank. This new line of policy was continued in 1986 with new devaluations and controlled wage-price increases in January and March.

The measures introduced in February 1985 differed from orthodox IMF-style stabilization programs in several important respects, including substantial wage increases, price controls, and multiple exchange rates. By early 1986, it remained to be seen whether the package would succeed in its overall objectives: stimulating the productive sectors of the economy, absorbing the excess money in circulation, reducing the speculative trade in goods and dollars, and inducing a shift in the labor force from unproductive to productive employment.

PROBLEMS AND PERSPECTIVES

In general, the revolutionary government managed the problem of external indebtedness with considerable aplomb in its first 6 years. The bad-faith borrowing of the Somoza regime was converted into a bargaining chip for successful renegotiation of the debt with private banks. Despite the financial blockade mounted by the United States, Nicaragua managed to tap a shifting composite of multilateral and bilateral sources for external financing. But the declining access to *liquid* foreign exchange and growing reliance on tied credits meant increased inefficiency. Economic policy after 6 years, although not without its problems, still avoided the extreme levels of disequilibrium that had contributed to the destabilization of the Allende government in Chile.

The outlook for significant improvement in Nicaragua's access to external finance in the near future is not particularly good. Despite a momentary boom in world coffee prices due to the 1985—1986 Brazilian frost, Nicaragua's terms of trade show no sign of sustained improvement. The Reagan administration demonstrated in the case of the 1985 IDB loan that it was willing to risk international opprobrium to shut off multilateral bank lending to Nicaragua. As long as the war goes on, a renewal of private bank lending is not likely either. The U.S. trade embargo announced in May 1985, followed by Congressional approval of another $27 million in aid to the counterrevolution in 1985 and $100 million in 1986, reflected a political climate in the United

States that translated into continued economic and military hostilities against Nicaragua.

In the immediate future, given the likely continuation of external constraints, the Sandinistas will continue to face the challenge of designing austerity measures that are compatible with the consolidation of revolutionary hegemony. This will require more active participation by the unions and other mass organizations—particularly the Sandinista Workers' Central (CST) and the neighborhood-based Sandinista Defense Committees (CDS), as the critical issues of food distribution and the structure of employment are confronted.

The Sandinista government will probably continue to pursue the general line of stabilization policies introduced in February 1985. These measures appear to be sufficiently respectful of the "national unity" pact with the capitalist sector to keep the loans flowing from Western Europe, but also sufficiently protective of popular living standards to exceed the bounds of "conditionality" typically imposed by the IMF (and, increasingly, by other multilateral lending institutions). Nicaragua participated with great interest in the 1985 Havana conference on Latin American debt and joined the growing number of countries that have denounced the *regional* debt burden as unjust and unpayable. But, barring a regionwide moratorium, the Sandinista government would have nothing to gain from abandoning its practice of making repayments according to very pragmatic criteria. In contrast to other Latin American countries, Nicaragua owes the bulk of its foreign debt to friendly governments rather than to private banks, so it is unlikely to take a leading role in efforts to organize a common front against the creditor banks.

The case of the Sandinista Revolution illustrates the particular difficulties of achieving financial stability in the process of social and economic transformation. In particular, the mounting costs of the counterrevolutionary war and financial blockade undermine the possibilities of creating a new economic model. However, popular mobilization—against decapitalization, in defense of the "social wage" of workers, in support of basic food distribution— opens possibilities for breaking free of the old model of external dependence and internal injustice. This popular mobilization holds hope for a revolutionary alternative to oppressive "stabilization" programs.

ACKNOWLEDGMENTS

The author is grateful for research support from the Doherty Foundation, the Institute for the Study of World Politics, and the University of California, Berkeley; and for helpful comments on an earlier draft from Trevor Evans and José Luis Coraggio of CRIES (Managua). None of these individuals or institutions, of course, bears responsibility for the contents.

Chapter 8

Patterns of Changing External Trade in Revolutionary Nicaragua: Voluntary and Involuntary Trade Diversification

MICHAEL E. CONROY

The United Nations Economic Commission for Latin American and the Caribbean (ECLAC) provided an unusually candid synopsis of the Nicaraguan external trade conundrum for the 1979–1985 period in an internal 1985 report. Departing from its normally sanitized prose and cautiously distant appraisals, the ECLAC staff wrote:

> The international trade policy of the Nicaraguan government, from the onset of the '80's, proposed an opening of trade with new countries and a diversification of trade across countries. This is an approach that Nicaragua has had to accentuate because of actions undertaken by the U.S. administration. These actions became apparent in diverse forms: on an economic level in the drastic reduction, among other measures, in the U.S. import quota for Nicaraguan sugar; on a financial level in the exercise of U.S. influence so that international financial institutions, such as the IDB, would not approve a 1984 loan for agricultural development; and, finally, on a political level by encouraging armed violence and supporting it with considerable resources.[1]

Two weeks after the report was published, the U.S. government announced a total embargo on commercial trade with Nicaragua. That dramatic step marks a logical delimiter for analyses of the transformation of patterns and levels of international trade set in motion by the overthrow of the Somoza regime in 1979.

The relative successes and failures of the Sandinista government of Nicara-

---

1. United Nations Economic Commission for Latin America and the Caribbean, "Notas para el estudio económico de América Latina y el Caribe, 1984; Nicaragua." (México: CEPAL, 17 April 1985), 35–36 (author's translation).

gua in the transformation of Nicaraguan external trade offer critical insights into the problems faced by small, peripheral, open economies in creating a position for themselves in the world economy that differs from their traditionally inherited roles. In those settings, one can see the role of international trade as a major determinant of national economic growth and as a major constraint on all dimensions of development. The concrete experiences of Nicaragua also demonstrate the potential that international trade contains for serving as a political tool in the hands of major trading nations. When policies are enacted to use that tool against a nation, the nature of international trade as a "weapon" is also clearly demonstrated. An analysis of Nicaraguan trade problems from 1979 to 1985 wreaks havoc with the traditional notions of the determination of trade patterns as the result of impersonal forces allocating international resources equitably under conditions of political and economic parity.

This chapter provides an overview of the nature of Nicaraguan international trade patterns over three distinct periods: the pre-1979 period under the reign of Somoza; the period of relative calm during the early years of the Sandinista government (1979–1982); and the 3 years following, through the end of 1985, when the full-fledged Contra war and a wide variety of other economic measures taken by the United States against Nicaragua, including the full embargo on trade decreed in May 1985, forced drastic changes in domestic policies, production, and trade. It provides responses to a series of questions about the political economy of external trade within the Nicaraguan revolution, including the following:

1. What has happened to Nicaraguan external trade over the period 1977–1985, especially merchandise trade, when seen individually and when placed in the context of broader Central American trends?
2. What were conditions prior to 1979 with respect to product composition and distribution of markets?
3. What have been the intentions of the Nicaraguan government vis-à-vis external trade and in particular with respect to trade diversification?
4. What had been accomplished by 1982, the end of the period of relatively "voluntary" control over foreign trade?
5. What then happened to the pattern of trade from 1983 to 1985, under increasingly stringent economic and financial pressures from the United States, under direct and indirect military attack, and, ultimately, under the trade embargo?
6. To what extent has there been (or had there been) trade diversification in either of those periods, both by product and across markets?
7. And what conclusions can be drawn from the Nicaraguan experience that may be useful to other nations that attempt to lessen their depen-

dence on one set of products or markets under the contemporary conditions of the global political economy?

THE POLITICAL ECONOMY OF TRADE DIVERSIFICATION

Diversification of trade patterns has long been a goal espoused by most small nations, although concrete definitions of the meaning of diversification and precise measures of levels of success at diversification have been slower to emerge. The fundamental notion, nonetheless, remains attractive. *Diversification* generally means a reduction in the concentration of exports and imports in a small number of markets or in a small number of products. Each of the two notions—market diversification and product diversification— has a separate rationale.

Nations seek to spread their markets across larger numbers of nations because of both structural economic reasons and political reasons. Structurally, the more that exports depend upon sustained demand conditions in a single market or in a small number of markets, the greater the likelihood that cyclical and other fluctuations in demand will throw the exporting economy through mirror-image fluctuations in growth and decline. For small, open economies such as that of Nicaragua where the export sector is the principal determinant of economic dynamism,[2] to depend too heavily on a small number of markets means chaining overall economic progress in one's own country to performance of the economies of those importing countries, a performance over which one has virtually no influence.

It is conventional wisdom with respect to diversification that one can achieve greater domestic economic growth and/or stability by exporting products to a larger number of smaller markets, rather than concentrating on a small number of markets, especially those within which one's products may or may not be competitive from period to period. The analytical acuity of that perception is not unchallenged, for it is relatively easy to postulate the preferability of a single large market if it is both growing rapidly and if it has been relatively stable. But recent developments in the political economy of international trade provide new and perhaps more telling justification for the pursuit of deliberate policies of diversification.[3]

2. Cf. Michael E. Conroy, "Economic Legacy and Policies: Performance and Critique," Chapter 10, in Thomas W. Walker, editor, *Nicaragua: The First Five Years* (New York: Praeger, 1985), 219–244.
3. For an analogous discussion of diversification relative to subnational regional economies, see Michael E. Conroy, "The Concept and Measurement of Regional Industrial Diversification," *Southern Economic Journal* 41,(3) (January 1975):492–505.

The political manifestation of interest in diversification relates to the growing politicization of external relations, in general, within the global economy. If the availablity of access to markets reflects not only the production of products of acceptable quality and at competitive prices but also the fulfillment of additional political criteria, it can become economically dangerous to concentrate one's exports in a small number of markets, especially if they are the markets most known for implementing political screening. At the middle of the 1980s, the exercise of such political discretion is equally true for both capitalist and socialist blocs, although there is very wide variation in the extent to which political criteria are used by different countries in each broad grouping.

The devastating economic impact that was experienced by Cuba after the almost total embargo of Western Hemisphere trade, organized and implemented by the United States, has been a constant reminder to new governments throughout the world of the potentially damaging consequences that can be wrought by trading partners who choose to use their economic leverage to do harm. But the 25 years that have followed the Cuban Revolution have produced changes in the global economic system such that the likelihood of an impact so severe as a result of deprivation of access to markets for critical *imports* is now significantly less. The growth of the semi-industrialized nations, the spread of production of formerly First World industrial products into numerous Third World areas, and the growing substitutability among imports from various regions have all lessened the potential dependence of any given nation upon any other single nation or bloc of nations for essential imported goods.

The elimination of the potential significance of critical *export* markets has been less clear. Most Third World nations produce and export relatively undifferentiated unprocessed or semiprocessed raw materials for which it takes great time and effort to develop market contracts and market penetration. In the event of a decision to use political criteria to deny a nation access to markets, it is relatively simple for importing nations to find alternative sources. Competitive pressures reduce the ability of the exporting nation to find alternative markets, especially in the case of perishable products. And brief delays or simple disruptions in the marketing of critical exports can have immediate and dramatic impacts upon the standard of living of small, open economies that cling tenuously to export-led growth that swings widely with variations in annual export earnings. As a result, diversification of export markets is sought unambiguously, especially by those nations that choose to intervene into laissez-faire processes in order to obtain growth or stability transcending those imparted by untrammeled markets.

Diversification of exports across products emerges from a completely different set of rationales. It has long been argued by structuralists in Latin

American development theory that the export-led growth dependent on unprocessed raw materials affords limited prospects for improvements in local value-added, productivity, and income.[4] These conclusions relate to the income inelasticity of demand for many traditional primary products (the fact that global demand for them grows less rapidly than global income) and separate price inelasticities of supply (the fact that it takes long periods of time to adjust to shortfalls in supply, leading to exaggerated cyclical swings in prices).

The solution to the limits placed on development by concentration on the export of a few unprocessed and semiprocessed raw materials is, first, to broaden the number and types of products that a country is exporting, and, second, to "diversify" into the production of more heavily processed, higher value-added goods. Ultimately, this means industrialization.

The quest for diversification of agricultural and other raw-material exports represents optimizing behavior within the constraints imposed by underdevelopment on potential immediate competitiveness in light industrial production. To the extent that a country can expand the production and export of "different," "less-volatile," or "more numerous" products, it is expected that longer term stability of export earnings will be increased.[5] To the extent that a nation's export patterns evolve toward greater concentration on a small number of export products, this is taken to represent "specialization," the opposite of diversification. And further specialization in traditional raw materials markets is expected to be deleterious over the long run.

Diversification of exports is an especially difficult task in laissez-faire economies, for the potential costs and benefits of diversification are generally not internalized by the many individual importers and exporters who engage in decentralized trade. The incentives for private importers and exporters are more closely related, institutionally, to the pursuit of short-term and immediate profits, except for the very largest multinational traders. It is not reasonable to expect that individual private sector traders will incorporate collective social concerns about "excessive dependence" upon a small set of markets or concerns about the "political risk" of the individual trading transactions when taken in the aggregate. It is for that reason that trade diversification policies in such countries have normally consisted of the creation of state-

---

4. See Albert Fishlow, "The State of Latin American Economics," Chapter 5 in *Economic and Social Progress in Latin America: 1985 Report*, Inter-American Development Bank (Washington, D.C.: IDB, 1985), 122–148.

5. There have been relatively few detailed studies of the phenomenon presupposed by this intuitive reasoning with respect to exports; there is, however, a body of comparable literature on subnational regional growth. See, for example, Michael E. Conroy, "Alternative Strategies for Regional Industrial Diversification," *Journal of Regional Science* 14 (1) (April 1974):31–46.

174 : **Michael E. Conroy**

sponsored incentives that stimulate the profitability of "new" or "nontraditional" exports. It was in part for this reason that the nationalization of imports and exports, as one of the first measures of the Sandinista government in 1979, raised hopes that greater social rationality with respect to trade diversification could be implemented.

PREREVOLUTIONARY PATTERNS OF NICARAGUAN EXPORTS AND IMPORTS

Prior to 1979, Nicaragua exhibited a pattern of trading relations that was somewhat more diversified than those of most of Central America at that time. As can be seen in Table 1, data for 1977 (the last full year prior to major economic consequences attributable to the subsequent insurrection) show that Nicaraguan commodity exports were sent to four principal markets:

TABLE 1
External Trade of Prerevolutionary Nicaragua 1977
Commodity Exports and Imports by Major Trading Partner
(Thousands of U.S. Dollars)

	EXPORTS		IMPORTS		TOTAL TRADE	
	AMOUNT	PERCENT	AMOUNT	PERCENT	AMOUNT	PERCENT
Total	632989	100.00	761927	100.00	1394916	100.00
United States	149254	23.58	219729	28.84	368983	26.45
Canada	681	0.11	5510	0.72	6191	0.44
LAFTA	16507	2.61	112287	14.74	128794	9.23
CACM	133986	21.17	164243	21.56	298229	21.38
Cuba	0	0.00	0	0.00	0.0	0.00
Rest of Caribbean	1684	0.27	12903	1.69	14587	1.05
Rest of Americas	2257	0.36	8102	1.06	10359	0.74
Japan	69806	11.03	77063	10.11	146869	10.53
China	21120	3.34	9208	1.21	30328	2.17
Other Asia	34482	5.45	1435	0.19	35917	2.57
Western Europe	197682	31.23	147274	19.33	344956	24.73
Soviet Union	0	0.00	202	0.03	202	0.01
Other E. Europe	6295	0.99	2065	0.27	8360	0.60
Australia, etc.	244	0.04	2036	0.27	2280	0.16

Source: U.N. Commodity Trade Statistics, 1977, 226–55.

Western Europe (31.2%), the United States (23.6%), the rest of Central America, through the Central American Common Market (21.2%), and Japan (11.0%). The largest share of Nicaragua's commodity imports came from the United States (28.9%), followed by Central American sources (21.6%), Western Europe (19.3%), and Japan (10.1%). Alternatively, if one groups LAFTA and the CACM, Nicaragua's trade with Latin America accounts for 24% of exports, 36% of imports, and roughly 30% of total trade. If one also views Western Europe as a statistical aggregate of nations with considerably independent policies, the level of diversification is even greater than these data would indicate at first glance.

Nicaragua enjoyed a surplus in its commodity trade relations with only two major trading partners, the People's Republic of China (to which it shipped cotton), and Western Europe. The largest share of the commodity trade deficit was incurred with other Latin American nations, both in the Latin American Free Trade Association (LAFTA) and in the Central American Common Market (CACM). The magnitude of the total trade deficit in 1977 ($129 million) and its relationship to total exports (20.4%) are indicative of the fundamental imbalance that characterized the Nicaraguan economy in the prerevolutionary years.[6] The imbalances by country groupings are primarily useful as indicators of the nature and direction of trade.

Nicaragua's deficit on services averaged $50 million per year from 1976 to 1978.[7] And it is conventionally assumed that a majority of those were provided by the United States, thereby increasing significantly Nicaragua's overall dependence on U.S. suppliers at that time. But reliable data on the distribution of imports and exports of services by country are not as readily available as the data on merchandise trade.[8]

The product composition of Nicaraguan exports in 1977 is given in Table 2. Coffee and cotton have been the principal exports of the nation since the early 1960s. By 1977, coffee accounted for 31.7% of all Nicaraguan export earnings, and cotton contributed 24.1%. Beef, chemicals, sugar, bananas, and seafood were the only other major contributing groups; but only one of them, chemicals, contributed as much as 8% of the total. The 56% of exports accounted for by just coffee and cotton in 1977 located Nicaragua

6. Cf. Michael E. Conroy, "External Dependence, External Assistance, and Economic Aggression Against Nicaragua," *Latin American Perspectives* Issue 45, 12 (2) (Spring 1985):39−67.
7. U.N. E.C.L.A., *Economic Survey of Latin America: 1978* (Santiago, Chile: United Nations, 1980), 391.
8. Nicaragua, like most Third World countries, has long maintained a very substantial deficit in the balance of payments for services. There are few nonindustrialized nations that can provide significant shares of the shipping, international telecommunications, insurance, management and consulting, and global financial intermediation that are listed under these accounts.

TABLE 2
Commodity Composition of Nicaraguan Exports,
1977 (Thousands of U.S. Dollars)

CATEGORY	1977	
	AMOUNT	PERCENT
Meat and preparations	38,983	6.16
Fish and preparations	23,584	3.73
Cereals and preparations	5,056	0.80
Fruits and vegetables	5,896	0.93
Sugar and preparations	31,171	4.92
Coffee, tea, cocoa, etc.	200,797	31.72
Animal feeds, etc.	11,533	1.82
Beverages & tobacco	7,470	1.18
Cotton fiber	153,094	24.19
Other crude materials	27,348	4.32
Mineral fuels	1,204	0.19
Fats and oils	5,460	0.86
Chemicals	50,968	8.05
Wood, cork, etc.	3,517	0.56
Textiles, yarn, & fabric	11,951	1.89
Iron and steel	4,035	0.64
Nonferrous metal prod.	8,602	1.36
Metal manufactures	1,274	0.20
Other basic manuf.	5,198	0.82
Machines, transp. equip.	3,941	0.62
Misc. manufactures	16,829	2.66
Other misc. exports	15,078	2.38
Total Exports	632,989	100.00

Source: Same as Table 1.

among the Latin American nations highest in dependence on primary product exports. Nicaragua's level of dependence on ten principal primary products exported by Latin America averaged 61.8% from 1972 to 1976, well above the regionwide average of 49.7%; this ranked Nicaragua among the top third of all Latin American nations in primary product dependence. During that same 1972–1976 period, no nation in the hemisphere depended so heavily on cotton, and only four depended to a comparable or greater extent on coffee.[9]

9. Inter-American Development Bank, *Economic and Social Progress in Latin America, 1985 Report* (Washington D.C.: IDB, 1985), 433–34.

EVOLUTION OF IMPORTS AND EXPORTS
FROM 1980 TO 1984 FOR CENTRAL AMERICA

The first 5 years of the 1980s brought Latin America as a whole its worst period of economic crisis in the entire twentieth century. Cumulative aggregate economic growth was a flat 0.0%; per capita growth of gross domestic product was −8.9%. The period began with unprecedented global interest rates and unprecedented levels of inflation in the industrialized nations; this implied unprecedented rates of increase in the cost of industrial imports for Latin America. And these first 5 years evolved into a period of deep global recession, with falling prices for Latin America's exports.[10]

For Central America as a whole, the period was even more critical. The exports of the region as a whole fell by nearly 15%, from 1980 to 1984 (see Table 3). The variation across Central American countries was great: Guatemalan exports fell by more than 30%; those of El Salvador by nearly 28%. Through all of its difficulties, Nicaragua's exports fared slightly better than the regional average, falling by only 13.3% over the period, although 1980 exports were particularly low due to the impact of the mid-1979 insurrection on planting of crops that would have been harvested in 1980.

The ability of a nation to meet the total demands of its population is given by its ability to supply, either through domestic production or imports. The level of imports of Central American nations fell by much more than their

TABLE 3
Total Exports of Goods and Services, Central America: 1980−1984
(Millions of 1982 U.S. Dollars)

	1980	1981	1982	1983	1984	PERCENTAGE CHANGE 1980−1984
Costa Rica	1359	1510	1428	1403	1488	9.49
El Salvador	983	810	690	732	713	−27.47
Guatemala	2047	1769	1604	1430	1403	−31.46
Honduras	799	817	715	751	797	−0.25
Nicaragua	593	681	626	658	514	−13.32
Central America	5781	5587	5063	4974	4915	−14.98

Source: Inter-American Development Bank, *Economic and Social Progress in Latin America: 1985 Report* (Washington, D.C.: IDB, 1985), 390.

10. U.N. E.C.L.A., "Preliminary Overview of the Latin American Economy during 1984," *Notas sobre la economía y el desarrollo*, No. 409/410 (January 1985).

levels of exports. There was an average decline of 29% in imports for the region from 1980 to 1984, but again there was wide variation (see Table 4). Guatemalan imports fell by more than 37%; those of El Salvador by nearly 29%. Nicaragua's imports fell by the smallest amount of any Central American nation over this period—23.6%. And this probably overestimates the real decrease; for 1980, imports were artificially high due to receipt of substantial worldwide assistance for reconstruction.

All of Central America suffered from similar external factors affecting the purchasing power of exports and the deteriorating terms of trade. The purchasing power of Nicaragua's exports, for example, fell by 49% in 1979–1980 and by a further 18% from 1981 to 1984. The terms of trade turned against Nicaragua by 19.6% from the start of 1979 to the end of 1980 and by an additional 26.6% from 1981 to 1984. This implies that Nicaragua had to export approximately 45% more of its principal exports in 1984 in order to obtain the same quantity of imports that it received in 1979.[11]

There was no apparent political component to the deterioration in the terms of trade and to the regional export and import declines, for the other Central American nations fared no better than Nicaragua. Costa Rica suffered a 20.5% decrease in the purchasing power of its exports from 1981 to 1984, and a 25.3% decrease in its trade-weighted terms of trade. Guatemala experienced a 33.3% decrease in terms of trade and a 37.9% worsening in the purchasing power of its exports.[12]

TABLE 4

Total Imports of Goods and Services, Central America: 1980–1984 (Millions of 1982 U.S. Dollars)

	1980	1981	1982	1983	1984	PERCENTAGE CHANGE 1980–1984
Costa Rica	1609	1185	971	1102	1207	−24.98
El Salvador	1030	922	723	716	734	−28.74
Guatemala	1387	1330	1051	846	866	−37.56
Honduras	1122	984	711	743	793	−29.32
Nicaragua	1058	1012	737	877	808	−23.63
Central America	6206	5433	4193	4284	4408	−28.97

Source: Inter-American Development Bank, Economic and Social Progress in Latin America: 1985 Report (Washington, D.C.: IDB, 1985), 390.

11. Ibid., 15.
12. Ibid.

NICARAGUAN TRADE POLICIES AND RESULTS BY 1982

The first requirement for the Nicaraguan government after the overthrow of Somoza was the reconstruction and reactivation of the economy. Decisions were made in 1979 and 1980 (and documented in the national plans published for 1980 and 1981) to focus upon established (and therefore traditional) agricultural production as the first priority for restoring domestic production and exports.[13]

FitzGerald refers to early concern with the relative strength of U.S. influence over imports as one of the factors that "determined the nature of accumulation" in the Nicaraguan economy, but there is little explicit reference in formal documents to an intention to diversify.[14] The official "Programa de Gobierno" disseminated widely in 1980 and 1981 notes that "Nicaragua must strengthen its capacity to function in diverse markets" all within the context of discussion of the continued importance of the private sector and joint public-private investment programs.[15] And a representative of the Foreign Ministry has written of the deliberate "diplomatic diversification," undertaken to attain greater economic independence, which resulted in a doubling of the number of nations with which Nicaragua held diplomatic relations by the end of the first year of Sandinista government.[16]

The principal instruments used to affect the composition of Nicaraguan foreign trade have been exchange controls for imports and direct state marketing programs for exports. By 1982, imports of nonessential goods had been virtually eliminated, in the middle of massive national campaigns to substitute Nicaraguan goods for previously imported goods. State participation in export markets has been more direct and more substantial.[17]

The nearly totally privatized import and export business in prerevolu-

---

13. Details of the early planning processes are still not plentiful. Useful information can be found in Junta de Gobierno de Reconstrucción Nacional (JGRN), *Programa de reactivación económica en beneficio del pueblo* (Managua: MIPLAN, 1980); JGRN, *Programa nacional de austeridad y eficiencia: 1981* (Managua: MIPLAN, 1981); and in E. V. K. FitzGerald, "The Economics of the Revolution," in Thomas W. Walker, editor, *Nicaragua in Revolution* (New York: Praeger Publishers, 1982), 203−23. See also the chapter by David Ruccio in this collection.
14. E. V. K. FitzGerald, 204.
15. JGRN, "The Philosophies and Policies of the Government of Nicaragua," Chapter 42 in *The Nicaraguan Reader: Documents of a Revolution under Fire*, Peter Rossett and John Vandermeer, editors (New York: Grove Press, 1983), 257.
16. Alejandro Bendaña, "The Foreign Policy of the Nicaraguan Revolution," in Thomas W. Walker, editor, *Nicaragua in Revolution* (New York: Praeger Publishers, 1982), 319−27.
17. Cf. George Irwin, "Nicaragua: Establishing the State as the Centre of Accumulation," *Cambridge Journal of Economics* 7(1983):125−39.

tionary Nicaragua was not atypical of Third World systems. As noted by Spalding, "prerevolutionary exports were dominated by a small number of large, internationalized trading houses such as Calley Dagnell [coffee] or Industrias Mina, S.A., the representative of Japan's Mitsui Co. [cotton]."[18] The change in this system was one of the most dramatic new policies implemented in 1979. Since then, the Ministry of Foreign Trade has exported Nicaragua's principal products through a series of state-owned trading monopolies. They purchase the agricultural products of both private and state producers at preannounced prices (often renegotiated if basic conditions change), offering originally a guaranteed minimum price that insulates domestic producers from international price declines and that shares with producers unanticipated price increases. The nationalization of the exports permits the state to capture a significant share of the export surplus as a basis for financing domestically subsidized programs. But when international prices fall, as they did from 1980 to 1983, the surpluses generated are minimal, and foreign financing of the internal deficit becomes critical.

The theoretical ability of the government to use these measures to diversify exports has, in fact, been quite limited in practice. The exigencies of reconstruction dictated the nature and magnitude of imports, and the origin of previously installed capital determined the origin of much of the newly imported replacement parts for industry, transportation, and equipment as mundane as the thousands of air conditioners installed in Managua hotels, homes, and offices. Limits on export diversification were related to production constraints as much as to marketing success. Introduction of new products was considerably more difficult during the period of reactivation and restructuring of the economy than expansion of agricultural production based on the use of existing equipment, agricultural skills, and prior work experience.

The deliberate interest in diversification did not mean elimination of trade with any partner. At no time, for example, does it appear to have been a policy of the government to reduce to zero its trade with the United States or with any other traditional trading partner. Personal interviews with many members of the staff of the Planning Ministry and of the Ministry of Foreign Commerce have indicated over the years that Nicaragua pursued an active policy of selling export products in the most favorable markets available while attempting to build nontraditional markets or to expand some of the traditional markets in a form that would lead to greater balance across markets. Agricultural policies have also attempted to stimulate the production of

18. Rose J. Spalding, "La expansión económica del estado en Nicaragua después de la Revolución," *Foro Internacional* 25(1) (Julio–septiembre 1984):20.

nontraditional agricultural export products (the most notable example is the expansion of sesame seed production) with the intention of lessening the relative importance of the cotton and coffee crops each year.

Total Nicaraguan exports increased dramatically from 1980 to 1981, and they have fallen irregularly since then (as seen in Table 3). The intermediate decline in 1982 is directly attributable to the devastating floods of May 1982 that forced more than 70,000 families out of their homes along the Pacific coast and that struck the farming communities at the moment of greatest vulnerability, immediately after clearing and planting. According to a United Nations report on the floods,[19] the damage was especially severe in the cotton-growing region and forced the abandonment of many fields and the reseeding of most of the rest. Because this was mostly rain-fed cotton, a probable decrease in cotton harvest and export was predicted. And it occurred.

By the end of 1982, as one can see in Table 5, Nicaraguan commodity exports had fallen to barely 60% of their 1977 nominal level.[20] The distribution of exports across markets, however, differed in several important ways from the pattern in 1977. Nicaragua's most important export market remained Western Europe, with an almost identical 30.3% of total exports. The U.S. share was a miniscule 1.5% higher, at 25%; and Japan retained an identical 11% share. But the share absorbed by Central American markets under the CACM fell from 21% to 13% as a natural result of the export and import crisis in the region described previously. China, the Soviet Union, and other Eastern European countries had purchased 4.4% in 1977; this share increased to 11.9% by the end of 1982.

The distribution of imports showed its greatest change in the proportion of imports procured in the United States. Nicaraguan imports from the United States in 1982 were nearly $75 million less than those of 1977; and this reduced the proportion of imports from the United States from 28.8% to 19.0%. By 1982, Nicaragua had shifted its sourcing of imports so that Latin America and the Caribbean (including the CACM but excluding Cuba) pro-

19. U.N. E.C.L.A., *Nicaragua: Las inundaciones de Mayo de 1982 y sus repercusiones sobre el desarrollo económico y social del país* (México: CEPAL, 22 June 1982).
20. Either 1981 or 1983 would have been a more "typical" year for evaluating agricultural export patterns, but by the end of 1983 the Contra war was beginning to dominate the entire economy, especially production out of Contra-affected highland areas. To use 1981 as an indication of the success of the regime in diversifying trade would reduce the period of effort to little more than 2 years, and most of 1982 represented a period of relatively "normal" production aside from the natural disaster embodied in the floods. Note also that Tables 3 and 4 provide data on trade in both goods and services and that they are there listed in 1982 real terms. There are no data available for decomposition by country and product that cover both goods and services and that are deflated to adjust for the impact of inflation. The data in Table 5 and all following tables are nominal or current dollars.

TABLE 5
External Trade of Nicaragua before "Contra" War, 1982 Commodity Exports
and Imports by Major Trading Partner (Thousands of U.S. Dollars)

	EXPORTS		IMPORTS		TOTAL TRADE	
	AMOUNT	PERCENT	AMOUNT	PERCENT	AMOUNT	PERCENT
Total	390,716	100.00	774,881	100.00	1,165,597	100.00
United States	97,861	25.05	147,556	19.04	245,417	21.06
Canada	3,187	0.82	12,587	1.62	15,774	1.35
LAIA	14,530	3.72	211,260	27.26	225,790	19.37
CACM	52,082	13.33	116,947	15.09	169,029	14.50
Cuba	1,272	0.33	30,500	3.94	31,772	2.73
Rest of Caribbean	98	0.03	8,391	1.08	8,489	0.73
Rest of Americas	1,430	0.37	12,258	1.58	13,688	1.17
Japan	44,949	11.50	18,510	2.39	63,459	5.44
China	19,428	4.97	197	0.03	19,625	1.68
Other Asia	8,194	2.10	12,885	1.66	21,079	1.81
Western Europe	118,503	30.33	141,996	18.32	260,499	22.35
Soviet Union	8,330	2.13	38,790	5.01	47,120	4.04
Other E. Europe	20,411	5.22	19,759	2.55	40,170	3.45
Australia, etc.	288	0.07	321	0.04	609	0.05

Source: U.N. Commodity Trade Statistics, 1982, 24–55.

vided the largest share—fully 45% of the total. The shares of total trade
undertaken with each of the countries or groups of countries in 1982 were
tangibly "more even" in 1982 than in 1977.

These trends in imports and exports are mirrored in shares of total trade.
The U.S. share fell by more than 5%; the CACM share fell by nearly 7%; and
the share provided by other Latin American nations (LAFTA in 1977 but LAIA
in 1982) rose by nearly 10%. Japan's share was reduced by half; and the
socialist bloc share in total trade rose from 2.8% in 1977 to 11.5% in 1982.

If the simple standard deviation of the shares is used as a measure of
dispersion around the mean proportion of trade with each of the groups listed
in Tables 1 and 5, the extent of the diversification can be quantified, albeit
roughly.[21] The standard deviation of shares of total trade was 9.85 in 1977,

21. Note that such an ad hoc quantification carries the implicit assumption that equal shares
across the fourteen groups listed in those two tables is a meaningful goal. The measure is

and it fell by 16% to 8.28 by 1982. This can be construed as an improvement of diversification across markets of 16%. Diversification of exports improved 7.7% in the standard deviation across principal markets, from 10.49 to 9.68; and the diversification of imports reflected the greater gain apparent in the data, a 9.7% reduction of the dispersion from 9.92 to 8.93. Although this is a rough measure, it provides a useful summary characterization of the changes.

THE CONSEQUENCES OF THE CONTRA WAR AND OTHER MEASURES TAKEN AGAINST NICARAGUA

The unfolding of U.S. policies against Nicaragua in late 1982 and after have fulfilled the worst forebodings of those who argued in Nicaragua in 1979 that the United States would attempt to "strangle" the revolution. It is not necessary to repeat here what has been documented elsewhere with respect to the nature of those policies.[22]

For purposes of the analysis of foreign trade patterns, it is sufficient to note that U.S. policies had several direct consequences, even prior to the imposition of the trade embargo:[23]

1. The 90% reduction of the Nicaraguan quota for sugar exports to the United States cost Nicaragua an immediate $23 million in trade with the United States in 1983, more than 5% of total exports for that year.
2. The mining of Nicaraguan harbors in early 1984 caused serious disruptions in shipping of both imports and exports, with exports more seriously affected because much of the previously contracted imports were off-loaded in Costa Rica and shipped overland, with delays of up to several months.
3. The blockage of Inter-American Development Bank lending for agricultural projects (such as farm-to-market penetration roads and new marketing programs) slowed the ability of the government to expand new agricultural production leaving further weight on continued production of traditional exports.

---

obviously sensitive to the number of groups and their composition; so its implications should not be extended unduly.

22. See Sylvia Maxfield and Richard Stahler-Sholk, "External Constraints," in Thomas W. Walker, ed., *Nicaragua in Revolution* (New York: Praeger Publishers, 1982), 245–64; M. E. Conroy, "External Dependence"; and "Devouring Nicaragua: Can Reagan Get Away With It?" *Mother Jones*, August/September 1985; and the chapter by FitzGerald elsewhere in this collection.
23. See also "Nicaragua's Foreign Trade: U.S. Tightens the Economic Noose," *Dollars and Sense* 107 (June 1985):6–8, and *Barricada Internacional*, June 20, 1985.

4. There were successful attempts by the Reagan administration to block short-term credits from U.S. banks for the financing of harvests and shipping of Nicaraguan exports.
5. There were direct attempts by the Reagan administration and by political groups in the United States that supported its position, to deter consumers from purchasing Nicaraguan products.
6. There were counterbalancing campaigns in Western Europe to expand public consumption of Nicaraguan products as a direct gesture of "solidarity."
7. There were a number of nations (including Algeria and Iran) that made state-based "solidarity" purchases of Nicaraguan exports as an indirect method of countering U.S. policies.
8. There were extensive campaigns by the U.S. Department of State to discourage other nations from providing trade credits for Nicaraguan purchases and short-term financing for assisting with harvesting and shipping of Nicaraguan exports.
9. The Contra war was heavily concentrated in the coffee-producing highlands of the Departments of Matagalpa and Jinotega and in the cattle-growing areas of Chontales and Boaco, creating serious reductions in the ability of those areas to contribute as usual to the nation's exports.

The consequences of all of these policies are just now becoming available in data relatively comparable to those of Tables 1 and 5. Table 6 presents an expanded version of those tables with comparable data for 1984 and 1985. The absolute amounts of exports in Table 6 can be interpreted more clearly in Table 7, which provides the distribution of specific products across markets, and in Table 8, which indicates the distribution of all exports across markets and products.[24]

Table 6 presents separate data on the distribution of Nicaraguan exports by major export commodity and by the market to which that commodity was sent. The "total exports" columns of Tables 6 and 7 indicate, product by product, the current value of exports of that product in each of the 4 years—

24. These tables display data that are not precisely equivalent to those of the previous tables because the principal data sources for the earlier tables, the U.N. Commodity Trade Statistics, are not published until nearly 2 years after the referenced year. No data for 1984 or 1985 were available as of the date of the last revision of this chapter (April 1986). The roughly comparable data from the Nicaraguan Ministry of Foreign Trade (MICE) are available in slightly different country and commodity groupings. Tables 6 through 8 focus on the most important commodities and the principal country groupings, without attempting to preserve the greater levels of detail found for each in Tables 1 and 5.

1977, 1982, 1984, and 1985. The interactive use of Tables 6 through 8 may be illustrated with an analysis of cotton exports.

Nicaragua's cotton exports in 1982 were only 60% of the prerevolutionary levels. They then rebounded in 1984, but by 1985 they were again back to the 1982 level. Japan has long been the principal market for Nicaraguan cotton. The share of Nicaragua's cotton exports purchased by Japan can be seen in Table 7. It rose from 38% in 1977 to 44% in 1982 and, then, to approximately 60% in 1984 and 1985. The relative overall importance of this cotton trade with Japan can be seen from Table 8. It accounted for only 9.2% of Nicaragua's exports in 1977, but it averaged 20% of total Nicaraguan exports in 1984 and 1985. The European Economic Community (EEC) has been the second most important market for Nicaraguan cotton, and its share has grown from 12.7% in 1977 to more than 20% of the total crop in 1984 and 1985. The market that has decreased its share of Nicaragua's cotton exports most dramatically is, in fact, the CMEA and China. Their share fell from nearly one-third of the total crop to less than 5% between 1977 and 1985.[25]

Nicaragua's coffee exports declined by 36% in total value from 1977 to 1982, but the volume shipped (not shown in the tables) in 1982 was only 4.5% lower than that of 1977. Then, total production fell from 1982 to 1985, and exports fell in total value even though prices improved slightly.[26] Western Europe markets for Nicaraguan coffee have also grown since 1977, increasing from 75% to 90% of the entire export production. The U.S. share fell from 17% to only 0.2% from 1977 to 1984, prior to the imposition of the embargo. The further loss due to the embargo was trivial. Because coffee exports have been relatively stable from 1982 to 1985, at a time of continuing deterioration of total exports, coffee trade has become increasingly important, accounting for more than 40% of total exports in 1985.

Tables 6 and 7 show how the United States dominated the purchases of Nicaraguan sugar and beef exports, with an average purchase of more than 90% of each in 1977. By 1984, the United States absorbed only 20% of sugar and 47% of beef. Although there have been increases in domestic consumption of both products in Nicaragua, total production of both is down. Their combined significance for exports has fallen more than 10% of total exports in 1977 to little more than 6% in 1985. The principal new market for Nicara-

25. The CMEA, or Council for Mutual Economic Assistance, is also sometimes referred to as the "Comecon countries." It consists of the Soviet Union, East Germany, Bulgaria, Czechoslovakia, Hungary, Poland, Rumania, Mongolia, Cuba, and Vietnam. The reference to China here is to the People's Republic of China; Taiwan is included under "Other Third World."
26. See the same sources as in Tables 1 and 5.

TABLE 6

Distribution of Nicaraguan Exports by Major Market and by Principal Product

Total Exports by Market and Product: 1977, 1982, 1984, 1985 (Thousands of U.S. Dollars)

PRINCIPAL PRODUCT		TOTAL EXPORTS	CACM	OTHER LATIN AMERICA	OTHER THIRD WORLD	U.S.	E.E.C.	JAPAN	OTHER OECD	CMEA & CHINA
Cotton	1977	153,092	2,662	581	16,583	1,393	19,507	58,219	5,611	48,535
	1982	89,095	2,171	97	7,634	—	15,270	29,324	41	24,560
	1984	133,815	5,098	—	10,482	—	28,120	82,241	—	7,874
	1985	91,017	5,052	—	10,176	—	18,498	53,138	55	4,098
Coffee	1977	200,797	—	—	260	34,766	151,638	9,872	4,261	—
	1982	128,404	115	22	713	6,692	72,966	4,199	23,649	19,890
	1984	121,812	—	—	98	6,985	103,038	8,358	2,390	943
	1985	117,934	—	—	3,102	14	105,748	4,527	2,989	1,554
Sugar	1977	31,171	357	19	—	30,795	—	—	—	—
	1982	39,267	—	14,078	—	21,361	—	—	33	3,795
	1984	20,940	—	6,616	10,217	4,107	—	—	—	—
	1985	6,920	—	—	5,592	—	1,328	—	—	—
Beef	1977	38,983	1,807	2,200	—	33,968	—	612	396	—
	1982	33,818	—	—	—	33,310	—	—	508	—
	1984	17,601	—	—	—	8,289	67	—	8,198	1,047
	1985	10,925	—	—	—	8,581	42	—	2,302	—

	Year									
Bananas	1977	4,474	—	—	49	4,425	—	—	—	—
	1982	9,802	—	—	8	9,794	—	—	—	—
	1984	11,907	—	—	—	11,878	29	—	—	—
	1985	16,458	—	—	2,402	4,086	9,970	—	—	—
Seafood	1977	23,584	486	74	66	22,941	—	—	—	—
	1982	22,315	—	97	—	19,826	2,392	—	—	—
	1984	12,607	35	5	—	10,738	—	—	1,834	—
	1985	12,854	391	—	—	6,051	372	6,035	—	—
Nontrad. exports	1977	106,315	95,419	1,706	2,985	4,712	756	—	—	—
	1982	30,320	27,744	950	132	236	172	326	1	808
	1984	65,169	n.a.	n.a.	n.a.	n.a.	n.a.	n.a.	n.a.	n.a.
	1985	35,536	n.a.	n.a.	n.a.	n.a.	n.a.	n.a.	n.a.	n.a.
Total Distributed	1977	558,416	100,731	4,580	19,943	133,000	171,901	68,703	10,268	48,535
	1982	353,021	30,030	15,244	8,487	91,219	88,408	46,241	24,232	49,053
	1984	383,851	5,133	6,616	20,797	41,997	131,254	90,599	12,422	9,864
	1985	291,644	5,443	5	21,272	18,732	135,958	57,665	11,381	5,652
Percentage of Total exports distributed	1977	88.22								
	1982	90.35								
	1984	99.75								
	1985	99.21								

Sources: For 1977 and 1982, the same as Tables 1 and 2; for 1984 and 1985, taken from Ministerio de Comercio Exterior, "Nicaragua Boletín Estadístico Comercio Exterior, 1983–84," Número 7 and from unpublished MICE data obtained by Richard Stahler-Sholk.

TABLE 7
Distribution of Nicaraguan Exports by Major Market and by Principal Product
Percentage of Each Product to Each Market: 1977, 1982, 1984, 1985

PRINCIPAL PRODUCT		TOTAL EXPORTS	CACM	OTHER LATIN AMERICA	OTHER THIRD WORLD	U.S.	E.E.C.	JAPAN	OTHER OECD	CMEA & CHINA	TOTAL
Cotton	1977	153,092	1.74	0.38	10.83	0.91	12.74	38.03	3.67	31.70	100.00
	1982	89,095	2.44	0.11	8.57	0.00	17.14	44.14	0.05	27.57	100.00
	1984	133,815	3.81	0.00	7.83	0.00	21.01	61.46	0.00	5.88	100.00
	1985	91,017	5.55	0.00	11.18	0.00	20.32	58.38	0.06	4.50	100.00
Coffee	1977	200,797	0.00	0.00	0.13	17.31	75.52	4.92	2.12	0.00	100.00
	1982	128,404	0.09	0.02	0.56	5.21	56.83	3.27	18.42	15.49	99.88
	1984	121,812	0.00	0.00	0.08	5.73	84.59	6.86	1.96	0.77	100.00
	1985	117,934	0.00	0.00	2.63	0.01	89.67	3.84	2.53	1.32	100.00
Sugar	1977	31,171	1.15	0.06	0.00	98.79	0.00	0.00	0.00	0.00	100.00
	1982	39,267	0.00	35.85	0.00	54.40	0.00	0.00	0.08	9.66	100.00
	1984	20,940	0.00	31.60	48.79	19.61	0.00	0.00	0.00	0.00	100.00
	1985	6,920	0.00	0.00	80.81	0.00	19.19	0.00	0.00	0.00	100.00

	Year									
Beef	1977	38,983	4.64	5.64	0.00	87.14	0.00	1.57	1.02	0.00	100.00
	1982	33,818	0.00	0.00	0.00	98.50	0.00	0.00	1.50	0.00	100.00
	1984	17,601	0.00	0.00	0.00	47.09	0.38	0.00	46.58	5.95	100.00
	1985	10,925	0.00	0.00	0.00	78.54	0.38	0.00	21.07	0.00	100.00
Bananas	1977	4,474	0.00	0.00	1.10	98.90	0.00	0.00	0.00	0.00	100.00
	1982	9,802	0.00	0.00	0.08	99.92	0.00	0.00	0.00	0.00	100.00
	1984	11,907	0.00	0.00	0.00	99.76	0.24	0.00	0.00	0.00	100.00
	1985	16,458	0.00	0.00	14.59	24.83	60.58	0.00	0.00	0.00	100.00
Seafood	1977	23,584	2.06	0.31	0.28	97.27	0.00	0.00	0.00	0.00	99.93
	1982	22,315	0.00	0.43	0.00	88.85	0.00	10.72	0.00	0.00	100.00
	1984	12,607	0.28	0.00	0.00	85.17	0.00	0.00	14.55	0.00	100.00
	1985	12,854	3.04	0.04	0.00	47.07	2.89	0.00	46.95	0.00	100.00
Nontrad. exports	1977	106,315	89.75	1.60	2.81	4.43	0.71	0.00	0.00	0.00	99.31
	1982	30,320	91.50	3.13	0.44	0.78	0.57	1.08	0.00	2.66	100.16
	1984	65,169	0.00	0.00	0.00	0.00	0.00	0.00	0.00	0.00	0.00
	1985	35,536	0.00	0.00	0.00	0.00	0.00	0.00	0.00	0.00	0.00

Source: Calculated from Table 6.

TABLE 8

Distribution of Nicaraguan Exports by Major Market and by Principal Product
Percentage of Total Exports by Market and Product: 1977, 1982, 1984, 1985

PRINCIPAL PRODUCT		TOTAL EXPORTS	CACM	OTHER LATIN AMERICA	OTHER THIRD WORLD	U.S.	E.E.C.	JAPAN	OTHER OECD	CMEA & CHINA
Cotton	1977	24.19	0.42	0.09	2.62	0.22	3.08	9.20	0.89	7.67
	1982	22.80	0.56	0.02	1.95	0.00	3.91	10.06	0.01	6.29
	1984	34.78	1.32	0.00	2.72	0.00	7.31	21.37	0.00	2.05
	1985	30.96	1.72	0.00	3.46	0.00	6.29	18.08	0.02	1.39
Coffee	1977	31.72	0.00	0.00	0.04	5.49	23.96	1.56	0.67	0.00
	1982	32.86	0.03	0.01	0.18	1.71	18.67	1.07	6.05	5.09
	1984	31.66	0.00	0.00	0.03	1.82	26.78	2.17	0.62	0.25
	1985	40.12	0.00	0.00	1.06	0.00	35.97	1.54	1.02	0.53
Sugar	1977	4.92	0.06	0.00	0.00	4.87	0.00	0.00	0.00	0.00
	1982	10.05	0.00	3.60	0.00	5.47	0.00	0.00	0.01	0.97
	1984	5.44	0.00	1.72	2.66	1.07	0.00	0.00	0.00	0.00
	1985	2.35	0.00	0.00	1.90	0.00	0.45	0.00	0.00	0.00

Beef	1977	6.16	0.29	0.35	0.00	5.37	0.00	0.10	0.06	0.00
	1982	8.66	0.00	0.00	0.00	8.53	0.00	0.00	0.13	0.00
	1984	4.57	0.00	0.00	0.00	2.15	0.02	0.00	2.13	0.27
	1985	3.72	0.00	0.00	0.00	2.92	0.01	0.00	0.78	0.00
Bananas	1977	0.71	0.00	0.00	0.01	0.70	0.00	0.00	0.00	0.00
	1982	2.51	0.00	0.00	0.00	2.51	0.00	0.00	0.00	0.00
	1984	3.09	0.00	0.00	0.00	3.09	0.01	0.00	0.00	0.00
	1985	5.60	0.00	0.00	0.82	1.39	3.39	0.00	0.00	0.00
Seafood	1977	3.73	0.08	0.01	0.01	3.62	0.00	0.00	0.00	0.00
	1982	5.71	0.00	0.02	0.00	5.07	0.00	0.61	0.00	0.00
	1984	3.28	0.01	0.00	0.00	2.79	0.00	0.00	0.48	0.00
	1985	4.37	0.13	0.00	0.00	2.06	0.13	0.00	2.05	0.00
Nontrad. Exports	1977	16.80	15.07	0.27	0.47	0.74	0.12	0.00	0.00	0.00
	1982	7.76	7.10	0.24	0.03	0.06	0.04	0.08	0.00	0.21
	1984	16.94	n.a.	n.a.	n.a.	n.a.	n.a.	n.a.	n.a.	n.a.
	1985	12.09	n.a.	n.a.	n.a.	n.a.	n.a.	n.a.	n.a.	n.a.
Total Distributed	1977	88.22	15.91	0.72	3.15	21.01	27.16	10.85	1.62	7.67
	1982	90.35	7.69	3.90	2.17	23.35	22.63	11.83	6.20	12.55
	1984ᵃ	99.75	1.61	2.07	6.51	13.15	41.08	28.36	3.89	3.09
	1985ᵃ	99.21	2.11	0.00	8.24	7.26	52.67	22.34	4.41	2.19

ᵃDoes not include "nontraditional" exports.

Source: Calculated from Table 6.

guan sugar was in the rest of Latin America (primarily Mexico) and in other Third World markets (primarily Algeria). With the exception of one shipment to Western Europe in 1984, there has been no significant development of alternative markets for Nicaraguan beef.

An average of 98% of Nicaragua's banana and seafood exports were consumed in the United States, even in 1982. Their continued high share in 1984 identifies them as major potential problems areas for Nicaragua at the time of the embargo. But Nicaragua appears to have had little difficulty expanding markets in Western Europe. Banana exports increased by nearly 400% from 1977 to 1985, and the reduction of sales in the United States after the embargo in 1985 was more than offset by increased sales to the EEC. And Canada (listed under "Other OECD") has replaced the United States as Nicaragua's principal market for seafood. Total seafood exports in 1985 were slightly higher than the 1984 level, although only half of the prerevolutionary 1977 level.

Nicaraguan chemical exports, a subset of "nontraditional exports," had fallen by 1984 to one-fifth of their 1977 level, and no data are presently available on their distribution across markets. The problem of chemical exports, however, was foretold in changes from 1977 to 1982. Ninety percent of Nicaragua's chemical exports were shipped to Central American markets in both 1977 and 1982. The draconian reduction in imports incurred by all of the Central American nations has left Nicaragua very exposed with respect to chemical exports. This is, perhaps, the best example of a level of prior specialization that was at risk of negative consequences because of concentration on a single market or interrelated set of markets.

The reduction of the importance of the U.S. market from 21% (of the products listed in Table 8) in 1977 to 7.3% in 1985 is apparent in the bottom rows of data in the table. The increasing shares went to Japan (from 10.9 to 22.3% of total exports), the EEC (from 27.2 to 52.7%), other OECD nations (from 1.6 to 4.4%), and other Third World nations (from 3.2% to 8.2%). This table further demonstrates that the socialist-bloc countries received only 7.7% of Nicaragua's exports in 1977, 12.6% in 1982, and 2.2% in 1985.

The increased concentration in commodity structure of Nicaraguan exports can be seen indirectly in Tables 6, 7, and 8. The extent of product diversification across this narrower set of seven categories can also be calculated from the data on percentage of total exports provided under the "total exports" column of Table 8. The standard deviation of the shares of exports concentrated in each commodity category was 11.82 in 1977. It fell by 8% to 10.87 by 1982, indicating a "more even" distribution of exports across these categories. But by 1984, the increasing relative importance of just two products, cotton and coffee, and the decreasing exports of sugar, beef, and manufactured nontraditional exports worsened the diversification tangibly.

The standard deviation of product shares increased to 13.83, 17% above the 1977 level. And 1985 saw a continuation in this specialization by commodity; the standard deviation rose to 15.15, an increase of 28% above the 1977 level.

Calculation of the standard deviation of export shares across countries for 1984 indicates that Nicaragua was nearly 20% less diversified in 1984 with respect to the distribution of its exports across markets than it had been in 1982. This is attributable to the fact that Japan had grown to occupy a position even more prominent than the position that the United States held in earlier years and that the shares of exports absorbed by both the CACM and the rest of Latin America had fallen—clear responses to the pervasive economic crisis throughout the hemisphere.

LESSONS FROM THE NICARAGUAN EXPERIENCE

Nicaragua's attempts to wrest control of its own destiny with respect to its entry in the international division of labor have not been encouraging. The diversification that it was able to achieve during the first years of the Sandinista government were impressive, especially when one considers the constraints of reactivation, reconstruction, private-sector control of export production, and limits on the rapidity with which new agricultural programs could be implemented.

The magnitude, ferocity, and persistence of the reaction of the United States, whether directly incited by Nicaragua's growing international economic independence via trade diversification or based upon other motivations, has wrought havoc with the external trade of the country. In fact, it is increasingly clear that the element of greatest coordination and cohesion in the "low-intensity war" being fought against Nicaragua may be its common impact upon export production and trade. But it is also clear that Nicaragua has been able to resist the full brunt of the economic measures taken against it by the U.S. government in large part because other Western, capitalist countries have absorbed increased shares and, in some cases, substantially increased absolute amounts of Nicaragua's export products.

The Nicaraguan experience redoubles the importance of trade diversification, especially with respect to diversification across "political" markets, for the prerevolutionary patterns of external trade and trade vulnerability have provided an Achilles' heel on which the attack upon the Revolution has been focused. For nations attempting to carve for themselves other new niches in the global political economy, the need for rapid and profound diversification of trading partners should now be, in the wake of the Nicaraguan experience, an objective of even greater importance than it was for Nicaragua.

Finally, the unprecedented increase in politicization of international trade, international assistance, and international finance, as seen in the case of Nicaragua, should serve to illustrate, once again, the increasing naivete of those who would argue that open and decentralized participation in the global laissez-faire trading system will bring the optimal forms and levels of social and economic progress to small, peripheral nations. The underlying nature of supposedly equitable and impersonal trading relations has never been so clearly demonstrated to this generation.

ACKNOWLEDGMENTS

This chapter has benefited significantly from data prepared and provided generously by Richard Stahler-Sholk and from the critical suggestions of Rose Spalding and Andrew Zimbalist. Errors of fact or interpretation, however, remain those of the author.

Chapter 9

An Evaluation of the Economic Costs to Nicaragua of U.S. Aggression: 1980–1984

E. V. K. FITZGERALD

This chapter is based on an extensive study of war damages prepared by the Government of Nicaragua, with technical assistance from the United Nations, for presentation before the International Court of Justice at the Hague in September 1985. A summary of the economic losses is also included in the 1984 annual ECLA report.[1]

THE NICARAGUAN ECONOMY: FROM RECOVERY TO RESISTANCE

In 1979, a popular insurrection led by the FSLN overthrew the Somoza dynasty. Since then, the revolutionary government has been engaged in a project to transform the previous economic model based on exploitation and dependency. This economic effort has three objectives: to raise the standard of living by providing for "basic needs" (health, education, nutrition, housing, etc.); to begin a process of balanced economic development centered in the agricultural sector (where land reform plays a fundamental role); and to rearrange foreign trade and international financial relations in order to reduce dependency and obtain better terms of trade. This was to be achieved within a mixed economy, with a third of production in state enterprises, a nationalized banking system, a growing cooperative sector, and guarantees for private

---

1. ECLA, *Informe económico sobre América Latina, 1984: Nicaragua* (México: CEPAL, 1985).

enterprise. It is also reflected in the nonaligned international policy of Nicaragua.[2]

During the first 3 years (1980–1982), this strategy began to produce concrete results and established the foundation for a future economic development different from the traditional model.[3] The volume of production to sustain social advances had largely recuperated following its collapse in 1979 (when it fell 30%). Between 1979 and 1983, the annual growth rate of the GDP averaged 5%, and investment averaged 20% of GDP. However, the deterioration in the international terms of trade (which fell 40% for Nicaragua between 1978 and 1983) and the growth of internal demand generated by these social programs created a foreign exchange deficit approximating half the value of imports each year.[4] Consequently, it was possible to sustain the economy only as result of extensive international financial assistance. Nonetheless, the outlook for the medium run (based on the expansion of primary sector exports) was considered encouraging by the multilateral agencies.[5]

The need to adjust economic and even social goals in order to maintain a realistic short-run external equilibrium was recognized by 1983, and the decline in labor productivity and administrative efficiency (common to most revolutionary experiences) of the first years was being redressed.[6] The economy was adjusting to difficult circumstances and the government was preparing to consolidate the considerable social advances in the expectation of sound, steady development, if not growth, while the world economy recovered.

U.S. military aggression, through the financing and direction of counterrevolutionary forces headed by and largely composed of ex-members of the Somoza National Guard, started as early as 1980. But it was not until 1983 that a considerable military force could be put in the field. Its strategic objective was to gain a territorial foothold in Nicaragua. Once Washington recognized that a military victory by the counterrevolution was not possible, a strategy was adopted of wearing down the economy and undermining the social base of the Sandinista Revolution.

2. See JGRN, Estatuto fundamental de la República de Nicaragua (Managua: JGRN, 1979); Ministerio de Planificación, Programa de reactivación económica en beneficio del pueblo (Managua: MIPLAN, 1980); and FSLN, Plan de lucha del FSLN (Managua: FSLN, 1984).
3. For a good survey of different facets of the Sandinista revolution, see Thomas W. Walker, ed., Nicaragua in Revolution (New York: Praeger, 1982), and Nicaragua: The First Five Years (New York: Praeger, 1985).
4. See ECLA, Informe económico sobre América Latina, 1983: Nicaragua (México: CEPAL, 1984).
5. See BID, Nicaragua: Análisis económico nacional (Washington: BID, 1983), and IBRD, Nicaragua: The Challenge of Reconstruction (Washington: IBRD, 1981).
6. See Jaime Wheelock, Entre la crisis y la agresión: La reforma agraria Sandinista (Managua: Nueva Nicaragua, 1984); JGRN, Política económica de Nicaragua, 1983–1987 (Managua: Government of Nicaragua, 1983).

From 1983 on, the economic cost to Nicaragua of the aggression rose rapidly (see Table 1), seriously affecting both production and the standard of living of the population. Even though the direct damages in 1984 were reduced by the increased operational effectiveness of the Sandinista armed forces, the production losses rose even higher. To place those figures in perspective, it should be noted that the total losses for these 5 years exceed total exports for 1984, the losses in that year being approximately half the value of exports.

To those costs should be added the financial value of the development projects that were negotiated with and accepted for their technical merit by the World Bank (International Bank for Reconstruction and Development, or IBRD) and the Inter-American Development Bank (IDB), only to be blocked by the intervention of the United States at the board level of those multilateral organizations. The total amount of the disbursements programmed for these loans between 1980 and 1984 would have been U.S. $200 million—one-fifth of the gross fixed capital formation during this period.

In addition, the direct cost of defense approximated one-third of the 1984 national budget, reducing the resources available for the health and education programs and productive investments that comprise much of the rest of the budget.

The objective of this chapter is to analyze the macroeconomic and macrosocial impact of the aggression, in order to be able to assess its effect more completely. The analysis follows four steps. It assesses first, the impact on the balance of payments, because the external constraint is crucial for the economy; second, macroeconomic effects that result from the scarcity of foreign exchange; third, the consequences for the standard of living of the population; and fourth, the consequences for long-term development.

TABLE 1
Damages and Economic Losses (Millions of U.S. Dollars)

YEAR	RAW MATERIAL AND CAPITAL DAMAGES	PRODUCTION LOSSES	TOTAL
1980	0.5	0.9	1.4
1981	2.7	4.3	7.0
1982	9.0	22.3	31.3
1983	41.1	102.4	143.5
1984	16.1	171.4	187.5
Total	69.4	301.3	370.7

Source: Evidence presented by the Government of Nicaragua to the International Court of Justice; see also ECLA, Informe económico sobre América Latina, 1984: Nicaragua (México: CEPAL, 1985).

THE IMPACT ON THE BALANCE OF PAYMENTS

The economic costs of the aggression, relative to the size of the Nicaraguan economy, are very large. The most direct impact on the macroeconomy is rooted in the loss of primary production. The effects[7] are summarized in Table 2, which illustrates the collapse of the forestry, fishing, and mining sectors, and the impact in coffee and cattle production that is concentrated in the war zones. The loss is large (almost one-seventh of primary production), and it affects disproportionately the economy in the border areas.

TABLE 2
Effect of the Production Losses on Exports and Domestic Supply
(Millions of U.S. Dollars)

CONCEPT	1980	1981	1982	1983	1984	TOTAL
Loss of production						
for export	0.9	3.5	6.1	65.3	102.8	178.5
Agriculture						
Coffee	—	—	—	32.1	37.0	69.1
Tobacco	—	—	—	1.9	1.6	3.5
Cattle	—	0.1	0.2	1.0	3.3	4.6
Wood	—	—	—	25.0	52.2	77.2
Seafood	0.9	1.2	2.8	4.0	6.6	15.5
Mining	—	2.2	3.1	1.3	2.1	8.6
Loss of production for						
domestic consumption	—	—	15.0	32.1	56.9	104.0
Basic grains[a]	—	—	—	0.4	11.3	11.7
Other crops[b]	—	—	—	1.7	0.6	2.3
Construction[c]	—	—	15.0	30.0	45.0	90.0
Total losses	**0.9**	**3.5**	**21.1**	**97.4**	**159.7**	**282.5**
Exports realized		499.8	405.8	428.6	381.6	

[a]Basic grains are computed as the negative effect of having to make up losses through imports; that is, entries are valued at "border prices," FOB for exports and CIF for imports. Input costs are not deducted because they were incurred before destruction.
[b]Coconut, yuca, cacao, and raicilla.
[c]Construction foregone through destruction of equipment, delay of projects, etc.
Source: Same as Table 1.
Note: Totals do not reconcile exactly with Table 1 because of the noncoincidence of agricultural cycles and calendar years.

7. The data were collected monthly by local representatives of each production ministry and then combined by the Ministry of the Presidency. The methodology and results were revised and approved by a special UN/ECLA mission in early 1985.

Table 3 summarizes the direct and indirect effects on the balance of payments. This estimates what part of the (lost) production would have been traded. Moreover, the greater availability of foreign exchange would have permitted an increase in the level of economic activity through the import of productive inputs, allowing a proportional increase in domestic production.[8] In this manner, a new hypothetical equilibrium in the balance of payments "without aggression" is calculated. For purposes of analysis, it is supposed that the lost resources would have been distributed between imports and debt payment in the same proportion as in previous years. In other words, this would have permitted greater industrial activity and better compliance with the foreign debt servicing. For example, Table 3 shows that in 1984 export earnings would have been $505 million instead of the actual $382 million, that is, 32% higher. This would have permitted increased imports and an improvement of $84 million in the trade balance.

To these effects of the military aggression, it is necessary to add the impact of the financial aggression (see Table 4). Without U.S. pressure on multilateral institutions, Nicaragua would undoubtedly have had access to "soft" loans (low interest rates and long repayment periods) for infrastructure, agricultural development, social sectors, and the like. In the short run, without U.S. military aggression, a positive outcome in the balance of payments would have been obtained with these credits because the long-term loans that were denied would have substituted for the "hard" short-term commercial credits to which it has been necessary to resort. In the longer run, and in financial terms, there would also have been a reduction in the weight of the debt service (which in 1984 absorbed almost 30% of the export earnings); in economic terms, the level of accumulation would have been more balanced on aggregate, causing less inflationary pressure.

If the direct effect of the military aggression on the balance of payments (Table 3) and the effect of the financial aggression (Table 4) year by year are added together, the magnitude of the impact, in relation to the few resources that Nicaragua has in this time of economic crisis in Latin America, can be appreciated (see Table 5). In 1984 alone, the total surpassed U.S. $213 million; that is, 56% of export earnings. The total for the 5 years was $521 million.

These losses made it impossible economically (and socially because it would imply an unacceptable drop in the living standard of the population) to service the foreign debt. This refers, in the first place, to the debt with the government of the United States inherited from the Somoza era ($223 million), and in the second place, to the commercial bank debt, principally with

8. For elaboration, see the third section of this chapter.

TABLE 3
Impact of the Damages on the Balance of Payments (Millions of U.S. Dollars)

	1981	1982	1983	1984
Trade Balance				
Actual	−499.6	−369.7	−378.3	−408.6
Without the aggression	−496.8	−368.0	−299.5	−324.8
Exports				
Actual	499.8	405.8	428.6	381.6
Without the aggression	506.0	424.5	557.0	504.6
Imports				
Actual	999.4	775.5	806.9	790.2
Without the aggression	1.002.8	792.5	856.5	829.4
Service Balance	−85.0	−152.7	−218.6	−226.8
Income	73.4	49.5	40.6	51.6
Expenditures	158.4	202.2	259.2	278.4
Donations	70.3	51.5	70.4	117.0
Current Accounts Balance				
Actual	−514.3	−470.9	−526.5	−518.4
Without the aggression	−511.5	−469.2	−447.7	−434.6
Net Capital Movements	572.0	371.4	610.1	507.7
Long term	599.1	454.3	659.6	512.3
Other movements	−27.1	−82.9	−49.5	−4.6
Balance of Payments				
Actual	57.7	−99.5	83.6	−10.7
Without the aggression	60.5	−97.8	162.4	73.1

Source: Same as Table 1.

U.S. banks. The amount of "inherited" debt of $2 billion ($1.6 billion in 1979 but with $400 million in interest capitalized through 1984) has been renegotiated several times. Nicaragua has not canceled the debt with U.S. nationals despite the actions of the Reagan administration, nor has it declared a general moratorium as is customary under these circumstances. On the contrary, Nicaragua has paid $234 million in service to these banks and $209 million to multilateral banks between 1980 and 1984, without any positive response in terms of new funds. The impact has been felt in the nonpayment of debts contracted after 1979 with friendly governments and in the lack of liquidity to clear $300 million in the unpaid balances with the *Cámara de Compensación Centroamericana*.

TABLE 4

Calculation of the Financial Aggression (Millions of U.S. Dollars)

	PROJECT DECISION	PROJECT AMOUNT	AMOUNT UNDISBURSED BY YEAR				TOTAL UNDISBURSED 1981–84
			1981	1982	1983	1984	
Bilateral U.S.-Nicaragua							
Partial blockade of U.S. $75 million that was already approved		15.0	—	15.0	—	—	15.0
Suspension of already approved wheat loan		10.0	5.0	5.0	—	—	10.0
Rural dev., education, and health program		11.4	2.2	2.3	2.3	4.6	11.4
Subtotal Bilateral		36.4	7.2	22.3	2.3	4.6	36.4
Multilateral							
IDB							
Abisinia-Valle del Cua	Vetoed	2.2	—	—	—	2.2	2.2
Hoyo Monte Galán-San Jacinto Tizate (energy)	Of. Jun. 80[a]	15.0	1.0	7.0	7.0	—	15.0
Global agricultural program II (agroind.)	Of. Jun. 82[a]	55.0	—	—	8.0	11.0	19.0
Livestock dev. program-Boaco-Chontales	Of. Sep. 82[a]	50.0	—	—	10.0	15.0	25.0
Agroind. rehab. program	Of. 1981[a]	98.0	—	6.0	23.0	28.0	57.0
Program of potable water, public service, and sewers for intermediate cities & rural communities, Phase II	Apr. 1981[b]	21.0	—	3.0	9.0	9.0	21.0
Preinvestment program	Apr. 1982[b]	5.3	—	—	2.0	3.3	5.3
Subtotal IDB		246.5	1.0	16.0	59.0	68.5	144.5
IBRD							
Agricultural credit program	Pres. Jul. 84[c]	50.0	—	—	—	10.0	10.0
Food prod. and export	Pres. Jul. 84[c]	90.0	—	—	—	9.0	9.0
Subtotal IBRD		140.0	—	—	—	19.0	19.0
Subtotal Multilateral		386.5	1.0	16.0	59.0	87.5	163.5

Source: Fondo Internacional de Reconstrucción, Managua.

[a]Officially approved on technical grounds on date shown.

[b]Approved but not implemented.

[c]Presented to IBRD formally but financial relationship with IBRD suspended in Nov. 84.

TABLE 5
Total Direct Impact of the Aggression on the
Balance of Payments (Millions of U.S. Dollars)

	MILITARY AGGRESSION	FINANCIAL AGGRESSION	TOTAL
1980	0.9	—	0.9
1981	5.6	8.2	13.8
1982	26.3	38.3	64.6
1983	167.0	61.3	228.7
1984	121.6	92.1	213.7
Total	321.4	199.9	521.3

Source: Military Aggression: Increased trade deficit (Table 3) plus the destruction of capital goods. Financial Aggression: Table 4.

THE MACROECONOMIC EFFECT OF THE AGGRESSION

The immediate impact on domestic economic production was felt through: (a) the direct production losses, above all in the primary sector; and (b) the decline in productive activity due to the scarcity of foreign exchange, above all in the secondary sector.

Taking factor (a) first, Table 6 illustrates the decline in primary output for 1983 and 1984—the years of greatest impact. It is clear that proportionally the effect is largest in the fishing and forestry sectors, even though the greatest impact in absolute terms is in the agricultural sector. Without the aggression, the primary sector in total would have produced 8% and 11% more, respectively, in the two years. When this direct production loss is translated into the availability of foreign exchange, it also generates an impact on secondary sector production (industry and construction above all) through the balance of payments by affecting the import of inputs.

Table 6 summarizes calculations by the Secretariat of Planning and the Budget of these results. These figures were derived by rerunning the macroeconomic planning model that the secretariat uses in constructing the annual economic program, using higher levels of production and foreign exchange availability than those which actually occurred.[9]

In 1984, secondary production would have been 10% higher in the

9. This is based on the standard ECLA planning model used in most Latin American countries. Foreign exchange availability from the primary sector determines industrial output because of fixed (and high) import coefficients for manufacturing energy, construction, and the like. It is assumed that tertiary output is not affected. Variations in GDP then generate a different investment level (determined by the marginal investment coefficient), and consumption comes as a residual.

TABLE 6
Actual Production versus Production under Normal Conditions without the Aggression (billions of córdobas at 1980 prices)

	1983			1984		
	ACTUAL	NORMAL	DIF.	ACTUAL	NORMAL	DIF.
Primary Sector	5.960	6.431	8%	5.647	6.292	11%
Secondary Sector	6.557	7.137	9%	6.526	7.160	10%
Tertiary Sector	11.321	11.321	—	11.332	11.332	—
GDP	23.838	24.889	4%	23.505	24.784	5%
Consumption	21.027	21.347	2%	22.101	22.222	1%
Investment	4.676	5.050	8%	3.901	4.017	3%
Exports	5.593	6.353	14%	4.374	5.796	33%
Imports	7.458	7.861	5%	6.871	7.251	6%

Source: Secretariat of Planning and the Budget.

absence of foreign aggression. Along with all of this, there would have been an expanded capacity to service the foreign debt. Table 6 also contains an estimate of this impact on the components of macroeconomic spending. As we have seen in the preceding section, without the aggression in 1984, exports would have been 33% higher, allowing imports to be 6% higher and the complete payment of the service on the debt.

National defense required considerable increases in the military budget in response to U.S. aggression. This implied both reductions in the budget dedicated to social services and new taxes. But in spite of these adjustments, the fiscal deficit grew to very inflationary levels. Because Nicaragua's defense is based on a massive mobilization of infantry, and the direct external expenditure for this is minimal, it does not have a great impact on the balance of payments. The increase in the deficit is entirely reflected in internal consumption demand, for the macroeconomic impact, in a situation of restricted supply, has inevitably been inflationary. In other words, inflation was used as a means of resource mobilization by the government to pay for the war.

In the absence of aggression and assuming that the "peacetime" defense budget would have been the same in real terms as it was in 1981, the relation between the fiscal deficit and the GDP in 1984 would have been approximately one-third what it actually was, and the inflation rate would have been proportionately lower, as Table 7 indicates.

Moreover, if it is taken into account that without the aggression, the GDP would have been higher and foreign financing more ample, the monetary deficit as a proportion of economic activity would have been even lower.

TABLE 7
Fiscal Deficit and Inflation

	1981	1982	1983	1984	1985
Fiscal Deficit as a proportion of GDP					
With the aggression	10%	14%	29%	24%	15%
Without the aggression[a]	10%	13%	25%	15%	5%
Inflation rate[b]					
With the aggression	12%	17%	15%	30%	70%
Without the aggression[c]	12%	16%	12%	19%	23%

[a]Assuming that in the absence of the aggression, the defense spending would have been the same proportion of the GDP that it was in 1981.
[b]GDP deflator.
[c]Proportionate to the decrease in the fiscal deficit because all of this increase is monetized.
Source: Secretariat of Planning and the Budget.

IMPACT OF THE WAR ON THE STANDARD OF LIVING OF THE POPULATION

The consequences of the war for ordinary Nicaraguan people have been more serious than the aggregate national accounts figures indicate. In the war zones, this is because it is precisely those new social services and supply systems that are attacked by the Contras. When these facilities are lost, it is the poorest strata of the population (mountain peasants) that are hurt most. Similarly, import shortages and inflation have hit wage workers hardest; the strata with an established standard of living, particularly businessmen who are better able to adjust their monetary income, are in a better position to defend themselves economically.

The war zones (Regions I, V, VI, and the Special Zones) are precisely those that have felt the greatest impact of aggression. They contain about a third of the population (a million people) of which one-third have been displaced by war, abandoning their peasant plots and homes for the security of the towns, the resettlement camps, or simply the roadsides. The government has made an enormous effort to provide health care, housing, education, and supplies for these displaced families, at the cost of necessary social projects in other parts of the country.

The attacks on the social services are concentrated in these zones. In education, 8 schools have been destroyed, with 149 teachers killed between 1980 and 1984 because they are a special target of the Contra. What is more, 231 schools have been abandoned because of the terrorism. Consequently, it has been necessary to suspend services to 25,680 students in elementary schools and 10,095 students in the adult education program.

In health, the effect has been similar. The physical destruction has focused on the new facilities that were beginning to raise the standard of living of the peasants. The counterrevolutionary bands, on arriving in a town, aim explicitly to destroy government facilities and assassinate those who cooperate with it. In consequence, the Ministry of Health has had to abandon fifty rural clinics and forty-five health posts. The population that has lost regular service from these units is approximately 225,000 people (that is, a fourth of the population in the war zone), requiring the government to devise new varieties of health services in order to avoid leaving this population completely unprotected.

Even more seriously, the war has impeded the extension and mobilization of preventive public health services, undermining the epidemiological advances that had been the pride of the revolution. In the war zones, the campaign to eliminate malaria has been halted, and polio, which was eliminated through a massive vaccination program in 1982, reappeared in 1984. The destruction of housing, lighting and telephone systems, and public transportation vehicles have all hindered advances in the rural standard of living.

However, it is the deterioration of the peasant economy that has most affected the standard of living in the war zones (if we exclude the human grief caused by the deaths, woundings, and kidnapping). The aggression has implied the loss of a third of the coffee and basic grains production in these zones, which are fundamentally produced by small producers. This loss is not so much caused by military destruction but by the impossiblity of planting or harvesting due to the risks to human life. To this more visible effect, we need to add two further factors that have dislocated the peasant economy.

The first is the growing scarcity of labor, owing to the flight of families or the entry of the young men into the war. This has reduced the commercial production of grains, cattle, and coffee, above all. The peasant family has retreated toward subsistence production or gone to the city. This urban migration has led to the growth of the Managua population from 600,000 before the Revolution to almost a million now.

The second effect of the war on the peasant economy is the disarticulation of its networks of commercial trade because the buyers or the state authorities that store the harvest, provide credits, and sell manufactured products (themselves in reduced supply and commanding high prices) cannot get into these zones. Thus the peasants are left without tools for production or a market for their corn, and they simply stop producing, reducing still further their own standard of living and the food supply of the urban population.

For the other two-thirds of the population located in the Pacific Coast area (Regions II, III, and IV), the impact of the war has been much less direct, even though thousands of families in this area have suffered the sorrow of having a son or daughter killed. Here the economic impact of the aggression has been (a) reduced imports; (b) diversion of budgetary resources to defense; and (c) reassignment of supply quotas.

The scarcity of foreign exchange has reduced the average basic per capita consumption (that is, food, clothing, etc.) in 1984 by 20% relative to 1982 owing to the stagnation of industrial production for lack of imported inputs, the difficulties of importing food to replace that which could not be supplied by the countryside, and the resources assigned to defense.[10]

As we have seen, this restriction of supply, combined with the monetary expansion caused in large part by the defense budget, produced a sharp rise in the rate of inflation. The real wage level fell by up to 50% between 1982 and 1984.[11]

The scarcity of foreign exchange for spare parts and essential inputs affected especially health and public transportation in the Pacific Coast area. At certain times in 1984, half of the operating rooms and buses were out of service for this reason. The scarcity of hard foreign currency derived from exports and available for purchases in the open world market (which is not compensated for by lines of credit, because these are tied to specific products) is particularly critical in this context.

The increase of the military budget at a cost to the civilian budget (which is primarily dedicated to health, education, productive investment, and consumption subsidies) has meant a quantitative halt in the expansion of, and to a certain point, qualitative deterioration in, these services. Although improved services only became available between 1979 and 1982, their loss is still serious for this population. Educational standards have also been seriously affected by the mobilization of students from high schools and universities for defense purposes and to replace drafted farm workers.

The supply of basic consumer goods has been seriously affected in the Pacific Coast area owing to the war. The loss of corn and beans was 15% of the total production in 1984, but this was equivalent to 30% of the flow to the cities once deductions for normal storage losses and producers' consumption are taken into account. Likewise, industrial production in 1984 was 10% lower than what it would have been without the decline of exports. It has been necessary to reassign marketed civilian consumption quotas away from the Pacific Zone toward the war zones to provide for the civilian population displaced or affected by the war. For example, the proportion of powdered milk assigned to Region III (Managua) was 60% in 1983; this was reduced to

10. Secretaría de Planificación y Presupuesto, *Programa económico 1985* (Managua, 1985).
11. ECLA, *Informe economico.*

40% in 1984.[12] Second, the mass mobilization of the infantry for defense drained off the same consumer goods (food, soap, clothing, etc.) that the civilian population required. In fact, provisioning the armed forces involves 45% of the manufacturing capacity of the shoe industry and 24% of the production capacity of the textile and clothing sectors. On average, this is equivalent to 10% of industrial production. Concerning basic food needs (sugar, rice, maize, beans, cooking oil, soap, and salt), the defense forces require approximately 10% of national consumption. All of this is deducted, logically, from the quota of the Pacific cities because the supply of goods for the rural area has priority.

The economic program for 1985[13] attempts to order this forced austerity within the new model of the "defense economy." The war zones were given priority in the provision of social services, infrastructure, and supply; the Pacific became a "rear-guard economy." This means that while the war continues, no new schools (except those in the resettlement communities) or hospitals will be constructed. There will be no new housing construction, paving of roads, or expansion of water and electricity services in the Pacific area. It has been necessary to discontinue the basic consumer subsidies, give priority to production workers for supplies in a commisary system, and place strict control on private commerce in order to fight inflation and defend the real wage. The consequence is that the cost of the war will fall, above all, on the informal urban sector.

THE EFFECT OF THE AGGRESSION ON THE FUTURE DEVELOPMENT OF NICARAGUA

It is extremely difficult to evaluate the effect of the war on the development of Nicaragua because this requires an estimation of what would have happened in its absence to investment, production growth, the transformation of economic organization, the formation of human resources, and international economic relations, among other things.

The development strategy of the Sandinista government is born of an appreciation of the roots of poverty and dependency in Nicaragua. The strategy was based on a transformation of the agricultural and natural resource sectors as centers of accumulation in order to insure a better standard of living (food security) and sufficient foreign exchange for the accumulation process (agroexports). This was to be achieved within the principles of a

12. MICOIN, *ABC del Abastecimiento* (Managua: Ministerio de Comercio Interior, 1984).
13. Ministerio de Planificación, *Programa de reactivacion*.

mixed economy and nonalignment by strengthening the state and cooperative sectors internally and obtaining balanced economic relations with the
different world trade blocs externally. As is evident, this development project
has been blocked materially by the war, yet its organizational principles have
not been abandoned.

The production losses, as we have seen, have a dramatic effect on the
scarcity of foreign exchange and thus the current performance of the economy. Furthermore, without U.S. pressure on long-term financing, it would
have been possible to dedicate more resources to current production, permitting much higher national production levels. The estimates presented before
imply that production would have grown over 6% per year between 1980 and
1984 rather than the average 2% achieved (see Table 8). However, this does
not take into account the positive effect that the postponed investments would
have had.

The last report of the World Bank before it suspended new loans to
Nicaragua reflected an encouraging perspective about the Nicaraguan
economy.[14] It recommended actions to overcome certain problems (like the
stabilization of the agrarian reform, the reduction of the budgetary deficit,
and profitability guarantees for producers), which were, in fact, implemented. It is reasonable, therefore, to cite the projection of the World Bank as
a balanced evaluation of what would have been the economic development
of Nicaragua without external aggression. As Table 8 indicates, production
between 1980 and 1985 was expected to increase by 39%, as compared with
the actual experience of 9%.

TABLE 8
Economic Expansion with and without the War (Billions of córdobas at 1980 prices)

	GDP							GROWTH RATE	
	1977	1980	1981	1982	1983	1984	1985	(1985/1980)	ANNUAL
Actual[a]	29.31	21.89	23.05	22.78	23.84	23.51	23.94	9.4	1.9
Without aggression and with normal foreign co-operation[b]	29.31	21.90	25.46	26.04	27.08	28.01	29.00	32.4	6.5
World Bank pro-jection[c]	27.92	21.34	23.26	24.88	26.37	27.98	29.65	38.9	7.8

Sources: (a) Secretariat of Planning and the Budget, *Programa económico 1985*; (b) calculations by the Secretariat of Planning and the Budget, Nicaragua (discussed in text; and, (c) IBRD, *Nicaragua: The Challenge of Reconstruction* (Washington, IBRD. 1981).

14. IBRD, *Nicaragua, The Challenge.*

Likewise, the World Bank report indicates that in 1984 the exports of goods should have risen to $1.1 billion, instead of the $382 million actually obtained.[15] Furthermore, it anticipated a net flow of $424 million between 1980 and 1984 on the part of multilateral lenders. In fact, Nicaragua received a *gross* disbursement of only $336 million. On the other hand, it paid $234 million between 1980 and 1984 for interest and principle on the debt Somoza contracted with these institutions. The net inflow, therefore, has been only $102 million.

The projects blocked in the World Bank itself and the Inter-American Development Bank (IDB) are precisely those that the World Bank had identified as essential for the stable development of the Nicaraguan economy, especially the agricultural production and social infrastructure. It is ironic that the major beneficiaries of these funds would have been the private sector, both the large producers (in the industrial rehabilitation project of the IDB, for example) and the small producers (in the World Bank livestock project, for example). All these projects were approved by the technical experts of these institutions as essential for development: Presumably they were blocked by the current U.S. administration for precisely this reason.

The United States has excluded Nicaragua as a trading partner, in disregard of its treaty obligations[16] and is using indirect pressure to isolate Nicaragua from its markets in Central America and elsewhere in Latin America. This is done with the objective of isolating Nicaragua politically and weakening her economically. It has produced a shifting of trade partners toward trans-Atlantic exchange, implying very high transportation costs and unbalanced relations with the socialist camp. Ironically, the latter would later be used to justify increased aggression, as was done in Cuba.

The consequences of economic isolation in the hemisphere for the future development of Nicaragua are very serious. First, the costs of trade would be much higher and likewise the difficulties of adapting the productive structure to other technologies. Second, Nicaraguan industrial development depends upon its integration into Central America, which is the only area that can provide a protected market of sufficient size.

The actions of the current U.S. administration undermine the same economic pluralism that underlies the Nicaraguan development model. The agrarian reform has distributed almost one-third of Nicaragua's productive land to peasants, individually or in cooperatives, without greatly affecting the

15. It is true that the IBRD did not anticipate the sharp deterioration in the terms of trade between 1981 and 1984 (see ECLA, *Informe económico*), but this would not explain more than a decline of 10% in export receipts.
16. Culminating in the trade embargo in 1985, which falls outside the chronological scope of this study. See, however, the chapter by Conroy in this volume.

productive private farms. Nonetheless, the counterrevolutionary violence in 1983 was unleashed on these cooperatives and in 1984 on the private estates.

Small industry and crafts that form large sectors in the cities and the vast majority of which have been grouped into service cooperatives have been hard hit by the scarcity of foreign exchange and the absence of imported inputs from Central America—both results of the war.

The development projects for the Atlantic Coast provide the material foundation for its eventual national autonomy within the Republic of Nicaragua. The destruction of these projects by the counterrevolutionaries not only deprives these people of health care, housing, and transportation but also impedes the development of their own ethnic society.

Perhaps the most serious impact of the war for the future development of Nicaragua is the impact on human resources. First, the flight of the population toward the cities and the military mobilization of up to one in every five young adult males has a serious impact on the agricultural production that is the center of development in Nicaragua. This affects production not only in the short run but also in the future because it will be difficult to reintegrate those workers into agricultural production. Second, a large number of professionals and technicians have emigrated, whether out of fear for their personal safety and that of their families in times of war or to avoid having their sons drafted into the army. This, combined with the necessity of mobilizing the remaining professionals, has seriously affected and will continue to affect industrial production, health care, energy, and other technical sectors. Third, a whole generation of young people are not completing secondary education or entering the university because they are being mobilized for defense. This affects up to half of the young male students between the ages of 17 and 25. Although to a certain degree they are replaced by women the future impact on technical and professional resources is highly troubling.

The final study that the World Bank did before it ended support projected a surmounting of current problems in the balance of payments and the achievement of stable growth for 1990, with the GDP 86% higher than in 1980. In contrast, the current tendency indicates a level only 15% higher (see Table 9) and, therefore, a notable deterioration in the per capita income. The forecast of a per capita income much lower than anticipated implies a radical redistribution of the income between the different social strata in order to guarantee the basic necessities to all the population, which logically implies a change in the existing social formation.

CONCLUSION

It is difficult to come to definite conclusions about the effect of a war that is not yet over and the consequences of which will be felt for decades even if the

TABLE 9
Outlook for Economic Growth

GDP	BILLIONS OF CÓRDOBAS AT 1980 PRICES			ANNUAL GROWTH	
	1980	1985	1990	1980–1985	1985–1990
Actual tendency[a]	21.89	23.94	25.16	1.9	1.0%
Original tendency[b]	21.34	29.65	39.66	7.8	6.8%

[a]Actual experience 1980–1985; the 1982–1985 trend (1% per year) extended from 1985 to 1990, assuming that external conditions continue unchanged.

[b]IBRD, *Nicaragua: The Challenge of Reconstruction* (Washington: IBRD, 1981).

efforts of the Contradora Group are successful. Moreover, the methodology used is relatively crude,[17] reflecting the difficulty of data collection and model building in this sort of situation. What is clear, however, is that the impact of the U.S. aggression on the external balances of a small economy that normally exports one-half of its material production has been sufficient to push development back to little more than a subsistence level. Extensive foreign aid, much of it a political reaction to U.S. policy, is a condition for survival.

Forecasting the future of the Nicaraguan economy, depending as it does upon the outcome of this war of attrition, is even more difficult and probably not even a meaningful exercise. Survival is itself a definition of sovereignty.

APPENDIX: DAMAGE TO THE ECONOMY IN 1985

Since this chapter was originally written (April 1985), U.S. aggression has continued, leading to heavy economic losses in 1985 as well. This was exacerbated by the imposition of a trade embargo in May 1985 and the continued blocking of development credit at the board level in the IBRD and IDB. In this Appendix, data for 1985 are presented based on the same methodology as for previous years; the original tables have not been revised in order to preserve the integrity of the original study. The source for all data is the Economic Advisory Service (Asesoría Económica), Ministry of the Presidency, Nicaragua.

As the first table indicates, the direct production losses in 1985 were considerably less than those in 1984, declining by about one-third to U.S.

17. The construction of a more complex partial-equilibrium model for the Nicaraguan economy (carried out by the government with support from the FAO and the technical asistance of Bill Gibson) based on a complete social accounting matrix and behavioral specification of the variables, is currently under way.

$107 million. This was due to the fact that there was considerable progress in defense during 1985: The Sandinista army had managed to push the counter-revolutionary forces of the Fuerzas Democráticas Nicaragüenses (FDN) back toward the northern frontier; the counterrevolutionary forces of Eden Pastora had disintegrated; peasant families had been relocated away from the frontier; and militia defense of rural production centers had been better organized.

A further result of this successful military campaign was to reduce the number of civilian deaths (from 289 in 1984 to 280 in 1985) and wounded (from 339 to 216). Counterrevolutionary losses, however, rose sharply from 3017 to 4334, whereas those of the Sandinista armed forces were stable at 1018 in 1985 compared to 1017 in 1984. The total deaths of Nicaraguans of all three categories between 1980 and 1985 was 13,443; about 0.4% of the population—a similar proportion to U.S. losses in World War II.

Production Losses in 1985 (Millions of U.S. Dollars)	
Agricultural production	
Coffee	18.2
Tobacco	4.5
Basic grains	5.6
Livestock	1.1
Others	0.3
	29.7
Nonagricultural production	
Forestry	41.5
Fishing	15.2
Construction	16.4
Mining	4.4
	77.5
Total production losses	**107.2**

Damages to property were also reduced in 1985 relative to 1984, due to the improved circular defense of villages, state farms, and cooperatives, and 1984 was itself a considerable improvement on 1983, as we have already noted. This, in a somewhat macabre way, indicates the military ineffectiveness of the counterrevolutionary forces.

Material Damage 1985 (Millions of U.S. Dollars)	
Inventories destroyed	1.2
Plant and buildings destroyed	19.3
	20.5
Production Losses	107.2
Total material damage	**127.7**

The "financial agression" in the form of blocked loan applications (see Table 4) continued in 1985; undisbursed credits that had been approved at a technical level and programmed for 1985 totaled U.S. $73.0 million.

The effect of the U.S. trade embargo in 1985 is difficult to gauge. The loss of export income due to shifting to new markets with higher transport costs is quantifiable, but the impact of shortages of spare parts, agrochemicals, and the like is much more difficult to assess. A preliminary estimate by the Ministry of Foreign Trade is of a loss of U.S. $50 million in 1985 based on the immediate differences in export (f.o.b.) and import (c.i.f.) prices.

If all these three categories are summed, the total foreign exchange loss for 1985 is U.S. $374 million, bringing the aggregate loss for 1980–85 to U.S. $1.23 billion. Compared to exports during the period, it is equivalent to roughly one-half of total foreign exchange income actually received.

PART IV

THE ECONOMIC OUTLOOK
FOR THE REVOLUTION

Chapter 10

The New Economic Policy: A Necessary Readjustment

ROBERTO PIZARRO

From an abstract or superficial point of view, it might seem surprising that a revolutionary government, committed to serving the interests of the national majority, has decided to adopt a package of rather restrictive economic adjustment measures that includes an exchange devaluation, the elimination of subsidies for basic consumer products, the reduction and rationalization of state investments, and a freeze on government spending. Although the new measures, announced on February 8, 1985, try to neutralize the negative effects of the devaluation and the spending curb with a readjustment of wages and a price policy that allows a reasonable profit, understandable doubts about the economic package exist. The task of explaining this decision, in which the government itself has taken the initiative, is critical in order to allow for the development of a national commitment to the restructuring of the country's economy.

This package was adopted after the external aggression intensified and became visible on the military, diplomatic, commercial, and financial fronts. The depth of the distortions of the economic system and the magnitude of the external and internal impact of the aggression have been evident since 1983—that is, from the beginning of the Reagan administration's overt war and its massive and open support for the counterrevolution. It is probable that the adoption of a readjustment package in 1981, when some of the recent problems were just appearing, would have partly relieved the economic tensions that have accumulated. However, the onerous Somoza legacy and the material destruction during the war of liberation sharply limited reconstruction and hindered the efforts to transform the economy. Later on, the need to concentrate resources on sustaining the revolution, most notably in

217

the realms of military defense and the electoral process, delayed the decision to provide a fundamental response to the country's economic problems.

The objectives of the new economic policy—to guarantee the country's defense, stimulate material production, and neutralize distortions in the economic system related to prices, salaries, the black market, shortages, contraband, and so on—can scarcely be questioned, given the present situation. The adoption of measures to meet these objectives could not be postponed. The urgencies of the war, the need to regain control over a mixed economy that was becoming less and less productive, and to achieve better relations with private producers are the fundamental issues that the package was designed to address. Nevertheless, the very character of these measures requires a realistic probing of the country's situation and an awareness of the structure of the economy in order to answer questions about possible alternative measures.

Every country undergoing profound transformation experiences economic upheavals. The "problems of the transition" are present in every society that tries to modify the logic of reproduction of a system based on the interests of a minority so that it favors the socioeconomic interests of the majority. The rebuilding of the state and the multiplication of its tasks, the flight of technicians, the difficulties of taking on entrepreneurial roles, the decreased productivity that accompanies the eradication of the dictatorship of capital, the uncertainty of the private sector as it confronts the new logic of economic and social life, and the decapitalization by those who apply the criterion of "every man for himself" are some of the most outstanding problems in every concrete process of transformation. And these problems have been quite obvious in the case of Nicaragua.

But they have been amplified there for other reasons, including the legacy of a country plundered by a long dictatorship and whose material base was affected by the war of liberation; the establishment of a new government when the sharpest world depression since the 1930s was just beginning; and the systematic aggression directed and financed by the United States. It is within the context of this complex set of problems that the state has intervened via economic policies and direct forms of control. Such intervention, however, has its own responsibilities.

The limitations of state policy, imperialism, and the unjust system of North-South relations have converged in a situation in which the distortions of the economic system have reached unbearable levels. Salaries lose purchasing power while inflation advances at a dizzying rate. The price of black-market dollars rises weekly while that of the official dollar remains fixed and the scarcity of exchange becomes a matter of daily commentary. The development of the informal sector of the economy reaches hitherto unheard-of levels, where the salary of a street vendor is higher than that of a government minister. These distortions have badly hurt the popular sectors, especially wage earners. They have withdrawn human and material resources from production due to the search for easier and greater profits in commerce and the informal sector. Ultimately, they have affected the very security of the country because the Contras and the forces of imperialism, taking advantage of these distortions, can more easily carry out their policy of destabilization.

The new package of economic measures, then, is a response to an extremely difficult situation. Nevertheless, one could argue that a more appropriate approach to resolving these distortions, striking back at those taking advantage of them and advancing the transformation of the country, would have been a policy of "radicalization," meaning a program of massive expropriation of land, industry, and commerce, placing all material economic resources in the hands of the state. This alternative, possible in the abstract and actually adopted in other societies, would be naive and irresponsible in the case of Nicaragua not only for reasons of internal politics and regional geopolitics but also because its economic results would be doubtful in a country structurally oriented toward land and cattle wealth and whose agricultural, industrial, and commercial properties are highly atomized.

The vast array of small and medium-sized agricultural producers, a significant level of artisan production in the industrial sector, the dispersion of commerce, along with the limited development of productive forces, objectively slow down nationalization. A proposal for "radicalization" involving large-scale expropriations and the establishment of a system of centralized planning would not only carry incalculable political and social costs; the economic benefits would also be uncertain, considering the country's technical backwardness, the limited training of the work force, and the atomization of economic units.

Furthermore, research during the years of the revolution has led to the rather surprising discovery that the economic power of Somoza and the big bourgeoisie was rooted only partly in the control of property and was exercised largely through control of the banking system and as intermediaries in foreign trade.[1] Thus the nationalization of the banking system and foreign trade in Nicaragua was an effective blow to the dominant interests, and it has given the revolutionary state powerful instruments for orienting the economy toward benefiting the popular sectors.

Recognizing the special character of Nicaragua's economic structure and

1. Regarding the exaggerated estimation of the scale of Somoza and the large bourgeoisie's property interests, see Eduardo Baumeister and Oscar Neira, "Economía y política en las relaciones entre el estado y el sector privado en el proceso nicaragüense," Paper presented at the seminar Los problemas de la transición en pequeñas economías periféricas, Managua, September 3–8, 1984.

the depth of the recent distortions makes it possible to understand the need for the government's package. Within the package is the implicit understanding that the price system plays an important role in economic behavior and that its normalization is fundamental to recovering control of the mixed economy and getting back on a productive path while halting speculative tendencies. Naturally, the vigilance of the state, backed up by the strength of its popular legitimacy and with the basic levers of control at hand, is needed to orient the price system in a way that benefits the majority.

THE ROLE OF ECONOMIC POLICY

The wide trade gap and high debt service obligations, along with the fiscal deficit and the excessive issues of paper money by the Central Bank, originate in a complex and varied cluster of external and internal factors, some of which are structural and some of which are more transitory.[2] They include the Somoza legacy, the destruction caused by the war of liberation, the international economic crisis, and the aggression of the United States.

Nevertheless, it would be wrong to blame all the economic difficulties on factors outside the control of the revolutionary government. The Somoza legacy, U.S. aggression, and the exploitative character of North-South relations are pieces on the game board, part of the "environment" of the revolution that has to be confronted and transformed by the appropriate strategy. The interests displaced by every revolution use varied mechanisms to recover their lost power, and imperialism is their strongest ally in that struggle. That has been the case in the past with imperialism's policy of destabilization elsewhere in the world. Today, Nicaragua is its target. Thus in the field of economic policy and the efforts to transform the state, Nicaragua has had to confront a hard reality. This is further complicated by the common desire of every country undergoing such a transformation to meet the urgent social and economic needs of its people. The Sandinista government's decision to satisfy them has collided with growing limitations in external and internal resources, thus making an economic readjustment indispensable.

The new Nicaraguan government's first 2 years were marked by the optimism of economic revitalization and national reconstruction. External resources were abundant at first, and the recovery of installed capacity for productive purposes sparked rapid growth. Nevertheless, by the middle of 1981, signs of grave problems began to appear; they became more and more

2. For a discussion of these issues, see Comandante Jaime Wheelock's speech of February 13, 1985 in *Barricada* of February 14.

pronounced. The fall in the GDP growth rate in the beginning of 1982, the difficulties in expanding production for export, the scarcity of foreign exchange, and the debt, inflation, and supply bottlenecks began to sound the keynote of the strains afflicting the economy. The effect on the country's macroeconomic equilibrium, involving internal and external factors, has been notable.

Foreign Exchange Policy

The scarcity of exchange, the most important restriction on agricultural, ranching, and industrial activity, began to appear in 1981. The need to raise foreign exchange through an aggressive policy of export production and the concomitant need to effect savings by adopting a policy of import rationalization were not met. Instead, the government deliberately overvalued the córdoba, thus contributing to a widening gap between its official value and its black-market value (see Table 1).

Criteria for ranking import requirements based on need were defined and implemented in 1981. High-level interministerial channels were set up to handle decisions on the assignment of foreign currency by economic sector. But a corresponding effort on the export-supply side was not forthcoming. Furthermore, exchange policy became an insuperable obstacle to increasing exports, just as it became a permanent stimulus to the demand for imports.

The maintainance of the overvalued córdoba in relation to the dollar inhibited export production, kept up the pressure for foreign exchange, and stimulated a contraband trade in goods for export and in products imported at the official rate of exchange. Simultaneously, this overvaluation and the difference between the rate of exchange for exports and that for imports resulted in financial losses for the Central Bank that were covered with more paper-money issues. Furthermore, one must not forget that a mixed economy itself puts permanent pressure on the dollar: The strong private sector, with considerable demand potential for códobas and with a pattern of luxury consumption, demands dollars that the government cannot provide. Moreover, the year-by-year growth in the differences between internal prices and those of bordering countries, like the difference between the official price of the dollar and its black-market price, was in a way indicative of the artificial character of the córdoba's overvaluation. Thus the rate of exchange stopped being an effective measure of the relation between internal and external prices, just as it lost meaning as an indication of the real scarcity of exchange.

In reality, neither the generous credit policy (with negative interest rates and 100% financing) nor the low price (owing to the exchange rate) for imported supplies was able to arrest the decline in profits from production for export that originated in the overvaluation. Setting guaranteed prices for

TABLE 1
Evolution of Exchange Rates (in córdobas per dollar)

YEAR	OFFICIAL MARKET	BLACK MARKET[d]
1980	10	21
1981	10	28
1982	10[a]	45
1983	10	78
1984	10[b]	212
Jan. 1985	10	480
April 1985[c]	28	700

[a]In February 1982, a 5-córdoba tax was established on every dollar sold for the purchase of imports considered nonessential. Thus the price of foreign exchange to import nonessential goods rose to 15:1. On the same date, Certificates of Exchange Availability (Certificados de Disponibilidad de Divisas, or CDDs) were established to stimulate exports. Theoretically, CDDs could be used in the following way: In the case of traditional export products, which were assigned a guaranteed price and marketed by state monopolies, a part of the exported value was liquidated at the official rate of 10:1, whereas the rest was paid at the rate of 28:1. The latter portion was delivered in the form of the CDD, which could be used to import products directly without going through official channels or could be negotiated at the Sistema Financiero Nacional. In reality, in a situation of exchange scarcity, the most important stimulant was the chance for producers to import some products without having to resort to the official procedure for obtaining foreign exchange. Nevertheless, this was only partially implemented, and in fact the CDD only served as an instrument to raise the implicit rate of exchange for exports. Thus a system of multiple exchanges rates for different products (28:1 and 10:1) was introduced that varied over time according to the guaranteed prices that continued in effect for traditional export products.

In the case of nontraditional agricultural products, 70% of earnings were exchanged at the 10:1 rate and 30% at 28:1. For manufactures, the percentages were 60% at 10:1 and 40% at 28:1. So in nontraditional agricultural products and in manufactures, the exchange rates were 15.4 and 17.2, respectively, whereas in the traditional ones, it varied in accord with changes in the guaranteed prices.

[b]In November 1984, the tax on the sale of dollars for nonessential imports was raised to 10 córdobas, making the real rate of exchange for these imports 20:1.

[c]In March 1985, the following devaluation was implemented: The exchange rate for earings on exports was fixed at 28:1; exchange resulting from donations was fixed at 50:1. In the sale of exchange, the following rates were in effect: imports and essential consumption goods—20:1; imports of nonessential consumption goods—28:1; imports of raw material and spare parts—20:1; imports of petroleum and its derivatives—28:1; and capital goods—40:1. In April 1985, "casas de cambio" for private-sector buyers and sellers of foreign exchange were opened to allow private buying and selling in accord with supply and demand at the parallel rate, at that time about 600:1.

[d]Based on information from the Banco de Datos INIES-CRIES, with original data systematized by Carlos Vilas.

producers as a compensatory mechanism was not enough to stimulate production for export, either because those prices did not adequately reflect costs and profitability or because they permitted only the most efficient producers to profit or simply because the prices were not announced in a timely way. The decision to issue Certificates of Exchange Availability in February 1982 in order to stimulate exports was never effective because the government did not have enough foreign currency to assign to producers (see Table 1, Note a).

Contraband grew in both nontraditional products and in some traditional ones, given the enormous differences between internal prices and those of bordering countries. In the case of nontraditional products, the petty trade of hawkers and peddlers (*buhoneros*) increased, undermining the state's efforts to regulate internal commerce. Operating virtually by barter, such petty traders overcame the differences between internal and external prices by selling directly in the open markets of neighboring countries and then buying products to be resold in Nicaragua at prices based on the black-market dollar rate.

On the other hand, the low price of imports at the official rate of exchange reduced any interest in substituting these imports with internally produced goods. These cheap imports even added to the pressure to buy new equipment instead of repairing the existing stock. Thus the government faced escalating demands for imported supplies from both state agencies and the private sector. In addition, the artificially lowered prices of imported spare parts and productive inputs did more to encourage contraband trade at the border than to advance production, and a similar process occurred with respect to imported medicine and basic consumer goods. Consequently, the low price of these imports, instead of increasing production and protecting workers' income levels, had a contradictory effect. It enriched a class of speculators who, taking advantage of the difference between domestic and foreign prices, made extraordinary profits by dealing in contraband.

Wages, Prices, and Subsidies

The Sandinistas' wage-containment policy, which had the laudable purpose of reducing inflationary pressures, nevertheless had counterproductive results. As a form of compensation to guarantee the real incomes of workers, the government generously subsidized basic grains, milk, sugar, drinking water, transportation, and "people stores" (*tiendas populares*). This policy added heavily to government spending in 1983 and 1984.

The government subsidy to some basic consumer goods meant low prices to the consumer, but the common consumer was not always the one who benefited. On the one hand, difficulties encountered by the state in exercising rigorous control over the marketplace allowed unscrupulous merchants to speculate in consumer goods through monopolization and arbitrary price increases that far exceeded the levels fixed by the government. On the other hand, agricultural producers, affected by considerable price increases for manufactured goods, sought compensation by selling subsidized products through parallel channels and making profits beyond those allowed through regulated channels. Moreover, price increases of basic, unsubsidized goods and especially of manufactured ones generated an inflationary and speculative spiral; the basic problem was limited production in a period of growing demand by those sectors (clearly not wage workers) who had acquired more cash.

The wage-containment policy encouraged migration from the countryside to the city. Incoming migrants became concentrated in diverse informal activities, any one of which was more lucrative than agricultural wage work. These higher incomes and the social services offered in the cities, particularly in Managua, have seriously aggravated the scarcity of workers for the harvests. One must recognize that agrarian reform and the human demands of the war have limited the availability of labor for productive activities. But low wages are clearly another disincentive for going into agricultural work, when alternatives exist in buying and selling, in performing services, and in other fields that pay more for what is probably less physically demanding work.

Investment Growth

Investments play an important role in any development strategy. They establish the bases for the future of a society by improving the material and human resources for the years to come. In revolutionary Nicaragua, investment is fundamentally a state responsibility. The state has taken massive investment initiatives, which in the 1980—1984 period meant a growth rate of more than 20% in gross domestic product, considerably higher than the Central American average.[3] Varied investment projects testify to the magnitude and diversity of the effort. Broad-scope projects include the sugar complex of Tipitapa-Malacatoya and the milk-production facility at Chiltepe; infrastructural ones include the Momotombo volcanic energy project and the Pacific-Atlantic railroad, and numerous investments have been made in health, education, housing, and even tourism. All of these efforts reflect the dynamic all inclusiveness of investment policy, in spite of the country's scarce resources.

Nevertheless, the multiplication of investment projects in different production and social-economic sectors has meant an excessively heavy burden on the treasury. Investment expenses have grown considerably, competing for resources aimed at maintaining production.

The Development of a Parasitic Economy

The black market in dollars, speculative trade, the expansion of the informal sector, country-city migration, contraband, and other distortions are manifestations of a parasitic or informal economy that strikes at the formal economy, with consequences that affect even the national security of Nicaragua.

---

3. See CEPAL, "Centroamérica: Bases de una política de reactivación y desarrollo" (México: CEPAL, marzo 1985) 30.

The government's efforts to increase production in the last 5 years have been hindered by the workings of this parasitic economy. Low interest rates and high levels of financing for agricultural and cattle production, along with low prices for imported productive inputs, have been unsuccessful as stimulants to producers when confronted with guaranteed prices that are unprofitable or whose profitability is substantially inferior to those offered by parallel activities. At the same time, governmental subsidies have been unable to protect workers' real incomes, precisely because this parasitic economy impedes the delivery of subsidized products into the hands of the workers.[4]

Meanwhile, middle-man and service activities have grown, giving rise to strong demand pressures. These pressures are derived from the purchasing power of a parasitic caste that has absorbed much of the expanded supply of money issued by the Central Bank. At the same time, the supply of goods for export and internal consumption has slackened, generating a scarcity of goods and foreign currency.

In the middle of such difficulties, imperialism's policy of destabilization finds fertile ground for its operations. Scarcities and the high price of the black-market dollar make it easier for the U.S. Central Intelligence Agency to finance its operations and for the Contras to foment discontent. Simultaneously, the lack of foreign exchange and the difficulty of raising it through exports under conditions of persistent military aggression not only make it harder to get goods needed for production but also reduce the government's ability to acquire resources needed for national defense.

THE NEW ECONOMIC POLICY

The main purpose of the package of economic measures announced on February 8, 1985, was to reverse the tendencies that had been taking shape and, in the medium term, to close the gap in the external and internal fronts of the economy. For the first time since the announcement of the 1980 economic plan, a complete package of measures embracing the entire economy was being proposed. The objectives as set out by the President of Nicaragua and the principal economic authorities of the country were as follows: to protect and stimulate material production, to neutralize distortions, and to

---

4. Carlos Vilas estimates that more than one-fourth of the official gross domestic product may have circulated through parallel (i.e., informal) channels in 1983 and 1984. Vilas points out that the difference between real salaries in the productive sector and in the informal urban sector has stimulated a transfer of labor toward the latter and resulted in the absolute reduction of the urban proletariat. About 30,000 workers went into self-employment and intermediary forms of work in 1982. C. Vilas, "Nicaragua año cinco: Transformación y tensiones en la economía," CIDCA, Managua, February, 1985, mimeo.

advance the military defense of Nicaragua. In the very presentation of these objectives, what stands out is the tight link between the economy and national defense. Let us examine the specific measures proposed for the completion of these objectives.

Production

Protecting and stimulating material production is to be carried out through an increase in the efficiency of state enterprises.[5] Resources are to be assigned in a way that strictly respects the priorities of production. Adjustments and stimulants induced by changes in prices, wages, and the rate of exchange are all part of the policy. Foreign exchange, external credits, and internal spending are to be allocated based on the following priorities: (a) the production of goods required for national defense; (b) basic general consumption and medical supplies; (c) export products; and finally (d) the basic infrastructure needed to support these priorities. Although these priorities also existed in the previous 2 years, they have now been made more explicit. The emphasis is on rigorously respecting them in order to give the necessary coherence to the new economic policy.

In addition, new producer prices and wage increases indicate the government's commitment to concentrating capital, labor, and entrepreneurial efforts in the production sector. It has been recognized that producer prices were too low to stimulate the expansion of production. Price adjustments have therefore been proposed that correspond to cost increases; they are to be made effective in a way that will trigger greater production. As for wages, the loss of real purchasing power is evident, and the increasing shift of labor from production toward the informal sector clearly reflects this fact.

The decision to direct external and internal resources fundamentally toward production will be reflected in diminished spending on health, education, and housing. In such social services, better organization and efficiency will be mandatory so that without increases in spending, the necessities of the poorest people can be attended to. Nevertheless, it will have to be understood that the demands of the war and production will require that priority be given to housing in rural areas.

The Fiscal Measures

The package's fiscal measures have the double purpose of neutralizing the distortions originating in the deficit and rationalizing spending. The measures

5. In a speech before more than 400 directors of state agricultural, livestock, and industrial enterprises, Minister of Agriculture Jaime Wheelock emphasized the government's desire and the country's urgent need for increases in productivity and efficiency. See *Barricada*, March 8, 1985.

propose curbs on spending in various areas and the adoption of new methods for raising revenue.

The spending reductions are mainly in the following areas:

1. The elimination of subsidies to basic consumer products and the reduction of subsidies to some public services. The policy of subsidies is therefore replaced, and one that favors money as a means of payment is stressed.
2. The freezing of hirings in the central administration of the state and cutting the number of positions by revising the programs that each institution is responsible for. This is intended to encourage technicians and professionals to orient themselves toward those productive enterprises given priority by the new economic policy.
3. A reduction, in real terms, of budgeted operational spending by state institutions.
4. A brake on indiscriminate investment spending and a coordination of investment policy. The investment program will concentrate on projects that generate goods and services in the short term and on medium-term projects that will soon be completed. In the first category are increases in the areas to be sown with burley tobacco, rice and basic grains, and in fishing. In the second are expansion of milk, cacao, coconut, sugar and vegetable production, and an increase in hydro-electric power production.

With respect to state revenues, the creation of new taxes, the devaluation, and the expansion of the tax base by including new taxpayers are among some of the most important additional sources of income. In particular, the Law of Presumed Profits (La Ley de Rentas Presuntivas), which affects profits obtained in intermediary operations, irregular trade, certain services, small businesses, and the self-employed professions is especially noteworthy. This law's purpose is to deal with the hefty profits of these kinds of activities, especially those concentrated in the informal sector of the economy, where a small export-import merchant or peddler can earn hundreds of thousands of córdobas in a single operation. (This contrasts with the earnings of a skilled director of a government program who, in 1985, would have made only 26,000 córdobas a month.) In each of these activities, an estimate of the profits will be made; this will be used to calculate the corresponding tax.

The New Foreign-Exchange Policy

The new rates of exchange are designed to deal with the complex of anomalies originating in the overvaluation of the córdoba. Clearly, the level of devaluation will be unable to immediately resolve the differences between foreign and domestic prices or between the official dollar and the black-market dollar. The fixing of the dollar for 5 years, at a price that did not correspond to the increases in internal prices, now impedes an adjustment in the parity levels because of the great impact that would have on the whole economic system. Nevertheless, the devaluation will tend to favor the restabilization of some economic relations, helping to reduce the pressure on imports and decrease the financial loss that the Central Bank suffered because of the overvaluation.

A single rate of exchange of 28:1 has been established for exports (although the point of reference for traditional agricultural and livestock exports will continue to be the system of guaranteed prices). Judgments about the possible effects of the new policy in terms of profitability and expansion of production in export activities will depend on the future increases in guaranteed prices. On the other hand, among nontraditional agricultural products and in manufacturing, the new exchange rate is insufficient as an instrument of stimulation; a system of additional incentives will be needed to make them competitive internationally.

Different rates of exchange have been established for imports, depending on the nature of the goods (see Table 1 Note C). Essential consumption goods, raw materials, and spare parts are purchased at 20:1, petroleum at 28:1, and capital goods at 40:1. This system of differential exchange rates, which in percentage terms represents a sharp devaluation, continues to favor those products necessary for production as well as basic consumer goods. There is no doubt that the wage and price policy will have to be alert to the effects of the devaluation on producers' costs and on the real income of workers and to make adequate compensatory adjustments.

Finally, the package includes the reopening of the private money-exchange business (*casas de cambio*), whose purpose is to allow the free buying and selling of foreign currency at prices determined by supply and demand in the parallel market.

Wages and Prices

The elimination of subsidies and the devaluation, although they seek to reestablish the logic of certain economic parameters, in the short term will generate inflationary pressures as the prices of basic products and imported supplies increase.[6] This is why compensatory measures have also been adopted. With respect to wages, readjustments have been implemented, and

6. It is necessary to keep in mind that consumers were not always paying the prices set by the subsidy or the official exchange rate. Scarcity and speculation pushed the price much higher than the official one. See Peter Utting's chapter in this collection.

the system of direct distribution of goods in the workplace will be strengthened to guarantee the purchasing power of wage earners. The readjustment induced by the wage restructuring under the Salary and Labor Norms System (Sistema de Normas de Trabajo y Salarios) has recently been complemented by an increase of close to 100% in agricultural wages. Compensation priorities tend to favor workers in the agricultural sector, the principal source of foreign exchange and of basic consumer products.[7] At the same time, a commissary system directly distributing goods to wage workers at controlled prices has been expanded.

As for producers, the increased prices of imports resulting from the devaluation, the increase in wages, and the reduction in the level of financing will require a very careful determination of new producer prices, taking as a fundamental criterion the need for expansion of production and of exports. When the central contradiction in the economy is the struggle between production and speculation, it is necessary to avoid prejudices or bureaucratic criteria in the fixing of prices and profit rates. The emphasis should be on the production increases and the reestablishment of economic equilibrium. In Nicaragua, the expansion of production and of exports is very much determined by the price policy. With the appropriate policies, every extraordinary profit that can be generated with higher prices for the producer can be converted into new investments in cultivation or into additional state revenue by means of taxation.

REMAINING PROBLEMS

The February package is a serious government effort to respond to Nicaragua's production problems. An indispensable part of this task was the recovery of the policy instruments that are used to direct the mixed economy. Both the space for direct action by the state as a property owner and the economic policy instruments for dealing with the price system are now to be used more fully to establish the bases for the expansion of production. Thus an effort is underway to impress on central state institutions and APP enterprises the need for efficiency and austerity, and incentives are also offered to producers and wage earners to concentrate on high-priority production activities—that is, foreign-exchange earners, mass consumption goods, and articles required for the national defense.

In contrast with the policies of the International Monetary Fund, this

7. The minimum wage in the countryside went from C$42 a day to C$82.20 (a 96% increase), whereas the minimum in the city rose from C$1700 a month to C$3000 (a 76% increase).

economic adjustment is not intended to be deflationary but to expand production. It also allows for wage increases and the direct distribution of goods to workers in order to alleviate the burden of inflation on the productive sectors.

Nevertheless, one must recognize that the economic readjustment is being implemented late, when the accumulated stress is excessive and when extra-economic pressures are extreme. The devaluation, for example, although apparently deep (the exchange rate went from 10:1 to 28:1) is actually modest, if one takes into account the acute discrepancy between internal and external prices. A devaluation that could actually normalize that relationship and stimulate exports would have to be much greater. But the timidity of the last 5 years has made it harder to effect a radical devaluation today because of the inflationary effects that could be unleashed.

In this sense, the adjustment proposed is not an immediate solution to the country's difficult economic situation nor a mechanism to diminish the workers' material sacrifices. In fact, neither scarcities nor inflation can be wiped out overnight. What is fundamental in this case is that the package seeks to close the doors to the parasitic economy and to eliminate the obstacles that have inhibited production. Under such conditions, a full understanding of the meaning of the measures on the part of popular social organizations and their direct intervention in the control and implementation of the measures is the strongest foundation for the success of the new economic policy. Sacrifice today for the sake of future investment becomes an effective instrument when it is clearly understood and accepted by the national majority.

At the same time, that popular participation, which is appropriate to a process of democratization, leads to increased demands whenever shortages become more severe. Furthermore, the new measures and the criteria for the rationalization of resources are not sufficient, by themselves, to drive production forward at the required levels. The trade deficit requires a sharp leap in the volume and value of exports, just as the growing demands of defense and basic consumption cannot be satisfied when production expands at a slow pace. The economic adjustment only establishes the bases for the thrust forward.[8] There are still at least three kinds of problems in the medium term.

8. *Author's Postscript, March 1986*
    After January 1986, the government announced new adjustment measures that continued the economic policy implemented in February 1985 and tried to compensate for the impact of 1985 price increases on the incomes of producers and salaried workers. In effect, salaries were raised 90% in January and then another 50% in March. The exchange rate was modified in February, reducing the value of the córdoba from 28:U.S. $1 to 70:U.S. $1. Nontraditional exports are to be compensated at a preferential rate; 75% of their export value will be liquidated at the 70:U.S. $1 rate, and the remaining 25% will be liquidated at the price of

First, boosting the supply of export and internal-consumption goods requires firm state action in expanding the area in agricultural production that will produce both in the short and medium term as well as in revitalizing the fishing sector and in using installed capacity more intensively in both industry and mining.

Second, a timely determination of producer prices for the agricultural season at hand and for the following ones seems absolutely necessary. As we indicated before, this kind of price-setting, if carried out with an expansionist perspective and in particular with a view toward increasing exports, must provide profits not only to the producers who are historically the most efficient but should include the widest possible range of producers.

Third, and as an indispensable complement to the expansion of both state and private-sector production, more seeds, fertilizer, insecticides, fuel and raw materials for industry, and spare parts are required. In other words, in an economy highly dependent on other countries, additional resources in the forms of technical assistance, productive inputs, and foreign exchange are needed as the basic "fuel" to spark an economy whose production is now rather limited. Because of the attempted strangulation from abroad, Nicaragua's normal foreign trade and external credit activities cannot provide the additional resources for expansion. It is necessary for the international community itself to provide new responses in support of the country's economic recovery. This should be expressed, among other ways, in a radical solution to the burden of the debt payments, in the coinvestment of additional resources for expansion of export production, in advancing preferential long-term credits, and in establishing price accords for exports and imports that go beyond the unfair logic now reigning in world markets.

---

the dollar in the parallel market (currently 850:U.S. $1). New guaranteed prices were announced for agroexport products, and additional adjustments are expected later in the year. The policy implemented in the middle of 1985, of providing dollars as an incentive for some agroexport production, will be continued along the following lines:

1. For coffee, the dollar incentive varies with the quality but on average is approximately U.S. $5 per quintal.
2. For cotton, the dollar incentive applies to yields that surpass the average traditionally obtained in the region where the farm is located.
3. For beef, the dollar incentive is from U.S. $9 for an animal of 210 kg. up to a maximum of U.S. $11 for the highest weight.

In March, new consumer price increases varying between 30 and 150% were announced for food, gasoline, basic services (water and light), and transportation.

In summary, the adjustments announced in the first months of 1986 continued to support the objectives announced in February 1985, that is, to raise the level of basic consumption and agroexport production and to reduce the distortions in the economic system. The orientation that guides this effort emphasizes using economic policy to shift resources toward production and away from unproductive sectors. Finally, these objectives are set within the broader framework of assuring the national defense.

The adoption of such initiatives by the international community would in the medium term help balance Nicaragua's external and internal accounts, would neutralize the aggression of the Reagan administration and its economic blockade, and would hasten the achievement of peace in the region. Naturally, such a course depends on a greater political will on the part of Europe, the Arab countries, Latin America, and Asia. In the present situation, the occasion for declarations on behalf of peace and solidarity with Nicaragua must open the way to the most concrete and far-reaching commitment in support of the country's economic resurgence.

ACKNOWLEDGMENTS

The author has benefited from the generous critical comments of E. V. K. FitzGerald and Eduardo Baumeister. This work was written in March 1985.

Chapter 11

Troubles Everywhere:
An Economic Perspective on the
Sandinista Revolution

CARLOS M. VILAS[1]

A PROBLEMATIC ROAD

Inquiring into the economic aspects of the Sandinista Revolution is a complex task. The Nicaraguan economy and the revolutionary process in general are going through a critical phase, one full of profound contradictions. This phase is undoubtedly part of the sharp crisis now affecting all of Central America, but it is also the result of factors specific to the Nicaraguan reality.

The revolutionary government had to assume a costly reconstruction prompted by the war against the Somoza regime in 1978–79. The economy was also affected by 2 years of abnormal rainfall—1982 and 1985—and by the impact of Hurricane Alletta in 1982. Furthermore, it has had to deal with growing restrictions on external financing, especially by multilateral organizations. The situation was aggravated in the middle of 1985 when the U.S. government imposed a trade embargo that affected about 15% of Nicaragua's foreign trade. Finally, there is the counterrevolutionary war, for which the U.S. government is providing the financing, equipment, propaganda, and troop training. In addition to the death and destruction that it has caused, the war also accounts for the fact that about half of the government's spending in 1985 went for national defense.

Yet the experience of almost 7 years of revolution shows that the Sandinista government is capable of sharp changes of direction in economic policy. The

---

1. The author is an Argentine social scientist who has been living in Nicaragua since 1980. The opinions expressed here are his own and not necessarily those of the institutions with which he has been associated.

revolution has committed itself in general terms to the principles of national unity, a mixed economy, and international nonalignment within the framework of a democratic, popular, and antiimperialist system. Within these parameters, there seems to be no principled commitments to particular economic policies nor to courses of specific action. Thus any effort to inquire into the probable course of future events will always have a provisional quality.

Furthermore, the development of every economic system is always tightly linked to political factors. The politicization of the economy is much greater during a process of revolutionary transformation because the making of a new political power precedes changes in the socioeconomic structure: In the building of a new society "politics cannot but have supremacy over the economy."[2] The new economy and the new society exist first as a political project—not necessarily finished or definitive—and later as an objective reality. More clearly than in other circumstances, the economy is, in a revolutionary process, *political* economy.

Finally, a very simple but important matter: Every speculation on the future course of the economy is based explicitly or implicitly on a diagnosis of its structure, external ties, and current functioning. The author of this concluding chapter does not pretend to summarize or synthesize the complex body of work presented in the preceding chapters. My diagnosis, presented more fully elsewhere,[3] is derived from my own interpretation of the dynamics of political and economic change in Nicaragua.

In spite of these complications, it is possible to draw some overall conclusions about the direction of Nicaragua's economic transformation. The revolutionary government has chosen an economic strategy of "agroexporting plus food" by means of (a) a broad transformation of the relations of property and production in the countryside that reduced the power of the landowning oligarchy; (b) a process of heavy investments in capital and technology by the state but with limited impact on the creation of jobs; (c) a rearticulation with the international market through diversification of exports, boosting the value added to its exports, and the capture of new markets in the Third World and the socialist countries. Up to now, the strategy has generated various effects

---

2. Vladimir I. Lenin, "Mensaje al VII Congreso de los soviets de toda Rusia," *Obras escogidas* (Moscú: Editorial Progreso, 1960), 527–553.
3. See especially Carlos M. Vilas, *Perfiles de la revolución sandinista* (Buenos Aires: Editorial Legasa, 1984 and La Habana: Casa de las Américas, 1984); "Unidad nacional y contradicciones sociales en una economía mixta," in Richard Harris and Carlos M. Vilas, editors, *La revolución en Nicaragua* (México: Ediciones ERA, 1985); and "Nicaragua, Año V: Tensiones y contradicciones en la economía," Paper presented in the VI Congreso Centroamericano de Sociología, Panamá, March 1985.

that, added to the elements noted earlier, contribute to a panorama that is complex, delicate, and even precarious.

One of the central problems at this juncture is inadequate export earnings. Within the framework of a slow recovery of production levels and of a marked economic slowdown in recent years, export income has fallen rapidly because of (a) erratic and basically negative trends in international prices; (b) stagnation and even reduction in export volume; (c) deterioration in the terms of trade, aggravated by an exchange rate that overvalues the córdoba; (d) recessionary behavior in broad sectors of private enterprise; and (e) the impact of the war, especially on coffee (the principal export), mining, forest products, and fishing. This situation is translated into a persistent deficit in the trade balance; it also drives up the deficit in the current accounts balance and has a heavy impact on the growing external debt.

The political commitment of attending to the most basic demands of the majority, the historic deficiencies in food, health, and education, and the need to develop the productive forces led to an expansionist policy financed initially with the income from liquid external resources. At first these resources were sufficient. Nevertheless, the slow maturing of investment projects and the problematical recovery of the levels of production led to sharp fiscal-financial imbalances—mainly a very rapid growth in the fiscal deficit, the money supply, and the coefficient of liquidity as well as to a heavy overmonetization of the economy. These factors, together with others, made explicit the economy's tendencies toward structural inflation and the associated phenomena of supply dislocations, surges in the black market, and speculative activities.

The policy of containing nominal wages was translated, in this highly inflationary environment, into a sharp decline in real wages. Material stimulants and compensation—what in the early years were called "social wages" and most recently "wages in kind"—improved the income of some small categories of urban workers but left out most of the labor force, including almost all agricultural workers. In any case, the result was a stronger black market and more inflation.

The policy of fixing price relationships between agriculture and industry and between agroexport production and production for the domestic market, combined with the imbalance in supply mechanisms in the countryside, discriminated against the peasantry. This reduced the impact of other policies aimed at improving the situation of the peasantry and created a space for the counterrevolution to operate politically.

The transfer of financial surpluses abroad and into speculative activities has been favored by the growing autonomy of the sphere of monetary circulation. A contributing factor is the low efficiency of the government's mechanisms of control. It is also the objective result of some of the government's own policies: the growing use of payments in dollars as an export incentive; the establishment of a free currency exchange market that amounts to an explicit recognition of black-market exchange prices; generous financing with negative interest rates; and the low recovery capability of the financial system's loan portfolio.

The state's capacity to directly control the development of the economy has been limited so far because the public sector of the economy represents a small share of productive activity and because the efficiency as well as the effectiveness of state enterprises still do not exceed those of capitalist enterprises. Results have also been disappointing in terms of more indirect control. By moving with the market to capture part of the surplus circulating within it and to reorient it toward productive public investment, the state has in practice (with some exceptions) strengthened and therefore stimulated the market system.

PERSPECTIVES ON THE AGROEXPORT STRATEGY AT WAR

The points we have just reviewed, combined with the growing burden of external aggression and especially of the war, make the prospects for the Nicaraguan economy and for society as a whole especially difficult. The crux of a strategy of agricultural exportation obviously rests on the capacity to export. From this standpoint, the outlook of the international market is not very encouraging. There is no reason to expect a substantial change in the tendency for the prices of Nicaraguan exports to decline except through the intercession of fortuitous events, such as frosts in Brazil or Colombia, that raise international coffee prices.

The slackness of private investment, in spite of the stimulants of economic policy and of the profits made in export production, weakens the agroexport strategy. Capitalist enterprises still produce between one-third and one-half of exports; we can safely predict that the economic withdrawal of the exporting bourgeoisie will continue in the near future, in spite of the active participation of some individual elements of the class. In spite of the incentives used to try to stimulate them to invest within the framework of a mixed economy, the political-economic system being promoted by the revolution is not attractive to most of the Nicaraguan bourgeoisie.[4] The existence of trade-union organizations with the capacity to oversee, or at least complain about, working conditions and production, and the broad regulation of economic activity

---

4. See, for example, Enrique Bolaños Geyer, "Nicaragua 1984: Situación económica," *Revista del Pensamiento Centroamericano* 186 (1985):11–41.

(notwithstanding its less-than-satisfactory effectiveness), among other things, collide with the subjective feelings of the Nicaraguan bourgeoisie, who are plagued with fears and prejudices.

Moreover, the restrictions placed on nonessential imports due to the growing scarcity of foreign currency and the rapid reduction in nonessential consumption in order to protect the masses' consumption of necessities make it less likely that the bourgeoisie's surpluses can be used as they prefer, and removes inducements to keep up the level of productive activity. The Nicaraguan bourgeoisie—subordinated politically, militarily disarmed, facing the possibility of total confiscation if they join the counterrevolution or flee the country, sneaking their children out of the country to avoid the military draft—live in real distress. It is not a situation that is propitious for productive investment or counting up profits.

Neither is it forseeable that the intensity of the counterrevolutionary war or U.S. government support for that war will diminish. Thus the deep and widespread dislocation that the war has provoked will undoubtedly be aggravated, independent of the ability of the Popular Sandinista Army to inflict successive military defeats on the counterrevolutionary forces. To the extent that U.S. financial and other kinds of support for the counterrevolutionaries increases, the Nicaraguan government's defense appropriation will have to rise, too. So one aspect of the enormous price that the country has had to pay in recent years for the maintenance of its sovereignty is a sharp deterioration in public services, education, and hospital care, which affects the popular classes most of all.

We have every reason to expect, therefore, a growing deceleration in most productive activities, a tendency for global GNP to fall, deterioration in the living conditions of most of the population, and a continuing decline in agroexport income. It is evident that the war is not propitious for the recovery of the economy and for an improvement in the social welfare indexes, when it is the territory itself—particularly territory in the heart of the productive zones—that is being used as a theater of operations.

Clearly then, the war is worsening the dislocation of the economy that began before the conflict reached its present magnitude. The dislocation is due in part to policy mistakes and partly to resistance from members of the former dominant classes that still retain neutralizing capacities on policy decisions.

One can legitimately argue that the situation is neither definitive nor irreversible and that it will surely be overcome in the next 3 to 4 years when the large agroindustrial investment projects begin to pay off, when the country becomes more active in the international market, and—above all—when peace has been achieved. But it is difficult to assess what the level of destruction and of attrition of society will be when peace finally comes.

In the immediate future and for the next few years, the economy will become more closed. Essentially, this is not incompatible with an agro-exporting strategy that, among other things, is based on the redefinition of its external linkage. The experience of other revolutions and proposals like the New International Economic Order indicate that every reentry into the world market always follows some previous withdrawal; this is one of the conditions for carrying out the internal transformations that will prepare the economy for its new external linkages.

Nevertheless, the cost of this withdrawal (even though it may be provisional) for an economy like Nicaragua's, which was traditionally very open to the international market, is quite onerous. In the first place, because of the heavy dependence on imports for the functioning of the productive apparatus, the reduction of those imports below a certain level might paralyze broad sectors of production and even threaten the agroexporting strategy itself. The scarcity of replacement parts for machinery and transportation equipment is acute; there is a lack of medicine as well. Nicaragua's situation reveals a perverse combination of external disarticulation in export income and yet a heavier dependence on the international market due to the foreign debt, external deficits, and the incorporation of international prices by means of the parallel market and foreign-currency speculation.

Moving beyond the withdrawal phase, what does "international reentry" mean concretely? Up to now, Nicaragua has achieved a relative diversity in its foreign markets, especially through the broadening of its relations with some Third World economies and, in lesser measure, with the socialist bloc (COMECON). A continuation of this tendency would not seem likely to generate broad transformations in the short term. Apart from the limitations involved in increasing the supply available for export (mentioned before), the capacity of Third World markets to absorb significant amounts of Nicaraguan exports seems rather problematic. This is due to the very conditions of generalized economic crisis that such markets face, to the erratic character of their trade policies, and to their vulnerability to the same harmful influences that affect the Nicaraguan economy. The prospects that some years ago seemed to be opening up in some Middle Eastern markets—especially in Iran and Libya—are today much less clear.

As for the COMECON countries, the reorientation of Nicaraguan foreign trade and the lines of economic cooperation are still relatively limited, in contrast with what the propaganda orchestrated by the U.S. government would suggest.[5] Real integration of Nicaragua into the COMECON area

5. See ECLA, *Notas para el estudio económico de América Latina y el Caribe, 1984: Nicaragua* (México: CEPAL, July 1985), Table 13; and Michael E. Conroy, "External Dependence,

could be beneficial for its economy, but it raises the question of short-term— and perhaps not so short-term—tensions and ruptures. In the first place, this is so because an economy like Nicaragua's would have to make profound changes in its structure, in the way it works, and in its regulative capacity that are still far beyond its reach or even beyond considering at this point. A broad integration into the COMECON area would imply a reorientation of the country's economic ties with the rest of the world that Nicaragua does not seem disposed to undertake while other alternatives remain. A decision of this kind would surely alter the whole network of international political relations—especially with Latin American constitutional regimes and Western European governments—that the revolutionary government, with some difficulty, is trying to maintain as part of its strategy of survival as it deals with the U.S.-backed war. It is illustrative that, in spite of the fact that the trade embargo decreed in May 1985 by the Reagan administration created the political conditions for a fuller orientation toward the socialist bloc, the decision taken by the Nicaraguan government up to now has been, without excluding new openings toward the East, to compensate primarily through reaccomodation within Latin America and Western Europe.

The strategy of national unity and mixed economy will almost certainly be maintained in the future. In particular, the "mixed economy" will continue to be interpreted in a way that centers on a broad alliance with the export sectors of the bourgeoisie. It is forseeable, therefore, that the present policy of establishing economic incentives will be maintained, even at a cost to other social sectors. The economic and financial measures adopted at the beginning of 1985, independent of their intentions, stimulated the market and, therefore, those who dominate the market as well. Measures to correct the undesired effects of this new policy—particularly the decline in real wages and consequent transfer of income—cannot be excluded, but they do not seem to be on the horizon.

Conceding economic stimulants to some capitalist strata is not new in the history of national liberation revolutions, nor even in socialist revolutions. The case of the New Economic Policy (NEP) in the Soviet Union is quite well known. But the NEP was introduced when the war against the counterrevolution had been won, to compensate for the maladjustments generated by the strongly centralist and collectivist policy of "war communism."[6] This is not

External Assistance and Economic Aggression against Nicaragua," *Latin American Perspectives* 45 (1985):39—65.
6. See Edward H. Carr, *La revolución bolchevique 1917—1923: El orden económico* (Madrid: Alianza Editorial, 1972); and Charles Bettelheim, *La lucha de clases en la URSS (1919—1923)* (México: Siglo XXI, 1976).

the case in Nicaragua; the war is not over, nor is the country emerging from a collectivist or even centralist experiment. Finally, "war Sandinismo," unlike "war communism," asserts as its most important element the continued broadening of alliances, even including sectors of the bourgeoisie that initially had been characterized by the revolution as the opposition, if not as enemies.

The position of the revolutionary government on this point is explicit. The bourgeoisie should restrict itself to production; politics is off limits. This is the condition for its incorporation into a system of national unity and for its reproduction as a property-holding class. But historical experience—and Nicaragua is no exception—teaches that the bourgeoisie does not produce unless it is the dominant political force or unless the political regime is one that inspires confidence. Thus in Nicaragua it accepts the apparent forms of the new situation that allow it to capture additional surplus by means of cheap credit and partial dollarization of agricultural and livestock prices. But it removes these resources from the production cycle and channels them into speculation and, to the extent that it can, abroad. Prolonged official tolerance of such notorious behavior has a political explanation. The issue is not just providing stimulants to control economic behavior but providing incentives to obtain the political compliance of the bourgeoisie—bonuses, as it were, for not having abandoned the country and for maintaining productive activities, at least at a minimal level.

The war, implemented by military means on the borders and in the mountains, is not separate from this economic dimension of the class struggle. The latter conflict is carried out in the fields of economic policy, inflation and the black market, profits and wages, and in general through the appropriation of the surplus still being generated in the Nicaraguan economy. The military and economic conflicts are two aspects of the same confrontation. The effective behavior of the bourgeoisie objectively supports the counterrevolution by contributing to the deterioration of the productive apparatus, thus supporting one of the explicit goals of the counterrevolutionaries. Four or 5 years ago, when the level of aggression was incomparably lower than it is now and the economy was still flourishing, this close relation was already obvious.[7] Today it is even clearer.

The costs of both dimensions of the war have been borne mainly by the same people: peasants and workers, artisans, the poor in the countryside and the city—the popular classes in general. Those are the ones who have felt most directly the impact of the deterioration of the conditions of life caused by the war and by the dislocation of the economy. They are also those who make

7. See Vilas, *Perfiles*, 281 ff.; *El Nuevo Diario*, June 13, 1981; and *Barricada*, June 16, 1981.

up the vast majority of the combatants of the armed forces, of the victims of the counterrevolutionary incursions, the dead, the wounded, and the mutilated.

This brings us to the question of the probable evolution of the social bases of the revolution. The continued deterioration of the conditions of life for the workers does not necessarily imply that they will become opponents of the revolution. Before arriving at this extreme, there is a tendency to resort to multiple strategies of adaptation and survival, of adjustment to the new circumstances. As for the working class, the decline in real wages and the growing gap between their wages and the incomes of the thousands of self-employed in the so-called informal urban sector have encouraged an alarming process of progressive deproletarianization of the urban and seasonal rural workforce. The adjustment measures adopted at the beginning of 1985 attempted to slow down this process through wage increases to those categories of workers most susceptible to the temptations of the informal sector and through the implementation of measures to control and contain its growth. It is still premature to judge the effectiveness of these measures.

In more general terms, one might suggest that the reduced levels of political and mass activism that one sees at present are related to the deterioration in the conditions of life and work. It is neither the first time nor the first procress in which the concentration of the masses' attention on particular adverse living conditions has translated into a declining participation in collective projects. In the case of Nicaragua, one could also note the obvious decline in the various kinds of worker participation in the management of their enterprises. This decline is a result of the greater emphasis on the centralization of decisions and of a notorious change in the predominant focus of the labor question. Worker participation now seems mainly to emphasize productivity and efficiency. This retreat, which is always serious for a popular power, is much graver in a situation like the present.

TOWARD A REORIENTATION OF THE STRATEGY?

The prolongation of the present situation brings with it an accumulation of pressures and tensions that affect the future of the revolution, its economy, and its social bases. One of the greatest political obstacles involved in reorienting the present strategy in order to overcome, or at least reduce, the impact of these tensions may be the effect such a reorientation could have on the internal and international alliances that are now helping to sustain the revolution. Still it is not fruitless to ask whether the impact of things as they are (and as they would continue to be without a change in strategy) is not already sufficiently onerous for those who are supposed to be the "motor force" of the revolution.

To change the present strategy does not have to mean tossing the whole strategy overboard, but it does mean to emphasize its second dimension—the production of food and the development of the economy on a more self-centered basis, given the problematic outlook of exports for the reasons already cited. A greater emphasis on production for the internal market means greater attention to the respective producers—fundamentally, but not exclusively, the middle and lower strata of the peasantry. What is implied, therefore, is a reorientation of policy regarding prices, credit, incentives, and technical assistance; better allocation of infrastructure and land; changes in investment policy; better attention to mechanisms for supplying the needs of the countryside; promotion of local incentives to satisfy the basic needs of the people at the community level; development of the capacity for planning on a small scale and at the local level; and encouraging an effective involvement of direct producers in decisions that affect them.

A reorientation of this kind, or something similar, but that in any case places more emphasis on the internal market, implies a parallel reorientation of the flow of surpluses, to the detriment of the sectors who have benefited so far, including a large proportion of the urban middle strata. A new matrix of conflicts and affinities thus arises. Is the Sandinista Revolution disposed to take this up?

This question once again raises the issue of the war and the way the war has reduced the margin for maneuvering. The position of Nicaragua in the present situation is similar in many ways to that of other Third World societies that try to initiate processes of national liberation and social transformation in a situation of marked underdevelopment. Backwardness itself, which the revolution seeks to overcome, becomes one of the main hindrances to the revolution's progress and makes the country more vulnerable to external aggression. By the same token, the war generates even greater complications when the economic foundation for the revolutionary process is precarious.

Nonetheless, a number of recent policy changes suggest a shift toward a more peasant-based, decentralized economic strategy. Throughout 1985, the priority given to national defense and the preferential treatment provided to the war zones brought the FSLN and the revolutionary government to modify the agrarian reform program, the rural development strategy, and the general treatment given to peasants and rural workers. As was noted at the beginning of this chapter, these modifications illustrate the capacity of the Sandinista Revolution to sharply shift its economic policy.

In contrast with the earlier emphasis on cooperatives and state farms, the agrarian reform has now been oriented in a more peasant-based direction. Between June and December of 1985, more than 136,000 mz. were distributed to landless peasant families; this is equal to around 75% of all the new land distributed to individual peasants since 1981 and to over 15% of all the new land redistributed under the agrarian reform. The land thus distributed was obtained primarily through the expropriation of private estates but also at the expense of some state farms. At the same time, a new price and commercialization policy acknowledged the peasants' primary demands. The new prices reflect the cost structures of the small producers more adequately, and these producers have been allowed to sell directly to consumers, without the requirement that they commercialize through the state channels. Credit and technical assistance policy aspires to provide these small family units with at least the minimum conditions necessary to generate a profit. Likewise, the supply system for basic and some industrial goods (machetes, clothing, farm tools, etc.) has improved in the countryside. Furthermore, the rural workers' salaries have been readjusted to reduce the gap between urban and rural salaries.

For the FSLN and the revolutionary government, giving priority to defense and the war zones does not just mean assigning an increasing portion of the government budget to military expenditures. It also implies giving preference in policymaking to the demands of the popular sectors located in the region of military conflict—peasants and rural workers—even though this requires modifications in development strategies that seemed unalterable.[8]

This reorientation of state policy was institutionalized in January 1986 with the modification of the agrarian reform law. The 1981 version of this law was directed against inefficient landowners and affected primarily land that was underutilized, abandoned, or illegally rented. It had a double objective: to modernize agricultural production and raise output and yield levels on the one hand and to eliminate the injustices associated with peasant landlessness and the exploitation of agricultural workers on the other. It was antioligarchical and antilatifundista, more than anticapitalist.

The 1986 law expanded the land susceptible to expropriation, lowering the legal "ceilings" from 500 and 1000 mz. (depending on the region) to 50 and 100 mz. This decision gave the state a much larger potential land pool to draw on. The text of the new law illustrates the decision of the revolutionary government and the FSLN to satisfy the land hunger of the peasantry but without breaking the alliance with the large capitalist landowners. For this reason, instead of targeting these large estates for redistribution, the state

8. See Fernando Quezada Pastrán and William Gomez Sóto, "Los asentamientos nicaragüenses: ¿Una nueva vía de colectivización?" Paper presented at the IV Congreso Nicaragüense de Ciencias Sociales, Managua, August 1985; and Manuel Ortega, "Tierra y lucha de clases," Paper presented at the IV Congreso Nicaragüense de Ciencias Sociales, Managua, August 1985.

opted for the potential expropriation of medium-sized properties (if they were not being efficiently used) and for reducing the holdings of the state. Another reason for this was that the peasant land pressure was not that intense in the zones where large capitalist estates were concentrated but was located primarily in the regions where the medium-sized properties predominated (such as the Departamentos of Masaya, Granada, Managua, Matagalpa, Carazo, Jinotega, and others).

It is still not clear how much the Sandinista Revolution intends to modify its original development strategy, which placed agroexportation at the center of the process of accumulation. As was indicated earlier, until now the performance of the agroexport strategy has been weak, but changing the strategy would require a modification in the social bases of the revolution. For the moment, the FSLN and the revolutionary government prefer trying to maintain the broad character of the social alliance in which they participate, introducing only those changes that are absolutely necessary. Nonetheless, to the extent that the new emphasis is maintained (as public declarations of the top leadership of the FSLN and government suggest),[9] it will have the impact of reducing the relative emphasis on agroexport and increasing the real incentives for production for the internal market. It remains to be seen to what extent this sector can make itself the new center of accumulation, capable of compensating for the limitations of agroexportation, within the framework of a progressive closing of the economy.

The new orientation is not without its own contradictions. The consumer price policy, for example, continues to discriminate against low-income groups. In 1985, the official consumer prices were raised 400% for rice, 300% for milk, 312% for eggs, 480% for sugar, and 300% for urban public transportation. In the same period, gasoline prices increased 150%, whereas prices for diesel—a heavy fuel used for transporting cargo and passengers—rose 225%. The increases decreed in March 1986 follow the same course. To illustrate the point, the price of a liter of milk went up 110%, whereas gas prices increased only 50%. The overt and accelerating deterioration in public transportation went hand in hand with the continued policy of subsidizing the importation of automobiles. The list could go on, but this sample is sufficient to illustrate the decision of the revolutionary government to maintain those economic incentives that reinforce the political loyalties of the urban middle class. After all, a substantial proportion of the staff and the rank and file of the FSLN come from that class.

In these times of rapid change, it is difficult to propose specific hypotheses about the future course that the complex Nicaraguan economic reality will run. The Sandinista style is to give priority to the short run and to focus

9. See, for example, *Barricada*, January 13, 1986, and March 4, 1986.

attention on the correlation of forces that shape the objective reality. All this suggests that the course of the war will define the orientation that will prevail. This is not in the sense that while the war continues the strategy of national unity will prevent revolutionary transformations. On the contrary, the national defense functions to deepen these revolutionary transformations and give priority to the satisfaction of popular demands.

The war of national defense is an inevitable stage for social revolutions in an epoch of imperialism. To the extent that popular power is consolidated and the socioeconomic transformations are developed, foreign domination, which previously was primarily economic and political, now assumes a military character. The experience of social revolutions of the twentieth century is that they are able to consolidate to the extent that they can advance their political and socioeconomic transformation in spite of the military attacks of the counterrevolution and imperialism.

It seems clear, nonetheless, that as far as the economy is concerned, the options that the Sandinista Revolution faces are quite reduced. In reality, this touches on a problem that Is common in other revolutionary settings where the society is impoverished and the economy is open to the international market. For a period that can be quite long, these economies in the process of restructuration—or if you prefer, of transition— *are not viable*.

An economy that specializes in agroexportation competes in the international capitalist market on the basis of an intense exploitation of the labor force, with authoritarian labor relations and salaries below the cost of reproduction of labor. Revolution ends this exploitation or at least visibly improves the labor conditions and living standards of workers and peasants. At the same time, it raises the cost of production above international prices; external competitiveness disappears or is drastically reduced. The alternative of changing the nature of agroexportation through intensive investments in capital leads, in the short run, to an increase in the foreign debt, deepening the inflationary tensions, and generalized disequilibrium. A blockade of funds in the multilateral lending agencies requires a country to resort to financing under increasingly unfavorable conditions, further impeding this transition. Moreover, even the international competitiveness of a capital-intensive agroexport model is questionable. In the case of Nicaragua, production of the major export product—coffee—cannot be mechanized.

On the other hand, a development strategy that emphasizes the basic needs of the working classes—rural and urban workers and peasants—suffers from important limitations. These include a reduced capacity to generate profits, the narrow scope of the internal market, the enormous size of the unproductive population, technical backwardness, and the heavy dependence on imported materials in the sectors that produce for the internal market.

As a result, *while these economies are in the process of being restructured, they need foreign subsidies. Without them, such economies collapse.* This, of course, was not the case in the Soviet or Chinese revolutions, which took place in closed economies of continental scope that were practically self-sufficient. But it is the case in the social revolutions in the rest of Asia, Africa, and in Latin America.

Analyzed carefully, this raises one of the oldest issues in the debate about the viability of socialism in less advanced capitalist settings. This question was first raised in the nineteenth century about the possibility of socialism in Russia. Marx's response to the questions raised by the *narodniki* on this issue was ambiguous; Engels, on the other hand, tied the possiblity of socialism in less-developed countries to a prior triumph of socialism in the West and the assistance that triumphant revolutions would provide to the poorer countries.[10] The revolution did not occur in the West, but in Russia. Still, the central idea remains: Assistance from the "advanced" revolutions is essential to guarantee the *initial viability* of social revolutions in less-developed and highly dependent economies.[11]

Questions about the viability of these economies during the restructuration are not simply technical but concern the very survival of these societies. As we indicated earlier, a central component of the transition is military aggression by imperialist powers. In such an unequal contest, the effort of the people is the most powerful weapon a poor nation has, but it is not enough. Unless it is complemented by international solidarity by an array of supportive countries, not just the future of the economy is compromised. In the final analysis, the very life and liberty of its citizens are in question.

10. Federico Engels, "Postcriptum acerca de la cuestión social en Rusia," in Marx and Engels, *Escritos sobre Rusia* (México: Siglo XXI, 1980), 89–90.
11. Along the same lines, see Vladimir I. Lenin, "Informe de la comisión para los problemas nacional y colonial, presentado al II Congreso de la Internacional Comunista," in Lenin, *La lucha de los pueblos de las colonias y países dependientes contra el imperialismo* (Moscú: Editorial Progreso, 1979), 409–410.

Index

Accumulation process, 4, 5, 76–80, 207
Africa, 246
Aggression, U.S., costs of: economic, 158–161, 167–168, 197–202; on future Nicaraguan development, 207–211; macroeconomic, 202–205; military, 196–197, 299, 218, 237; on Nicaraguan standard of living, 205–207
Agrarian reform. See Land, reform
Agrarian Reform Law (1981), 130
Agrarian Reform Law (1986), 243
Agriculture, 3, 6, 53, 66, 70, 74, 81, 228; constraints on, 129–140; co-operatives, 114–115, 141, 209–210, 242; credit policy, 112–122; labor shortages, 134–137; production, 20–21, 73, 127–147, 225, 231; redistributive policies, 140–146, 181–182; reform, 30, 38–39, 90; during Somoza era, 16–22, 25, 106–112; state farms, 120–121, 242. See also Agroexports
Agroexports, 3, 16–20, 22, 30, 38–39, 89, 152; banks and, 107–118; elite, 119–120; perspectives on

strategy for, 236–241; reorientation, 241–246
AID (Agency for Intenational Development), 111, 157
Algeria, 184, 192
Allende, Salvador, 167
Alliance for Progress, 56
Angola, 158
APP (Area of People's Property), 66, 67, 74, 75, 76, 77, 79, 120, 123, 124, 229
Arab countries, 232
Asia, 232, 246
"Austerity" measures, 80–81

Balance of payments, 9; crises, 6, 26, 27, 37, 53, 92, 175; impact of U.S. agression on, 198–202, 203
"Banana republic," 15, 15n
Bananas, 15n, 18
Banco de América, 107
Banco Nacional de Desarrollo, 113, 116, 117
BANIC (Banco Nicaragüense), 107
Banking system, 16, 32, 105–125, 219; administrative reorganization,